Is Catholicism Reformable
Copyright © (Michael Winter 2021)

ISBN: 978-178456-766-8
Paperback

First published 2021 by UPFRONT PUBLISHING
Peterborough, England.

An environmentally friendly book printed and bound in England by www.printondemand-worldwide.com

Dedicated to my wife Alison
and to our sons
Ben and Max

I wish to express my gratitude to the
graphic artist, Christine Ayre
for her brilliant design of the cover,
incorporating Giotto's fresco in Assisi.

IS CATHOLICISM
REFORMABLE?

MICHAEL M. WINTER

CONTENTS

ABBREVIATIONS

Abbott Walter M. Abbott, The Documents of Vatican II.

A.A.S. Acta Apostolicae Sedis.

Alberigo Joseph, Alberigo, Conciliorum Oecumenicorum Decreta.

MPG Migne, Patrologia Graeca.

MPL Migne, Patrologia Latina.

S T St. Thomas Aquinas, Summa Theologica.

INTRODUCTION

At the beginning of the new millennium, the Catholic Church is experiencing one of the worst crises in the whole of its history.

In any nation where reliable statistics are collected, the numerical decline is unmistakable. Cradle Catholics are abandoning active membership of the Church in unprecedented numbers. The first wave left in the 1960/70's, apparently as a result of the exposure of the birth control encyclical's faulty theology. The next wave are leaving in the early years of the new millennium, seemingly when the full extent of the sexual abuse of children by Catholic clergy could no longer be hidden. Most recently the absence of adolescents has indicated a unique problem. It is the purpose of this book to explore the deep causes of these massive demographic migrations, from the Church to which these Catholics formerly showed allegiance, and also to suggest realistic remedies.

In one representative nation Germany, the numbers are totally reliable. In June 2020 the German Bishops' Conference published disquieting statistics of Catholics who had deliberately left the Catholic Church. In 2019 there were 272,771 departures, which is an ominous increase on 216,000 in 2018, and 218,000 in the year 2014. The numbers are completely trustworthy since they are taken from the government's taxation records.

In Germany, when a baby's birth is registered, the child's religion is also recorded. About twenty years later when the same child has become a wage-earner, a proportion of his or her tax, is diverted by the government to the Church to which the individual was affiliated at birth. This is known as the Church Tax (*Kirchensteuer*) which the government hands over to the central authority of that Church, in Germany.[1]

For Great Britain, reliable figures have been carefully researched by Professor Stephen Bullivant for the year 2016. His results are as follows. In an adult population of 50.3 million, there were 7.2 million cradle Catholics, of whom 3.2 million were disaffiliates. The term disaffiliates covers those who have abandoned Catholicism in favour of another Church, or non-Christian religion, together with those who have given up religion altogether. The numbers speak for themselves and require no further elucidation.[2]

Another important factor, noted by Professor Bullivant, is that the phenomenon of disaffiliation is not confined to the Catholic Church. American estimates suggest that the mainline Protestant denominations lost between a quarter and a third of their members between the 1960's and 1980, and in Britain the Anglican Church lost about a quarter of their communicants between 1960 and 1980.[3] These are important observations, since it means that the disaffiliation of Catholics cannot be blamed on the Second Vatican Council.

As to the causes of this on-going crisis, I am competent to speak only about the shortcomings on the Catholic scene and indeed principally in Great Britain. But I am aware that the same influences and results on the Church are much the same for the whole of Europe, and indeed for all Christians. In the course of this book I will examine those causes carefully and suggest practicable remedies and reforms.

The causes of this crisis are complex, and they can be divided roughly into four main categories: historical, sociological, psychological, and theological, but those are not water-tight compartments. Historical factors are present in all of them, and theology is the principal factor of reform, but institutional changes are also indispensable. Moreover, history is also useful in elucidating how things went wrong.

As far as young people are concerned, the principal cause would seem to be the absence of an appropriate opportunity for them to ratify their baptism, by a deliberate personal act of faith. This is compounded by the contemporary Church's lacking of an inspiring public purpose.

On the wider canvass of the life of the Church as a whole, one can say that the Second Vatican Council raised high expectations which have not been fulfilled. This is a complex question. A serviceable model is the aftermath of the Council of Trent, since that council grappled with the same problem, successfully! The task facing that council was in a sense clearer than for Vatican II. In reply to Luther's revolt, and blatant immorality in the Catholic Church, Trent divided its decisions into doctrinal definitions and disciplinary rules. To ensure the implementation of both categories of commands, a new Congregation was established in Rome called The Congregation of the Council. In the post-conciliar period it pursued its mandate with persistence and patience.

The programme of Vatican II was somewhat different. In the second half of the 20th century there was no heresy threatening the Church's unity and orthodoxy, nor was there any obvious blatant immorality. (The child sex abuses by clergy came to light at the end of that century). The documents of Vatican II were visionary ideals for the modernisation of a Church whose practices had remained basically in their late mediaeval pattern, such as Latin as the language for all public worship. Significantly the reformed liturgy has been the most successful benefit of Vatican II, because it did have an on-going commission to supervise the implementation of its reforms. Other projects did not, and after the Council, the Roman Curia dragged its feet as to implementation, and in all too many instances, worked against those objectives, as will be seen in the subsequent chapters of this book.

In some areas of post-conciliar activity, the opposition was more serious than merely dragging their feet. During the pontificates of John Paul II and Benedict XVI, more than 110 progressively minded theologians were penalised. If they were in Catholic institutions, (universities or seminaries for instance) they were summarily dismissed. If they were in other institutions they were penalised in different ways, always with the aim of reducing them to silence.[4] Measures like that were of limited effectiveness in the present time, because it encouraged the persecuted theologians to resign from their religious orders, or from the clergy, in order to pursue writing and publishing in the more broad minded ambience of secular institutions.

Another field in which the Council's implementation was impeded, was the extension of the existing pattern of the erosion of decision-making competence of the bishops, by the excessive power of Roman Curia.

There is also a serious lack of recruits to the secular clergy and religious orders. Of more positive influence are factors like the vigilance of public criticism of Church policies, thanks to Vatican II, and free speech for lay people to discuss everything. These two highlight the absence of really practical structures and procedures, for the Church to engage in areas of social justice, such as workers' rights, the amelioration of the worst cruelties of warfare, the advancement of the rights of women, and overshadowing everything else is global warming. All of these issues should be the rightful concern of the Church's message, but the mechanisms for delivering its contribution are absent.

As a result of all these factors, young people find the activities, which the Catholic Church does undertake, quite literally uninteresting and irrelevant to their lives. One glaring example is the obsession by the British and American bishops, with denouncing the evils of abortion. It should not surprise us if young people cease to attend church services.

Those topics and others like them will occupy the subsequent chapters of this book. In case some readers may not like the tone of how I will be presenting them, let me state that I am, and have always been a totally committed Catholic. In the present state of the Church's ineffectuality, the situation is so serious, that considerations of politeness and deference towards those in authority cannot be regarded as of over-riding importance. The authorities in the Church must be prepared to face up to the sort of frank criticism and questioning that members of Parliament, for example, accept as a normal part of their responsibilities in the service of the nation. It is not the first sign of a revolution, but the normal pattern of accountability, which is the accepted norm of political responsibility in mature democratically governed nations. It fits in quite naturally to the pattern of life in societies where universal literacy, and free speech are the norm.

The theological principles, which have guided me in this study of reform, are principally those which are developed in the late Yves Congar's masterpiece, *Vrai et Faux Réforme dans l'Église.*[5] His basic schema is that a true reform, as opposed to a superficial re-orientation of policy, must fulfil four conditions. Firstly it must be motivated by charity and apostolic zeal. Secondly it must be a return to the sources. Thirdly it must proceed with what Congar describes as *patientia*, for which 'patience' is a misleading translation, as I will show below. The fourth and last condition is that the Church's unity must be preserved.

To amplify the full significance of those four conditions, a few lines will be necessary. Charity and apostolic zeal is a deceptively simple, since it comprises the core of the Christian message including its uniqueness. In the first century A.D. it was a complete innovation for a religion's primary purpose to be the love of the one and only God, and one's neighbour, who might be a total stranger. Apart from Judaism, most religious activities in all societies of that epoch, were forms of bargaining with the gods for favours, of which elaborate sacrifices were the 'quasi-currency' of such dealings. Moreover they were definitely national gods, whose worship cemented patriotism. It was equally unique for the Christians to invite people of all countries, to join them in their world-wide community, which owed no special ties to any particular nation.

Congar's programme of such thoroughness, contrasts sharply with some initiatives in later centuries by Catholic rulers, to reform the Church in their territories, with such goals as greater administrative efficiency.

The second condition, a return to the sources, means that the intellectual content of a reform, must derive primarily from the writings in the New Testament, for obvious reasons. It also comprises the practices of the early Church, because the first few generations of Christians can be presumed to have remembered the instructions of Jesus, of which only a small proportion were recorded in the writings of the New Testament. A good example is the fact that the early Christians always celebrated the liturgy in the spoken language of the people. But no written instruction about it is recorded in the New Testament. The same outlook motivated them to translate the whole bible into the local language when new regions had been evangelised. This can be seen because very early manuscripts have survived, in part at least, of the translations into Syriac, Armenian, Georgian and more than one dialect of Egyptian.

Thirdly it must move with "patientia," to use Congar's own term, which means tenacity, as well as enduring the passage of time. There is an interesting parallel in the modern world with the long drawn our struggle to secure the rights of women. That campaign covered a wide programme, of which the central components were the granting of the same voting rights as men enjoyed in national and local government, and the right to stand as candidates for election in those same areas of government. Then, admission to the civil service, universities and professions, also on the same terms that men enjoyed. Although the suffragette movement started in the latter half of the 19th century, it was not until the 1930's that its principal objectives had been achieved.

Needless to say, that programme met with bitter opposition, since history shows that groups who have any sort of privilege of wealth, influence or power, do not relinquish it without a struggle. Possibly the most disedifying group of opponents were the governing bodies of the ancient universities of Oxford and Cambridge, who could have been expected to exhibit greater enlightened understanding.

In the twenty first century the wide consensus among enlightened Catholics, to seek the ordination of married men, as well as women, is a clear example of where "patientia" is required. In the immediate aftermath of the Second Vatican Council, perceptive Catholics realised that the Council had nullified the theological basis for obligatory celibacy, but by the year 2020 the Vatican was still resisting the repeal of the law.

Fourthly a true reform must preserve unity. In communities like political parties, Trades Unions, and religious bodies, it is relatively easy for an enthusiastic elite group to flourish. Whether it hives off and forms a new Trades Union, or stays to re-invigorate the parent organisation, is of little consequence. Among Christians that is not the case, because the teaching of Christ is so clear that his followers must remain united.

The Anglican Church has been enriched by zealous movements such as the Methodists and the Salvation Army. What was problematical was whether they would stay within the parent body and influence it, or whether they would hive off, full of zeal, but leaving the original community relatively unchanged. Without seeming to be smug, I would suggest that had John Wesley been a member of the Catholic Church, his movement would probably have been institutionalised as a religious order. It would have preserved his original charism, but it would have continued to nourish the larger, perhaps less enthusiastic parent body.

The historical factors which provide the background to Congar's masterpiece were firstly the Lutheran reform in the sixteenth century, which shattered the unity of Western European Christianity. The second factor was the positive ecumenical movement in roughly the same geographical area, which was trying to repair the ancient divisions after the Second World War.

In Luther's favour, it must be acknowledged that he fulfilled the second condition that of a return to the sources, when he restored three important practices, which were genuine resumptions of those in current use in the very earliest period of the Church's life. They were that the liturgy should be in the spoken language of the people. Next that in the eucharist the laity should receive the sacrament in the form of the consecrated wine, as well as the consecrated bread. And finally that the clergy should be family men. That last stipulation was written into the New Testament in the letters to Titus and Timothy. One cannot help being baffled as to how the Church authorities could have so blatantly defied the explicit instructions of those two Epistles, which were inspired and formed integral parts of the New Testament. More than half a century since the Second Vatican Council, the Church is still waiting for the Pope and Vatican to do justice to those stipulations, particularly as the Council demolished any possible theological justification for demanding celibacy as a condition for priestly ordination.

Sadly, Luther and his followers, did not keep to the two conditions of preserving unity or observing "patientia". They pushed ahead, may I say it, recklessly. It was equally sad, and culpably so, that the Catholics over-reacted to Luther. Roughly, their stance crystalized into an attitude that since Luther was a proven heretic over doctrines like justification and the theology of grace, everything that the Lutherans taught was to be treated as falsehood. The speed with which Pope Leo X excommunicated him was disastrous, compared with the admirable patience that was displayed by the Emperor Charles V, in his years of negotiations with Protestant principalities within the Empire, in an attempt to preserve unity, both of the Empire, and the Church, because the two were so closely bound together.

In the 1960's the Second Vatican Council reversed much of that negative hostility to Lutheranism. An extremely successful liturgical reform has been achieved. Unfortunately though, Pope Paul VI withdrew the matter of married priests from the Council's agenda. Several years after the Council, he published his own encyclical letter on the subject of Priestly Celibacy, which singularly failed to present a theologically convincing case for its retention. This gave rise to widespread agitation for its abolition as a compulsory condition. It was tragic, but foreseeable, that literally thousands of secular priests resigned from the ministry, because it was clear that Vatican II had demolished any possibility of justifying the obligation theologically.

In addition to those four conditions, and to bring clarity into such a complicated field of reform, Congar also divided the faults which needed correction into two comprehensive categories. These can be translated colloquially into "the Church gone churchy" and the "Church gone worldly".

The first of those categories supplied ample material for the reformers in the area of the liturgy, for example. By the twentieth century, details of ceremonial were described ad nauseam in dozens of books, while the laity could not understand a word of what was taking place, unless they were fluent in Latin. For example, whole volumes were filled with directions for such matters as to when the celebrating priest should wear the biretta, and when he should remove it. For those who have never seen a biretta, let me explain. It is a four-cornered hat, which has evolved from a mediaeval prototype. A priest walking from the sacristy to the sanctuary was instructed to wear the biretta until he was inside the sanctuary, and he was to hand it to the altar server when he was in front of the altar, but before he genuflected.

In the middle of the twentieth century, numerous volumes had been written about such inessentials. The use of incense was another example. It was used only at high mass, i.e. that which had a large amount of music, almost all of which was sung by the choir, for obvious reasons. At the offertory of the mass the incense holder (thurible) was presented to the priest who put more incense on the red hot charcoal blocks inside, as the smoke rose up, the priest incensed the chalice. That is to say he performed two circular swings round the chalice in a clockwise orientation, and another two in an anti-clockwise direction. Then he walked to the corners of the altar and performed two circular swings to each corner of the altar. I remember being on holiday in South Africa shortly before the end of apartheid. Riots were taking place on the outskirts of the city where I was staying, and in the church one could hear the sound of shots being fired by the police. Yet the young priest celebrating the mass carried out the incensing meticulously and without a fault, as if it were the most important activity in the world.

Looking back on it after an interval of more than half a century, it reminded me of the famous novel by Herman Hesse, *The Glass Bead Game.* In which he described a community of men who devoted their lives to the correct performance of complicated board games, rather like chess.

The second category described by Congar was "the Church gone worldly". The career of the sixteenth century Cardinal Wolsey exemplifies that deviation perfectly. Thomas Wolsey was born c. 1474 of fairly humble parents, but he was educated at Oxford, and was elected as a Fellow of Magdalene College, c. 1497, which was a sign of his abilities. He was ordained priest 1498, and became one of the chaplains to the Archbishop of

Canterbury in 1501. After that he became a chaplain to the king, Henry VII c. 1507. After that king's death, he was retained in the same capacity by Henry VIII, who noted his abilities, and appointed him as a member of the Privy Council in 1511. From that year onwards he started collecting wealthy benefices. In 1514 he became bishop of Lincoln, and in the same year he was also appointed as Archbishop of York. Significantly he never set foot in that Archdiocese until after his fall from power in 1529, when he was dismissed from the post of Chancellor. Needless to say, he had also been living with a mistress, and had an illegitimate son by her.

Writing in the 1950's Congar deliberately limited his field of necessary reforms to those of the category of "Church gone churchy", observing that there was no heresy threatening the Church, nor widespread immorality of which Wolsey was such a classical example. Congar was spared the painful exposure, after his death, of widespread sexual corruption of the clergy in the latter part of the 20th century. Their extent and depravity, particularly the sexual abuse of children, were even worse than the moral failings in the 16th century clergy. Nevertheless, the principles for authentic reform, which he had elaborated, apply to the eradication of those disgraceful practices too. In this particular book, the reform is mainly that of institutions, as will become apparent in the chapters which follow.

In subsequent chapters I will refer frequently to Vatican II. Its documents presented a re-invigorated and creative vision of the Church's mission. Although the participating bishops could not have foreseen it, their programme hit the Church at the same time as secular society was undergoing far-reaching changes of traditional attitudes in the late 1960's. For some backward looking Catholics the double impact on their childhood certainties was just too much, and they became resentful of the post- conciliar Church's direction.

CHAPTER ONE

ADOLESCENTS ABANDON THE MASS

Readers will grasp that the title of this chapter is something of an over-simplification. However in a very complex problem, it serves as a point of entry to the subtleties of their acquiring, retaining or abandoning a coherent philosophy of life, based on spiritual values. Since roughly the start of the new millennium, regular mass goers have observed a diminishing proportion of teen-agers and young adults in the average congregation on Sundays. Does it mean that they are rejecting belief in God? Did they ever really have such belief in the first place? Is it no more serious than their finding the liturgy boring? Or of no apparent relevance to their lives at present? Will they return to community worship later in their lives, when they have worked out where they stand in relation to God and religion? It must be borne in mind that teen-agers are not the only ones who have given up attending mass. Their presence or absence is more obvious than that of the adults who have followed the same path.

The absence of the young adults is the more serious problem because with them lies the future of the whole Church.

Fortunately, one element in this complex problem is clear, namely the starting point. Faith is a free choice made by the individual, to commit his or her life to God in personal loyalty, in response to the invitation of Christ, announced by the Church. In that context it is important to remember that baptism was given to infants, since ancient times, only on the understanding that the individuals would personally re-affirm it in their own lives, when they were sufficiently mature to make such a decision. It is well known that St. Ambrose, bishop of Milan, and St. Augustine of Hippo, were still un-baptised catechumens in adult years.

However, with the passage of time, the personal re-affirmation in adult years seems to have disappeared, possibly because no practical means of inviting it seems to have been established. After the collapse of the Roman Empire in northern Europe, the nascent Christian communities there seem to have vanished. Famous missions like that of St. Patrick, St. Augustine in England and St. Boniface in Germany had to introduce Christianity as something new. That of St. Augustine is a typical example. As is well known, at the end of the sixth century he converted and baptised Ethelbert the king of Kent, and the whole of that tiny kingdom followed their sovereign into the Church. From that point onwards the other small kingdoms in England followed that pattern. Once the king had accepted Christianity, the whole nation followed suit. In several instances it was connected with success of the Christian kingdom in battle. In short, it seems clear that any individual decision was out of the question. It is difficult after so many centuries to discern their motives. Those small Saxon kingdoms still had the tightly knit bonds of a tribal society, where conformity was the essence of their social system. It should also be remembered that in a basically religious society, the dignified monotheism of Christianity could not have failed to impress serious minded people of that epoch. The contrast with Thor, Wodin and others of the Teutonic pantheon could not have been starker. From then onwards, it appears that the children born to Christian parents adopted their parents' religion, as automatically as they inherited their fathers' surname and nationality. In other words, it involved no free and deliberate decision. Yet it was not a totally mechanical response to the king's decision, because the culture of society was thoroughly religious.

In this context, and for the first generation of converts, there is a charming incident, recorded by Bede in his Ecclesiastical History. The bishop Paulinus had spoken to Edwin, the king of Northumbria, inviting him to adopt Christianity. After surviving exile and many dangers, once the king was secure in the possession of his kingdom, he summoned a council of his chief men, to seek their advice about conversion to the newly arrived religion. Here I quote Bede's own words, reporting the speech of one of the king's advisors, "Your Majesty, when we compare the present life of man with that time of which we have no knowledge, it seems to me like the swift flight of a lone sparrow through the banqueting hall where you sit in the winter months to dine with your thanes and councillors. Inside there is a comforting fire to warm the room; outside the wintry storms of snow and rain are raging. This sparrow flies swiftly in by one door of the hall, and out through another. While he is inside he is safe, from the winter storms; but after a few moments of comfort, he vanishes from sight into the darkness whence he came. Similarly, man appears on earth for a little while, but we know nothing of what went before this life, and what follows. Therefore if this new teaching can reveal any more certain knowledge, it seems only right that we should follow it." On the strength of that persuasion the king and the whole of Northumbria accepted Christianity.[1]

That basic pattern, of following the king's example, and command, seems to have been universal in the conversion of northern Europe in the latter part of the first Christian millennium. Charlemagne is perhaps the most powerful example, in more senses than one. The popes and bishops seemed to have accepted such mass conversions without any misgivings, and after the lapse of so many centuries, it is difficult for us to draw any firm conclusions, as to individuals' sincerity. In the long term, and in the cultural sphere, it was certainly effective in producing the remarkably rich homogeneous Christian culture of mediaeval Europe.

In trying to understand the attitude to religion displayed by teenagers and young adults in the 21st century, we should bear in mind that the period in which St. Bede wrote his description of the bird flying through the king's banqueting hall, was a time when the mental framework of the whole population was culturally religious. It governed their outlook on everything, including the weather! As I noted above, and I repeat now, to serious minded people in such societies, the Christian vision of God would have been much more satisfying than the lives and legends about pagan deities, such as Thor, Wodin, and other inhabitants of the Teutonic pantheon. Yet those considerations are irrelevant today.

However, in the modern world of universal education, freedom of speech, democratic government, and every other expression of autonomy, such paternalistic methods are useless. I use the word 'paternalistic' advisedly. Neither heads of state, nor parents, nor teachers or priests can control the religious choices of the children in their care. Before the modern period, when children still followed the pattern of their parents' lives, such a decision could be made gradually over the years. Perhaps first holy communion or confirmation would provide a non-dramatic opportunity to affirm their faith in God. Or they might have conformed uncritically to religious practices throughout their lives, without any deep convictions. One serious consideration must be borne in mind here, namely that in the first decade of the 20th century, the age of first holy communion was reduced from about fifteen to about five or six. That innovation was problematical. What was even more complicated was that the first confession was made obligatory before the eucharist. One cannot help reflecting, that in the third century the sacrament of Penance was given only once in a lifetime, and that was for really serious sins, such as murder, adultery, or apostasy. Frequent confession for children as young as six, carries with it a very real danger of trivializing the sacrament, and that attitude could well remain with them into adult life.

Returning to the present time, I think that it is fair to say, that adolescents will cease to attend mass because they always found its language and underlying ideas too difficult to understand and hence boring. At about the age of 15 or 16, their parents will realise that to compel them to attend, does more harm than good. So they allow them to remain at home, in the knowledge that further disciplinary pressure will merely drive them further away psychologically, by introducing a measure of resentment into their coming to church under duress.

By that time in their lives, many young people will look at the various Churches (and I am particularly concerned with Catholicism), and see nothing relevant or helpful in those Churches' activities and programmes. The sufferings of the sick and the poor are catered for effectively, by the National Health Service, and other provisions of the welfare state. Workers' rights are safeguarded by the Trades Union movement. As for warfare, the Church has done nothing to abolish it, nor to ameliorate its cruelties. In the two world wars of the 20th century, the Catholic hierarchies of France, Germany, Austria, Italy, the United States, and England tacitly supported the military policies of their respective nations. There was no protest from the bishops in Germany about the extermination of the Jews, or about the testing of atomic bombs on civilian targets from the American bishops. Likewise, the indiscriminate night bombing of the residential areas of large cities like Hamburg or Dresden drew no censure from the English bishops.

The English theologian, John McDade spoke about the problem in the 2018 conference of the Catholic Theological Association of Great Britain. He stated: 'The consensus among the young people whom I have taught in courses dealing with the tension between the religious and secular identities is that formal religious practice is being replaced by personally focussed quasi-religiosity that never issues in social expression. Nor does this mutated form of religious identity take seriously the demands of justice and the rights of the poor... The divine is occluded; artificiality rules; celebrity worship pervades all forms of social communication and religion is banished to 'uncivilized' lands: a dark vision indeed, but not without its truths'.[2]

Some readers may find this description of adolescents' attitudes rather too simplistic. I am aware that it is a generalisation, but I would ask my critics to reflect on just what does Catholicism have to offer them, to counterbalance the disgraceful scandals of sexual abuse of children by priests, which has been exposed since the beginning of this century. I will have much more to say about all these issues in subsequent chapters.

To make the Mass more intelligible, many parishes organise alternative religious activities for young children, in another room during the first part of the liturgy, and bring them back to join their parents after the sermon. Unfortunately that is point at which the eucharist becomes really difficult for a child to understand. Basically, that part of the mass is a symbolic re-enactment of the Last Supper, which in turn was based on the Jewish Passover Supper, which commemorated symbolically the first deliverance of God's people from the evil of slavery. The Christian eucharist, gives to that supper meal the extra dimension, that it commemorates the crucifixion and resurrection of Jesus, which brought about the definitive deliverance of the whole human race from moral evil. In other words, it is an amalgamation of gigantic historical and theological realities, couched in language which must be difficult in order to do justice to those mysteries.

Then there is the sermon. While the children of primary school age were being given an informal and relaxed lesson about God and religion, their older brothers and sisters were still in the church with their parents. For them the experience consisted of listening to three passages from the bible, followed by the sermon. Modern research has shown that a verbal monologue with no opportunity for questions, or discussion, is the least effective way of communicating ideals, or arousing enthusiasm. Most church-goers will agree that most of the sermons that they have heard are boring. In antiquity, and in parts of Africa where most people are still illiterate, sermons are popular. The problem in England, for example, is that little care in the seminaries is devoted to the difficult task of how to write a satisfactory sermon. Priests who can perform it are very rare. So perhaps the best advice to the majority is to keep it short; which is almost a counsel of despair. To put it briefly, it is highly probable that the older children who stayed in church with their parents, will have been bored even by the first part of the Mass.

Although the weekly Mass presents serious problems of communication in conveying religious values and conviction to children, there has been another sphere of opportunity, to which the Church has devoted considerable energy, namely education. Education for all but a tiny elite, became feasible some years after the invention of printing, since this discovery heralded the time when the price of books would be within the purchasing power of skilled artisans. In the Catholic Church that opportunity was grasped positively by the creation of religious orders of men and women who devoted their lives to the work of educating children free of charge.

In the 19th century progressive nations like France and Germany introduced universal, free, and obligatory education for all children. The governments accepted the responsibility for financing the vast scheme, out of tax revenues. Initially it was only for a few years, to ensure that all future citizens could read, write, and cope with simple mathematical calculations. The reason for this was that the industrial revolution, and the increasing use of machines required elementary education so that the workers could cope with the machines.

In Great Britain the establishment of free universal elementary education had to cope with a problem of having so many different denominations. Church leaders realised that in country villages there would be only one school, and whichever Church controlled the school would have an overpowering influence on the religious attitudes of all the young people, in that village. Eventually, in the second half of the 19th century, various compromises were effected, and universal elementary education was established. Religious susceptibilities were respected and even the small Catholic minority secured the legal right to control Catholic elementary schools, which were largely financed out of tax payers' money. Within the sociological framework of the times it was a reasonably satisfactory arrangement. However there was a danger that children would accept the religious programme at a cultural level, and the necessity of their free and deliberate commitment to the Catholic faith was overlooked. At one well known boarding school, at a later date, an intelligent boy recounted to me what one of the monks had said in an R.E. class, "We do believe this boys, don't we". The young man in question did believe it, but he was sufficiently sensitive to realise that the monk who was teaching them, was not entitled to take that for granted.

Since the introduction of universal schooling, the Catholic Church in Great Britain has deployed more money and human resources into education, than to any other branch of its activities. It is therefore extremely important to remember that children should not gain the impression that Catholicism is not just a school subject, which can be left behind with geography and algebra when they leave school.

In a still wider context it is also important to try asses the success or failure of the whole Catholic schools' enterprise since about 1870, when it was possible, for the first time in history, for practically every Catholic child to attend a Catholic school. Some exceptions were inevitable, for example children who lived in remote rural areas, where there was insufficient concentration of Catholic families to constitute a quorum for even a small Catholic school. It is sad to have to admit it, but there has never been a satisfactory evaluation of the success rate of Catholic schools in ensuring that their pupils keep the faith into adult years. This is all the more surprising as for the last few decades the purely cultural achievements of the schools have been inspected, monitored, and assessed ad nauseam. Results in the public exams like GCSE are pored over in the press and discussed at length. Some educationalists argue that the competitive effect of all this publicised evaluation puts pressure on the schools to educate their pupils towards exam results, rather than to the overall enrichment of their minds. Doubtless debates over the balance will continue in the future, but one thing is clear. Although the development of children's minds cannot be measured like their height and weight over the years, some valuable information can be deduced about their intellectual progress. Similarly in the realm of religion, the degree of their conviction is even harder to asses, but there are significant markers which can indicate the general orientation of their loyalty or hostility towards the Church and its spiritual message.

In the absence of the Church authorities' conducting any systematic evaluation of the schools' spiritual influence on their pupils, one has to rely on anecdotal evidence. As an approximative assessment, it would seem that up to the time of the World War II, the majority of pupils from Catholic schools, maintained the minimum of Catholic practice in adult years. After that war, there were far reaching social and psychological changes in British society. Universal adult suffrage was firmly embedded in political life, freedom of speech was spreading into every area of life, including criticism of the Royal Family and the Churches. Materially, people had a large measure of financial and other security, such as legal protection against unfair dismissal, and peace of mind about doctors' bills, thanks to the N.H.S. In short, life for the majority was no long dominated by constant anxieties about poverty, ill health, or homelessness. In this more relaxed frame of mind, peoples' attitudes to Church authority became more relaxed too, and from the post- war years onwards, there are a variety of indications that increasing numbers of pupils from Catholic schools could no longer be described as practising Catholics.

I noted above that no official surveys have ever been conducted at the instigation of the bishops. However there are other sources of information. Prof M. Bullivant has conducted painstaking research in recent years. I have quoted from his book *Mass Exodus* in the Introduction. During World War II, chaplains to the forces were supplied with the religious denomination of all new recruits, which was a routine question in those days, like next of kin, in case they should they be killed. It soon became apparent to the Catholic chaplains that approximately 10% of the servicemen were Catholics. As the population was approximately 50 million at that time, it meant that there were five million Catholics living in Great Britain at that period. That figure was far and above what anyone had imagined. The implication was that vast numbers of those five million Catholics were no longer active in their religion. Had the Catholic schools failed vast numbers of their pupils?

Similar conclusions can be deduced from other sources, such as numbers published in the statistical section of the national Catholic Directories year by year. For example, baptisms are recorded with great care in every parish register, and the national totals were published year by year. Confirmations are also recorded carefully, but as the bishops' visitations were not conducted on a regular basis, it was difficult to make an accurate comparison as to how many of the baptised children received confirmation ten or eleven years later. In spite of such limitations, and making due allowance for families moving from the parish where their children were christened, there was a gap of about one third. That is to say, only about two thirds of baptised children received confirmation ten or eleven years later. It was possible to glean a similar picture from the Registrar General's Statistics of Marriages, since the registrar was present at all Church marriages, and the denomination of the religious element was duly noted. In the decades after World War II there was a steady decline in the number of marriages nationwide, which were accompanied by a Catholic religious ceremony.

In addition to these crude large-scale indicators, there is a wealth of anecdotal evidence. I will cite just a few typical examples. At one period of my life I lodged for a year in the Catholic chaplaincy of a well-known university. Every week day I celebrated the early morning mass at 7.30. Not many students came, but two young men were there every day. Both of them were the former pupils of non-Catholic schools. At another period of my life I was a chaplain at another large university. Among our most loyal supporters were two young men who had been pupils at Catholic schools immediately before coming to university. One was at a boarding school and the other was at a day school. Both of them informed me, on different occasions, that during their last two years at school they were the only ones in their respective classes who were still practising Catholics. All the rest of their immediate contemporaries had ceased to attend regular mass on Sundays. This ties in with the situation in the second decade of the new millennium, which is the title of this chapter, namely that widespread anecdotal evidence indicates that young people in vast numbers are giving up on Catholic practice.

The Quest for a Relevant Presentation of Catholicism

So, how should we present Catholicism to children as a vital influence in their lives, as they grow towards of adulthood and the fulfilment of their personalities.

31

Quite simply it could be presented to children as an international community, whose bond of worldwide unity is based on our belief system, and not any other political or commercial ties. The objectives of this community are to be an effective opposition and practical remedy, to injustice and other forms of wickedness in the world, with a view to overcoming evil altogether.

That description needs some careful unpacking and elucidation. Children from about the age of 12 onwards have many ways of discovering the world's wickedness, namely TV, radio, mobile phones, newspapers, in addition to history classes at school. They are sensitive to issues of justice and fairness. While confining my narrative to Great Britain, they do not have to be exceptionally clever to become aware of evils like knife crime in big cities, the poverty of people who are unemployed, which is often compounded by their being evicted from their homes by ruthless landlords if they cannot pay the rent. At the same time they can hardly fail to be aware of the sickening inequalities of wealth. How is it that some people are exorbitantly rich in the midst of all this poverty, and seem to be getting richer every day. Before long they will become aware that much of this is produced by grossly unfair government policies, such as the refusal to increase taxes on rich people, for fear of losing their political support at the next election.

With a basic political and social awareness, such as I have sketched above, it would not require undue expectations for them to be educated to see that the injustices are mostly created by insensitive, biased or downright wicked decisions by people in power. In other words, the root causes are dependent of free choices, i.e. morality. This outlook will undoubtedly be fortified if they have some sort of experience of warfare. Television coverage of the long drawn-out civil war in Syria will surely make an impression on the minds of adolescents. They will have seen pictures of children who have been killed or maimed, by the violence of political leaders who thirst for power, and who can rely on the cruelty of soldiers to help them achieve it.

The practical question is, how do we translate the kind of awareness that I have outlined above, into religious commitment? It is a two-stage process, which was elaborated by Liberation theologians, mostly in Latin America, after the Second Vatican Council. What one might call the background orientation of mind and attitudes to life, is that sincere Christians (including Catholics) must be fully committed to the political struggle for social justice. This is of particular relevance in all free democratic nations, enjoying universal suffrage. In every city in this country, all adolescents will have seen impoverished people sleeping on the streets. The first stage of conscientization as formulated by the Liberation theologians, is to discern whether such occurrences should be regarded as normal, or if they are aberrations in human affairs. In the example above, the precise cause is that for more than ten years central government has not built a sufficient number of council houses or flats. It has been a simple political decision by a government that does not want to alienate the support of rich people by raising taxes.

The second stage of conscientization is to bring young people to the realisation that all important political decisions entail moral choices, and morality must be based on religion. Common sense and ordinary decency are just not strong enough to sustain the generosity and hard work needed to pressurize the politicians to pursue policies of justice, rather than short term decisions which will favour their own continued grasp on power, which will be directed to their personal advantage. In other words, all Christian Churches, in a democratic nation like Great Britain, must be fully involved in the political process, to ensure that religious values are brought into the political debates, and programmes.

Then comes the most delicate decision of all, in the life of an adolescent. How, when, and in what circumstances, do we convince an adolescent to give his or her personal commitment to a Church which will promote the cause of social justice.

We can learn something from the different staging posts in the ordinary life of children, and discern how those turning points are negotiated. For example, at the age of five children will have been prepared by their parents that they will leave home every day to go to an exciting place called a school, where they will be guided to interesting and enjoyable activities, and meet other children to make new friends. The vast majority of them make this separation from the security of home, quite effortlessly.

At about the age of 14, they will become aware that their years at school are drawing to a close, and they must decide on what to do at the next stage of their lives. This imminent and challenging change provides the parents with a period of painless and unselfconscious discussions about their future careers. The young people realise that the ultimate decision is their responsibility, and that school and parents will give them a great deal of positive help in making that choice. For example, do they want to start work right away, and in that case what sort of career will suite their temperament and abilities? Also in that situation how do they find, for example, a relevant apprenticeship? or a job into which they can enter right away without a lengthy training. On the other hand do they feel the inclination to carry on with further study at university, possibly because they really enjoy expanding their knowledge, and because it will help them to find satisfying and well paid jobs. In that case, which university offers an attractive programme for the area of study, which interests the young person.

Sadly, in the field of religion, none of the Christian Churches have devised what might be called a rite of passage, which contains a programme of what choices the young person might make, about the definitive adoption of religion into his or her life. This is all the more regrettable because theologically infant baptism demands it at some time in early adult years.

Fortunately, there is one ready-made solution at hand, in the bible, although the Church has never made use of it. I refer to the annual Passover supper of Jewish families. It was initiated about 3000 years ago by the command of Moses, when the Israelite people were escaping from Egypt. The details are laid out clearly in the Book of Exodus (chapter 12: vv. 1-18). From that first enactment right up to the present day, Jewish families all over the world, commemorate that historic event, by the same ritual supper in the spring, (near the equinox), and it is the high point of the Jewish liturgical year. As far as young people are concerned, there is one really significant point in the celebrations. One of the young children, who is old enough to understand it, asks the time-honoured question, "Why is this night different from all other nights?" At that point the parents explain the history behind the Passover night, and their ancestors' escape from slavery, so that they could become a free people, worshipping the one true God in the promised land.

With careful reflection, something similar could easily be worked out for Catholic use, on the night between Good Friday and the morning of Holy Saturday. The fixed elements would have to be copied from the Jewish practice. (Obviously in these ecumenical times, it would be a courtesy to our spiritual cousins, to ask their agreement for our copying such an important institution from their tradition). That is to say, the whole event would take place in the home, and not in church. It would be organised and led by the parents and not the clergy. In addition to the serious religious question and its answer, the meal should be a relaxed and celebratory occasion, similar to a Christmas dinner, and there should be presents too. Easter eggs are the obvious essential gifts, others could be given as well. The theological core of this relaxed and homely gathering would be the parents' answer to the child's question as to why this night is different from all other nights. The explanation would have to take in the crucifixion and resurrection of Jesus. It is for the parents to work out how much detail, and how deep the explanation should be, since they know best how much "theology" their own children could cope with. As the years go by, such explanations could become steadily more sophisticated, in relation to the children's intellectual and emotional development.

Some parents would find this kind of instruction extremely difficult, especially if their own religious education had been uninspiring. In that case other parents, or the clergy could give them guidance. It would be a useful educational activity for a parish, to organise informal discussion groups for parents precisely to help them with this task. However, it must be stressed time and time again, that the priests and other "experts" must not supplant the parents, in this unique responsibility, in relation to their own children. In some form or other they must be guided into explaining to their children how the heroic death of Jesus and his rising from the dead were instrumental in producing reconciliation with God the Father, from which all the spiritual richness of Christianity develops.

An annual gathering such as I have described, perhaps with grandparents present too, could provide a focus for a child, or young adult's embracing faith as a personal responsibility. Above all, it would avoid the pitfalls of an obviously contrived artificial dialogue, such as is sometimes necessary for parents to engage with their children over disciplinary measures, if for example, they might have seen their children smoking.

If and when children were to express a serious desire to embrace Catholicism, then some carefully planned discussion groups could well be organised for them in the larger community of a parish. Such meetings should not be designated as classes, or instruction, but they must be in the form of open-ended relatively informal discussion groups.

It seems to me that measures such as I have outlined in the preceding paragraphs, would have the best chance of enabling young people to affirm the assurances made on their behalf by their godparents, at their christening as infants. In this way they could adopt adult membership of the Church, by their own free choice and decision. I realise that the scheme, which I have outlined briefly in the preceding paragraphs, could be "fine-tuned" or modified with other details. Nevertheless, I wish to repeat that some kind of ceremony, like the one that I have sketched out, is absolutely essential, if the young person is to accept responsibility for his or her future religious development. It does not happen automatically even in the families of the most strongly committed Catholic parents.

CHAPTER TWO

CATHOLICISM'S LOST OPPORTUNITIES

Abolition or Toleration of Widespread Injustices

I concluded the previous chapter describing a scenario in which young people could pledge loyalty to Christ and his message, in the context of Catholicism.

The time has now come to outline the positive ideals of the Christian proclamation. The practical implementation of these ideals should form the day-to-day tasks, of the working life of the Catholic Church. In the course of this chapter, I hope that it will become clear that the Christian contribution to the world's well-being is essential, because no other organisation has a sufficiently comprehensive vision of reality, or the motivation which is strong enough to achieve it.

In this chapter I will outline some of the worst cruelties and injustices of the human race, in such a way as to show how they are all motivated by perverted moral decisions. That being so, the remedy must also be in the area of enlightened moral choices, and not varieties of self-interest. That is where the Catholic Church has a great opportunity to serve the legitimate expectations of the human race for an enriched life, rather than a constant struggle against exploitation. For centuries this area has been neglected by the Church authorities, principally the Roman Curia. If the Catholic Church could re-enter this world, entailing full participation in politics and social issues, its moral and spiritual remedies would be obvious, and could persuade doubting youngsters that active membership of such a Church is a worthwhile enrichment of their lives.

To illustrate this statement in a practical fashion, I will draw attention first of all to the process by which the abolition of slavery was accomplished. That achievement can serve as a case study for the way in which other gigantic injustices to the human race could also be remedied. The eradication of slavery has been described by one of the most famous rationalists (Lecky), as one of the few really noble achievements of the human race.

The institution of slavery can be traced back to the beginnings of recorded history, in many societies. As is well known, it was so widely accepted, that Aristotle regarded it as natural. The practice of slavery took a significant turn for the worse, when the element of trade became predominant in the whole process. That development occurred soon after the European explorers discovered America, and set about exploiting its potential wealth.

At about the same time as that development took place, a number of high-minded reformers came to the conclusion that the institution itself was intrinsically bad, and required abolition. As far as the Christian programme is concerned, the abolition can be divided into four stages, namely, amelioration, protest, enablement, and institutional (legal) change.

The first stage exemplifies authentic Christian charity. It would not have produced the abolition of the system without the other three stages. But those three stages would not have succeeded without the strong motivation of charity which was exemplified in the lives of those who sought to mitigate the hardships endured by the slaves.

The cultivation of sugar cane was one of the earliest of the activities which the colonists adopted in central America. The finished product was brought back to Europe and sold for such high prices that the trade became immensely profitable to those who owned the plantations. However the Europeans found the climate of the Caribbean islands too hot and humid for them to do the manual work on the plantations. Accordingly they imported African slaves to carry out the exhausting labour.

The process soon became systematised on a notorious three-stage journey. In the first section, ships set out from the western seaboard of Europe, (Liverpool, Bristol, Brest, Lisbon, Seville, Cadiz, were all involved, as well as many other smaller ports). It is disedifying, but undeniable, that the Catholic nations had the largest share of that trade, with Portugal topping the list. According to recent research, between the years 1440 and 1870, Portugese ships made 30,000 journeys taking 4,650,000 slaves from Africa to America. In the same period, ships from France and Spain made approximately 4,000 voyages each, carrying a total of nearly 3,000,000 slaves. In that period British ships made approximately 12,000 voyages transporting 2,600,000 slaves. In total it has been calculated that approximately 11,000,000 human beings were transported across the Atlantic, and sold into lifelong slavery. These statistics are taken from the indispensable modern study by Hugh Thomas, *The Slave Trade.*[1]

On the outward bound journey the ships carried cargoes of cheap trinkets like glass beads, small metal boxes, which were manufactured in Europe, but not in Africa. So they could be exchanged profitably for prisoners of war, who would be purchased just like chattels. The transactions were carried out in places now bearing the names of Senegal, Liberia, Ghana, Nigeria, and the Gulf of Guinea in general. Since these regions had a climate similar to that of the Caribbean, the traders calculated that the prisoners whom they were purchasing, could cope with the hard manual labour in the Caribbean, which was too taxing for the Europeans. If the local African rulers had not produced a sufficient number of prisoners of war to fill their ships, they would send out their own raiding parties, to capture their own prisoners.

The second stage of the journey was to sail westwards across the Atlantic to the Caribbean, where they would discharge their human cargoes in the slave markets of the islands and the mainland, such as Colombia and Mexico. That second stage of the journey was the cruellest, as the slaves were manacled to prevent mutiny, and their allocations of food and water were the very minimum to keep them alive, and not to eat into the traders' profits unnecessarily. In the course of the voyage across the Atlantic, their conditions were so harsh that many of them died, and the survivors arrived at their destinations in a state of exhaustion, and often seriously ill as well.

It was at their ports of disembarkation that some committed Christians tried to help them physically, and spiritually. One of the most famous was the Jesuit missionary priest St. Peter Claver, who was based at Cartagena in Colombia. He had been ordained as a priest in that city in 1615, and worked there among the slaves, until his death in 1654. When the slave ships arrived in port, he tended the wounds and the illnesses of the new arrivals, and procured reasonably adequate food for them. His devotion to their spiritual well-being extended to his accompanying condemned men to the gallows. His reputation was so highly respected that at his death, the Jesuit house where he lived was literally invaded by hundreds of his devotees, desperate for just one more glimpse of the man, who had given them the assurance that they had not been exploited by the whole human race.

His life-long work of charity was literally heroic, but without being cynical one has to be realistic, and bear in mind its limitations. The cruel trade continued unabated. From one point of view Claver made them ready for work on the plantations. The root of the evil had not been eradicated.

The second stage in the process of abolition was that of protest, which is significantly different from theological repudiation. During the period when the slave trade went into "top gear" (if one may describe it thus), several theologians and church leaders expressed disquiet. The first such criticism came from the pen of the Dominican theologian de Soto, who wrote a book against slavery in 1557. In 1569 another Dominican, Tomas de Mercado, published a further book against the practice, drawing on his own experiences in Mexico. In 1639 Pope Urban VIII issued an encyclical letter against slavery, and in the following century Pope Benedict XIV also condemned it.[1] None of those theological criticisms were backed up by practical measures, nor did they inspire, any kind of realistic solution.

A different kind of protest, authentic Christian protest, can be traced to roughly the same period and locality as the work of Peter Claver. The term protest speaks for itself, and it is a necessary stance to be adopted in circumstances where practical abolition of a social evil is impossible for the present time. It is one of the manifestations of Christian witness to the truth. If anyone should undervalue that activity, they would do well to reflect on Christ's words when he was being interrogated by Pilate: "For this I was born, and for this I have come into the world, to bear witness to the truth." (John 18: 27). It is the opposite of silent distress, shading off into supine acquiescence, which can so easily lead into co-operation, as was sadly the case in the Nazis' campaign of extermination of the Jews in the Second World War. That abominable process would not have been possible without the co-operation, in Germany and the occupied countries, of thousands of nominal Catholic and Protestant policemen and soldiers.

The inspiring genius of this kind of protest was the famous Dominican friar Bartolomé de las Casas.[2] His contact with the slave trade extended back to the very beginnings of the colonization of America. He was born in Seville in 1484 and a few years later, his father and one of his uncles accompanied Columbus on his second voyage to the Carribean. In 1502 Bartolomé himself went to Haiti as a soldier. He also served in the invasion of Cuba, and like so many other soldiers he was rewarded with a grant of land, in what was known as the *encomienda* system. The natives who were living on the land which the colonizers received, were obliged to work for their Spanish masters without payment. It was not the total form of slavery, because they were not reduced to the level of merchandise, who could be bought and sold. But their loss of freedom and the compulsory unpaid labour constituted a serious injustice. Bartolomé himself underwent a profound spiritual conversion during this period, culminating in his being ordained a priest, the first ordination in America. He also freed his own natives and resolved to put an end to the system of their enforced labour.

To this end he returned to Spain and spent the next six years writing against the treatment of the natives, and lobbying the King of Spain and his ministers. In 1516 he published his *Memorial de Remedios*, in which he advocated the abolition of the *encomienda* system. In its place he urged that the natives should be paid wages, they should not be allowed to work for their Spanish masters for more than two months a year, and this work should not be too far from their homes. It is interesting to note that at this stage of his career, he supported the use of black slaves as labourers, because he believed that all of them were condemned criminals. At that time enlightened opinion tolerated and even advocated such treatment for criminals. In *Utopia*, Thomas More envisaged that convicts would be put to useful public work rather than remain incarcerated in prison, and therefore be idle.

In 1524 Bartolomé returned to America, and entered the Dominican order in Haiti. After missionary work in

Nicaragua and Mexico, he returned to Spain again in 1540. In 1543 he was back in central America, armed with considerable powers, granted by the central government in Spain. In the same year he became bishop of Chiapa in Mexico.

In 1552 he wrote his famous *Bresvissima Relacion de las Destrucion de las Indias.* This book and his persistent lobbying had the effect of changing the Spanish legislation for the colonies. The New Laws required that the native labourers must be freed from the *encomienda* system and must be paid wages. Bartolomé followed up the new legislation by denying the sacraments to the Spanish settlers, who refused to give their indigenous workers the benefits of the new laws. It was that practical step which differentiated his programme from that of the theoretical writings of the theologians, alluded to above. He could not enforce the law, because he was not a colonial administrator, but he entered the public arena with a practical policy. Sadly the vested interests in the slave trade were immensely strong, and king and his advisors in Spain were too far away for the laws to be enforced realistically.

In 1552, Bartolomé sailed to Spain, yet again, to continue his work of protest. He died at Valladolid in 1556 without ever seeing the end of the system, for the abolition of which, he had devoted the major part of his life.

It is significant that in the last period of his work in America, he also condemned the trade in slaves being imported from Africa. It is also worthwhile noting that five centuries later the Indian reformer Gandhi, adopted a policy, which was essentially the same as Bartolomé's, namely non-violent political protest. Gandhi's success was greatly assisted by the evolved social systems of the twentieth century, namely democratic government in Europe, as well as total freedom of the press, radio, and other media, which shaped public opinion.

The third stage in the abolition of slavery was the process of enablement. The essence of this process was described succinctly, by the famous Brazilian bishop Helder Camara. He stated simply, "If I give a fish to a poor man, he can feed his family for one day. But if I give him a fishing rod, and teach him how to fish, he can feed them all his life. If I enquire into the causes of his poverty, people call me a communist". The gift of one fish was an example of amelioration. Enabling him to catch fish was one stage more effective.

An early example of the application of the principle of enablement to the slave trade, took place in the Quaker community of Philadelphia, in the eighteenth century. That decisive change of policy came about initially by the initiative of one man, John Woolman. He was born at Ranconas in New Jersey, the fourth child in a family of thirteen. As a young man he tried his hand at a variety of jobs, being at one time or another a tailor, shopkeeper, surveyor, and schoolteacher. Eventually he gave up work in order to free himself from the quest for money. His spiritual gifts were manifest, and at the age of 23 the local Quaker community acknowledged in him the gift of 'vocal ministry'. He became an itinerant preacher, speaking out against slavery. With this message he toured the English-speaking colonies of North America. In 1745 he published a book entitled *Considerations on the Keeping of Negroes.* 1758 marked a decisive achievement in his work, because he persuaded the Quaker community of Philadelphia to give freedom to all their slaves. Many other communities were persuaded to do the same. After that he came to England preaching the same message and died in York in 1772. The publication of his journal two years later, caused a considerable stir, and ensured the continued dissemination of his campaign against the institution of slavery.

During this period, namely the latter part of the eighteenth century, it is fair to acknowledge that Christian philanthropists were being supported by influences, coming from the largely French-inspired enlightenment. Their ideas about human rights and equality, associated with Voltaire, Rousseau, Diderot and others, which ultimately unleashed the French Revolution, also influenced peoples' attitude to slavery. Slavery was abolished in France very soon after the revolutionary government took control of the nation. However it is difficult to estimate what effect this had in England, on account of the long war against revolutionary France, which engendered in this country an antipathy towards anything French.

The anti-slavery movement in England continued to be inspired almost exclusively by Christian principles. Moreover it is useful to reflect on the basic Christian influences on the principles of the Enlightenment. During a lull in hostilities in the English civil war, Cromwell's soldiers were discussing similar issues in the well documented debates in Putney parish church. They discussed topics such as the equality of all people before the law, and the real source of political authority (not force). For the soldiers in the Parliamentarian army, all of those issues drew their authority from the New Testament. It is a subject which merits further research. Innovative political reforms sometimes retain more of the former systems which they replaced, without realising it.

The fourth stage in the implementation of the practice of charity is that of structural or institutional change, which is mainly the legal alteration of practices or organisations, enshrined in custom or law, which produce injustices. The abolition of the slave trade, and thence the institution of slavery itself is the classical example of this stage of implementing charity into the life of nations or large institutions. It could give rise to the objection that compulsion destroys the freedom of virtue, in the same way that paying taxes under threat of legal penalties, nullifies the charity in the handing over of money which the government will devote to running hospitals. The answer to that objection is that in some situations compulsion has to accompany persuasion, according to the circumstances of the crisis in question. If the organisers of the slave trade could not be persuaded to relinquish their institutionalised injustice, then it would not be an act of virtue for good people to refrain from seeking the legal suppression of their infamous trade. From another perspective, one could say that this fourth stage (institutional change) is the most complete act of charity to poor, or victimised people, since it removes the causes of their poverty.

Until quite modern times, with the advent of economics and sociology as sciences, people simply did not understand the complex causal processes which produced wealth and poverty. They realised that hard work sometimes made a person rich, and they also adopted an unsympathetic attitude to idleness, which was regarded as morally reprehensible, to which they attached the derogatory label of "sloth". Conservative minded Church leaders have a tendency to fear social change. When food banks are distributing food to starving families, high ranking ecclesiastics do not feel threatened. But if the causes of poverty are discussed they feel uneasy. Possibly the connection with Marxism has something to do with it. In his *Theses on Feuerbach,* Marx published his famous dictum "In the past the philosophers have been at pains to understand the world: the important thing is to change it".[3]

Within the present case study, in England, it was the work of Thomas Clarkson and William Wilberforce that illustrates how this stage was achieved. The two men were almost exact contemporaries, Wilberforce being born in 1759, and Clarkson a year later. Wilberforce was rich and brilliant, and he was confidently expected to attain high office after his election to parliament in 1870, perhaps even the premiership. Clarkson was the son of a rural clergyman, who was also the headmaster of the grammar school in Wisbech in Cambridgeshire. Like Wilberforce he also studied at Cambridge, and he gained a First in mathematics. More significant for his future labours, was his winning a university prize for an essay entitled 'Is it right to enslave men against their will'. On the way to London in 1785, to arrange for the publication of the essay, he underwent a profound religious experience. It was so clearly etched on his mind, that he was able to describe it as having taken place on the road near Ware in Hertfordshire. It was so powerful that he abandoned his original intention of following his father into the ranks of the clergy but resolved to devote his life to the abolition of slavery. Wilberforce experienced a similar religious conversion while on holiday in France, also in 1785. Thereafter he changed his manner or life, devoting the early hours of each morning to prayer and study, and deliberately looking for a good purpose to which he could devote his life. Providentially the opening was provided for him, when the Committee for the Effecting of the Abolition of the Slave Trade invited him to become their parliamentary representative.

Thenceforth the work of both men was characterised by a combination of disinterested love, and hard-headed realism. Clarkson toured the seaports of England collecting evidence from seamen working on slave ships. Eventually he interviewed a total of 20,000 sailors. Wilberforce made the all-important practical decision of pursuing a limited objective. He realised that the eradication of slavery was too diffuse an objective. So he persuaded his collaborators to aim for a more restricted, but precise goal, namely the abolition of the trade. He argued that once this had been achieved, the other ramifications of the practice would inevitably collapse.

Needless to say, the campaign stirred up powerful opposition from many influential people, who had vested interest in the trade itself, and the indirect benefits of profits on the merchandise, which the slaves produced. It is surprising how many good people had remained blind to the role of slavery in the apparently innocent items of trade, in sugar for example.

In 1798 Wilberforce put before Parliament a bill for the abolition of the slave trade. It was defeated. Opposition came from many quarters. For example, in1791, Colonel

Tarleton, one of the M.P.'s for Liverpool, stated in Parliament that the abolition of the trade would bring an end to the work of 5,500 sailors and 160 ships, bringing in imports, with an annual value of six million pounds (at values then current). Even allowing measure of hyperbole, one can understand how commercial interests felt seriously threatened. Threats of other kinds were aimed at Wilberforce and his supporters, who for nearly twenty years were obliged to endure vilification, hostility of all kinds, including death threats, and for Wilberforce himself, the loss of any prospect of promotion in his political career. The social historian Trevelyan was of the opinion that 'Wilberforce could probably have been Pitt's successor as prime minister if he had preferred party to mankind'.[4]

The conduct of those campaigners illustrates the virtue of 'patient endurance' which is perhaps the best translation of *hupomone,* prominent in St. Paul, which has been identified as a specifically Christian virtue.[5]

After several unsuccessful attempts, a bill to abolish the slave trade was passed by Parliament in 1807. Slavery as such, was outlawed in Britain and its colonies in 1833.

The abolition of slavery by legislation, illustrates a well-known principle concerning the competence of governments in general. Namely that governments and their powers, exist to provide for the citizens benefits and safeguards, which they could provide by themselves. In primitive times that meant organising an army to defend the citizens from external invasion, and then law courts so that disputes could be settled without recourse to blood feuds and vendettas between families.

With the passage of time, and the progress of science, the necessity of government interventions has increased. The most striking example within living memory is the establishment of national health services, in wealthy and advanced societies, because scientific medicine is now intrinsically expensive. It is deplorable that the United States, the wealthiest nation in the world, does not have such an institution. This means that only rich people can enjoy adequate medical care, while poor people die of preventable diseases, although all the remedies are available in their own towns. Hilary Clinton and then President Obama attempted to create a state funded nation-wide health service, but they were thwarted by the vested interests of the pharmaceutical industry and insurance companies. The Republican party was bitterly opposed to it, since it would have entailed raising taxes. However, both plans could have succeeded if they had been supported by the Catholic bishops. Catholicism is the largest single religious community in the nation, comprising, in those years, more than 40 million members. The bishops opposed Obama's plan because the scheme included guidance on contraception, and availability of abortion. Their decision was wrong, because no one would have been compelled to take up the availability of those two measures against their consciences. The same applies to the availability of divorce in the majority of nations, including Great Britain.

Is Legislation the Remedy for All Major Evils?

The success of the anti-slavery legislation, and the present impasse over a national health service in the USA, prompts the question as to, what are the capabilities and limitations of legislation, in the abolition of widespread social evils. Moreover, is there a place for personal morality, and if so, how should it be deployed? Should political involvement be a central plank in the programmes of religious communities? Finally, can the good sense of a well-educated society produce the good life?

To clarify this problem, I will draw attention to one of the world's most successful political systems, where religion was not obviously a major influence, namely the culture of the ancient Greek city-states. The visible evidence of their achievements is with us to this day. Their architects had produced the Parthenon in Athens, which is still an object of beauty, even in its semi-ruined state. Their sculptors had created representations of the human body, which were so beautiful that they have not really been improved upon subsequently. Their literary geniuses produced poetry and drama that have scarcely been equalled in later centuries. With democratic government and a rational legal system, they had devised a scheme for the regulation of human conduct, which has not yet been achieved by many nations in the present century. Yet all of that achievement was brought to a halt, largely as a result of warfare. First of all, came the internecine wars of the Greek city-states (the Peloponnesian War). Some centuries later there was the steady progress of Roman imperial expansion, which eventually incorporated Greece into its worldwide empire.

Despite the tragedy of Greece's being subjected to the Roman Empire, their achievements were not forgotten. For two and a half millennia the human race has been in possession of a valid example, of how to establish a just and efficiently functioning society. Yet somehow it has only been implemented in limited regions of the world, and for only a small proportion of that two and a half thousand years. As the philosopher Thomas Hobbes declared in his *Leviathan,* "The lives of most people are short, brutish, and nasty". If this should seem to be an exaggeration, I would invite the reader to consider several recurring patterns of cruelty in our history, and to reflect on where Christianity could have alleviated or abolished them.

The first is the widespread and almost incessant phenomenon of warfare. Humanly speaking, killing is the worst evil that one person can inflict upon another, because it admits of no possible form of restitution. For many people alive in England at the time in which I am writing, warfare may seem somewhat unreal, because for more than seventy years, there has been no war between the major European nations. It is an all-time record, and it must rank as one of the major achievements of the European Union to have brought it about. As far back as one examines the history of this continent, there has never been another period of seventy years duration, which has enjoyed such peace.

However, people in their eighties retain vivid memories of the Second World War, because air raids were so widespread. In addition to the industrial cities, small towns in the country, and even villages were bombed. Those who were children during that war, remember vividly how their parents and grandparents, were still traumatised in the 1930's by the memories of the First World War. Basically, warfare in the whole of the twentieth century had been transformed in its cruelty, by the technical advances of industrialisation. In addition to that, during the Boer War the British invented the concentration camp, in which they imprisoned the women and children of the rural Boer colonies. The men had disappeared into the bush, from which they conducted highly successful guerrilla operations against the much larger British army. Yet they had to return to their farms quite frequently to obtain food, and to recuperate. In those camps, thousands of women and children died as a result of exposure to the elements, inadequate food, and unhygienic living conditions. The British government tried its hardest, but unsuccessfully, to conceal their disgraceful treatment of the civilians.

A few years before 1914, the Ottoman Empire conducted the first genocide of the modern period. They exterminated approximately one million Armenian Christians within their borders. Modern Turkish governments have constantly tried to conceal the truth of that atrocity.

During the war of 1914-18, the front-line conflicts assumed a new level of cruelty and callousness, on account of the increased power of the high- tech weapons such as machine guns, tanks, poison gas, and field guns of greater range and destructive power than ever before. For the infantry it was a process of unmitigated slaughter, which the higher command continued to pursue, in spite of its repeated failures to achieve proportionately worthwhile results.

During the war, in 1917, Pope Benedict XV proposed a peace plan, but it was rejected by the warring nations. Sadly, he had neither the personality nor the prestige to inspire confidence. The reputation of the papacy had suffered irreparable damage in 1773 when Pope Clement XV had suppressed the Jesuits. He yielded to political pressure from the leaders of Spain, Portugal, France and Austria, (Catholic nations!). All the popes in the 19th century opposed the re-unification of Italy because it entailed the loss of the Papal States. Benedict XV's plan stood no chance at all.

The attitude of Church authorities, in all the belligerent nations, and in all the major denominations, was one of pained regret, but unprotesting acquiescence to the policies of their respective governments. Token gestures were adopted from time to time, such as prayers for peace, and food parcels for prisoners of war. There was one edifying exception, namely the Quakers. Their young men refused combat duties, but the Society of Friends arranged with the government that they would operate an ambulance brigade. That unit included stretcher bearers who used to bring back wounded men from where they lay in no-man's land, and carry them back to where the ambulances could convey them back to the field hospitals. In other words, those men faced just as much personal danger as the combat troops, but they were unarmed, and resolved never to kill anyone.

The Second World War witnessed an extension of the mechanised cruelty which had occurred in the first one. This time the carnage included millions of civilians, on account of the development of aircraft, and aerial bombardment. During the first year of hostilities, the British government roundly condemned the Germans for bombing the residential areas of cities such as Warsaw and Rotterdam. Our claim to the moral high ground was short lived. By 1941 the British air force was doing the

same. Daylight raids had proved to be prohibitively
dangerous on account of the efficiency exhibited by
German anti-aircraft fire, and fighter planes. As a result
night bombing was adopted. But once again, to avoid the
anti-aircraft fire the planes had to fly so high, that the
margin of inaccuracy was roughly four miles from hitting
any specific target, like an armaments factory.

By 1943 the bomber planes and the bombs were much
larger, but no more accurate at night. Instead, the RAF
perfected a method of carpet bombing of unbelievably
indiscriminate cruelty. Technically it was described as
creating a fire storm. High explosive and incendiary
bombs were dropped roughly in a circle of about four
miles in diameter. The rising of the hot air in that circular
pattern, created a furnace effect drawing in more air and
fanning the existing flames. Survivors described the force
of the artificially created gale, as being so strong that they
could not remain standing in its path. It was fuelled by the
timber in the houses of closely built city dwellings, and the
fires went out only when everything combustible in the
area had been burned, and all the oxygen had been
consumed as well. People sheltering in their cellars were
asphyxiated in their thousands. Hamburg suffered the
worst effects of that technique. Four such raids were
carried out on successive nights between the 25th and 30th
of July in 1943. According to the most reliable estimate, a
total of between 34,000 and 38,000 civilians were killed.
The acceptance of indiscriminate bombing of civilian
targets reached its horrific logical conclusion with the use
of atomic bombs on the Japanese cities of Nagasaki and
Hiroshima in 1945.

Another refinement of cruelty in that war was the killing of perhaps as many as six million Jews, by the Nazis, drawn from all the countries which they had occupied. After more than seventy years of disclosures of the horrors of that operation, new facts keep coming to light indicating the utter depravity and cruelty displayed by the perpetrators, and the silent acquiescence of untold millions of passive collaborators. For example, in occupied France it is now clear that the Jewish people were arrested and deported to the extermination camps, not by the German SS, but by the French police. One incident, recorded in the journal of Hélène Berr, is almost incomprehensible, on account of its cruelty and cowardice. In 1943 a family of thirteen children had been entrusted to an orphanage, when their parents (being Jewish) disappeared, in order to evade arrest. Months later, a train destined for Auschwitz, needed a few more Jewish people to complete the number of one thousand, which was the standard complement of such trains. The train was scheduled to depart next morning, but the French police simply did not know where to find the necessary extra half dozen Jewish prisoners, at such short notice. However, there was a record of the fact that the children of the couple who had evaded arrest, had been entrusted to a local orphanage. That orphanage was soon traced, and a police inspector was despatched there late at night to arrest the necessary number of children, whose ages ranged from thirteen to five. His words to the director of the orphanage are significant: "Sorry about this, lady. I am just doing my duty". And the children were duly handed over to him to complete the train's requisite quota for the extermination camp![6]

Centuries earlier the Catholic Church had elaborated a reasonably coherent theology of a just war, which had been generally adopted by other Christian Churches after the Reformation. A war was deemed to be morally justifiable, if the cause was just, if all peaceful means had been tried to resolve the dispute, and if the foreseeable loss of life was proportional to the end being pursued. So much for the theory.

The descent into war in 1914 by all the major powers in Europe is a useful case study, because the preliminary negotiations are so well documented. For this section I am mainly dependent on the brilliant study by Christopher Clark, *The Sleepwalkers: How Europe Went to War in 1914.*[7]

As is well known, the immediate cause of the crisis was the assassination of the Archduke Franz Ferdinand, heir to the Austrian throne, at Sarajevo in Serbia, in the summer of 1914. The immediate reaction among all the nations of Europe was of shock, indignation and uncertainty as what might follow. Some high-ranking officers in the Austrian army advocated immediate mobilisation, with a view to making war on Serbia. Quite what such a war might achieve was unclear, since within a few days the Serbian police had arrested all but one of the conspirators. That individual had escaped into Croatia and was beyond the power of the Serbian government. The conspirators who had been arrested were tried in court, condemned and imprisoned.

That situation limited the scope of what an Austrian invasion of Serbia might achieve. Further confusion can be detected in the way the crisis was spoken about. One reads of almost meaningless slogans such as "learning to tolerate Serbian impertinences without resorting to war", and "the final wish for a thorough settling of accounts with Serbia".[8]

At the other extreme there was disquiet at the prospect of provoking Russia to war on behalf of Serbia, since the Russian Emperors regarded themselves as the defenders of the Orthodox Christians in the Balkans, and especially the Slav people. The possibility of Russian military intervention raised the even more serious possibility that France would support Russia, since a treaty existed between those two nations.

The policy which was adopted eventually was an ultimatum to Serbia from the Austrian government, demanding a thorough investigation into the alleged supporters of the conspirators inside Serbia. The ultimatum consisted of ten high-handed directions to the Serbian government as to how the investigation should be conducted. Points 5 and 6 of the ultimatum, demanded that Austrian officials should be allowed into Serbia to supervise the investigations. That requirement was clearly incompatible with Serbia's status as a sovereign State.[9] Not surprisingly Serbia refused the ultimatum. Austria invaded, the various alliances among the European powers clicked into activation, and shortly all the major nations in Europe were involved in the war. The rest is history!

What concerns this study is the fact that the Catholic Church made absolutely no effort to deter the Austrian government from going to war. The same acquiescent silence was the policy of the Catholic bishops in all the other nations swept up into that war.

A similar vacuum of leadership occurred 26 years later. In the summer of 1940, when the French army was on the point of imminent collapse, the Italian government under Mussolini's control, declared war on France. Clearly he wanted to share in the supposed glory. None of the theological conditions for a just war was present, yet not one Italian bishop, from the Bishop of Rome downwards, is known to have protested.

In a slightly different context, the European and American bishops had been presented with an earlier opportunity to protest against war's cruelties, when the terms of the Treaty of Versailles were published in 1919. The financial demands imposed upon Germany were so severe and unreasonable, that in the foreseeable future the nation would have no chance of re-building its economy. Effectively it was an act of vengeful collective robbery. Morally it was so indefensible that the famous economist, Maynard Keynes, resigned from the British Peace Delegation.

In spite of all this, not one single bishops' conference made any public protest. Their collective silence is incomprehensible, particularly as these same episcopal conferences, and the Vatican, have never been reticent about making public pronouncements on matters such as abortion, and birth control. With the passage of the years, it is possible to perceive a depressing connection, between the Church's unwillingness to address important matters in public life, and the declining influence of all Christian Churches, after the First World War. The general public could be forgiven for concluding that they had nothing relevant to say about the urgent issues of everyday life, such as the vengeful nature of the Treaty of Versailles.

Before leaving this brief exposition of the evils of warfare, there is one factor which needs to be discussed, namely, how do governments persuade rational human beings to kill their fellow men? Many years ago, a friend who had served in the British navy during World War Two, recounted to me a conversation that had taken place on the bridge of a battleship where he happened to be present, as a very junior officer, but within earshot of the discussion. The admiral, looking down on the crew working on the deck, asked his fellow officers the question, "Do you think that these men will fight to kill the Germans?" A polite silence ensued, and the admiral continued, "They will fight, if they fear their own side more than the enemy". That seemingly improbable contention was demonstrated beyond doubt by the German army. In order to keep the conscripted soldiers fighting it was necessary to instil in them a greater fear of their own superior officers, than of the enemy. The well-known German author Gunter Grass claimed that in the course of the war, 20,000 German soldiers were court-martialled for alleged cowardice, and sentenced to death.[10] Precise numbers are difficult to find, on account of the chaotic state of Germany in the last months of the war. A recent historian has claimed an even higher number. Andrew Roberts maintained that on the Russian front alone, in the last year of the war, the German military courts condemned 30,000 men to execution for desertion or cowardice. He adds that two thirds of these sentences were carried out.[11] This final component to the cruelty of warfare has received no censure from any Bishops' conference. The silence of the Catholic Church and other Christian Churches implies acquiescence.

The next phenomenon which I would invite my readers to reflect upon in assessing humanity's propensity to evil is akin to warfare, namely colonialism. The pattern has been constant over the whole period of recorded history, namely that militarily powerful nations have invaded and effectively stolen, their weaker neighbours' land, if those neighbours had wealth in raw materials which the plundering neighbour lacked. The most prominent enticements have been minerals, especially precious metals like gold and silver, but also those that have more pedestrian values, like iron ore, coal, and oil. The list of desirables does not stop there. For a nation with a population that is expanding beyond the resources of its own agriculture, good agricultural land and a benign climate have also acted as motives for annexation. In other words, it was a large-scale operation of theft, which was socially acceptable in the estimation of the predatory nations.

The famous voyage of Columbus in 1492 marks the beginning of the modern form of colonialism. In one sense his success was a sheer accident, as is well known. He had set out to find an alternative route to India and other sources of the lucrative spice trade, against the advice of the experts. That is to say, the professional geographers, who knew roughly the circumference of the world, calculated correctly that the size of the ships which were available to him, simply could not carry sufficient fresh water and food for such a lengthy voyage, entailed in sailing westwards from Europe to India. He was saved from disaster, when he chanced upon the islands of the

Caribbean, about one third of the distance to India. This lucky chance inspired other merchant adventurers to set off on similar voyages. In that context modern colonialism was born. The national governments back home in Europe, could not reasonably prohibit them from setting off, but once they had settled so many miles from the country of origin, it was almost impossible for the home governments to control their selfish and violent excesses, in the plundering of the natural resources of the newly discovered lands. The history of the Spanish American colonies bears ample testimony to that situation of practical impotence. The stage was set for exploitation on the largest scale imaginable. Even worse were the situations where the governments of the predatory nations actually initiated the enterprise, and carried it out with the nations' armies and navies.

The actual seizure of the territory required military superiority in organisation and weapons. The Spanish annexation of most of South America was closely connected to their steel armour and weapons, including firearms, and also the domestication of the horse, and its training for warfare. When they confronted societies like the Aztecs and Incas, their possession of firearms and war horses must have been psychologically overwhelming. Initially, firearms must have been perceived as killing by a loud noise. Since horses were not native in the whole of the American continent, their impact must have been even more disorientating. Still worse for the locals must have been when they saw the rider dismount, and reveal himself as a separate living creature. The initial perception as they galloped across open country, must surely have been more like perceiving the centaurs of classical antiquity. Factors such as those can account for the subjugation of vast territories, initially by a small number of invaders.

A similar pattern can be traced in the 19th century scramble for Africa. In the sub-Saharan half of the continent the horse was not known. But worse cruelty resulted from the Europeans' employing long range field guns, and even worse that was the invention of the machine gun. As a result, the whole continent was colonised by the European nations by the end of the 19th century, resembling the Spanish and Portuguese activities three centuries earlier. Being possessed of such military and organisational sophistication, relative to their victims, it seems that the colonists simply disregarded the human rights of the Africans, and in effect, plundered their minerals.

The so-called "white highlands" was another variant on the disregard of the rights of the local inhabitants. It is clear that in British colonies, like Kenya and Northern and Southern Rhodesia, only white people were allowed to own the best agricultural land, known as "the white highlands". The name derived from the skin colour of the possessors, not any natural feature of the landscape! Such was the arrogance of the colonists that no one tried to advance any justification for the practice.

During the 1940's and '50's colonialism came to a relatively rapid ending. Initially it was due to the non-violent activity of Mahatma Gandhi. His achievement is so well known that little need be said here, apart from recalling the distinctive elements of his philosophy. He was determined that he would not lead India to political freedom, along the path of violence. Accordingly, he was the originator of a powerful instrument, that is to say, non-violent protest. His inner conviction is summed up in the remarkable principle which he formulated early in his career, when he was still in South Africa, namely "I am prepared to die for my convictions, but not to kill for them."

In the preceding pages, I have analysed different scenarios in which human beings have exploited one another with irrational greed and cruelty. In the examples which I have described, namely slavery, warfare, and colonialism, a constant pattern is discernible. It is when stronger societies have coveted more than their fair share of the world's natural resources, and if denied acquisition of the extra quotas, they resort to violence. It is a form of collective robbery, but in practice there is nothing like an international police force, which is large enough and strong enough to prevent them carrying out their policies.

What was the role or relevance of the Catholic Church in all this morass of cruelty? The answer is shameful. Apart from a few creative protest actions, the Church in each nation acquiesced meekly to the governments' policies. The Church leaders had completely failed to discharge their duty of prophetic protest. Even if they saw little likelihood of their being listened to by the rulers, their own moral integrity was at stake. It is reasonable to account for this moral lacuna, as one of the consequences of the clergy having become a privileged class. Failures like this may well explain why the young adults of the present day, see little relevance of Catholicism (or other Christian Churches) to their own lives.

The exceptions were the protests by Bartholomé de las Casas against slavery, followed by powerful and effective agitation by Wilberforce and other Christians, whose activities brought an end to that trade. To their credit, the Quakers have been opposed to warfare since their foundation. And that is about the sum total of Christians' activities in this sphere.

Having discussed the motivations, and cruelties of warfare, and other pro-active patterns of injustice, the time has now come to turn our attention to another slightly different, but vast area of heartless cruelty, namely the exploitation of manual workers. Up to the 19th century, it was taken for granted that a farm labourer's work was hard and poorly paid. During the 19th century, advances in technology made industrial production and mining far more productive. This in turn generated higher profits for the owners of the mines and factories, but the crucial moral questions concerning the sharing of those profits with the workers, were completely ignored by those in control.

At the risk of some over-simplification it can be asserted reliably, that initially the owners of the means of production made vast profits on the industrial operations, whereas their workers received payment which was just about sufficient for the food to keep them alive and capable of working. Moreover the workers faced dangers far more serious than those which farm labourers had faced, particularly in the mines. From the middle part of the 19th century there was constant unrest, and strikes by industrial workers, as well as political pressures to extend the parliamentary franchise. It lies outside the scope of this study to pursue those conflicts in detail. With the passage of time, trade unions acquired legal recognition, industrial wages improved somewhat, and the parliamentary franchise was gradually extended to include all adult men. Every step in those developments was bitterly contested by those in control, namely those men who wielded the ultimate power in politics or commerce.

What is depressing for committed Christians is that the organised Churches made so little creative contribution to the improvement of the workers' wages, working conditions, or housing, not to mention political advancement, during the 19th and 20th centuries. There was one laudable exception, namely the Methodists. John Wesley, the founder of the Methodist movement, had always intended that the movement should stay within the ambit of the Anglican Church. However, after his death in 1791, the movement soon became an independent Church. It seems that it was his personality that kept it within the Anglican family. At that early period of Methodism many of the preachers were laymen, many of whom had full time jobs in mines and factories. Those men were extremely influential in the creation and development of Trades Unions. It has been said, and rightly, that Trades Unionism in Great Britain owed more to Methodism than to Marxism.

Sadly, the Catholic Church, along with most other Churches in Britain, did not contribute to the progress of Trades Unions. Personal interventions, like that of Cardinal Manning in the London Dockers' strike of 1889, were conspicuous by their rarity. During the depression of the post war period, Cardinal Bourne declared that it would be sinful for Catholics to take part in the General Strike of 1926. The enduring classical image of industrial protest at that period, was the series of marches by unemployed men from places like Jarrow and Glasgow, walking to London to present their protests about unemployment to Parliament. Early in the 1970's I had the privilege of meeting an elderly man who had taken part in one of those marches. Meals were organised for them along the route, and overnight accommodation was provided in village halls and similar places, but nothing could spare them from the overall discomfort and hunger of the whole exercise, not to mention cold weather and pouring rain. The man who described it to me, declared that they were so constantly close to exhaustion that he "cursed his Maker". I listened to what he said and preserved a genuinely respectful silence. But I thought to myself, where were the clergy and religious orders? Why did none of them walk with those men as a gesture of solidarity? In the terms of Christian morality, it would have been a form of witnessing to the truth. What were the Franciscans doing? I do not wish to be judgemental, but I can only assume that they were sitting in their centrally heated friaries, secure in the knowledge that hot meals would be available in their refectories, as on every other day. I will return to this theme, later in the book, when discussing the harmful effects of the clergy having become a privileged class.

The Churches were not the only organisations at fault. Legislation for a nationwide compulsory minimum wage was mooted in Parliament before the First World War, but not implemented for a century! However a significant improvement in the working and living conditions of manual workers took place after the Second World War, during the time when Attlee's Labour government was creating the National Health Service, and other elements of the welfare state. Those measures are indications of the necessity for enlightened legislation to control the exploitative tendencies of employers, and the shareholders of their companies.

At the start of the 21st century further evidence of excessive greed was revealed, thanks to the researches of various institutions. At the risk of some over simplification, it has become apparent that many of those who direct international commercial organisations, avoid the taxes and other regulations of national governments, and have devised methods to enrich themselves astronomically. I quote from one researcher: "For example, the average pre-tax income of the top 10th of Americans has doubled since 1980, that of the top 1% has more than tripled, and that of the top 0.001% has risen more than sevenfold – even as the average pre-tax income of the bottom segment comprising 117 million Americans has remained static. Globally, over the same period, according to the World Inequality Report, the top 1% captured 27% of the new income, while the bottom segment of humanity, presently more than 3 billion people, saw 12% of it. Across much of the world, the system has been organised, to siphon gains upward, such that fortunes of the world's billionaires grow at a more than double the pace of everyone else's, and the top 10% of humanity have come to hold 85% of the planet's wealth. New data published this week by Oxfam show that the world's 2,200 billionaires grew 12% wealthier in 2018, while the bottom half of humanity got 11% poorer".[12]

All of this prompts the question, Why is it that history has so many examples of exploitation, greed and violence? Why should that be so?

Chapter Two

Writing as a committed Christian, I have no hesitation in tracing the tendency to Original Sin. This factor is rarely spoken of in sermons, and also widely misunderstood. The failure to appreciate it properly, or explain in adequately, is linked to the perfectly reasonable modern reluctance, to accept the former fundamentalist interpretation of the sin of Adam and Eve in the Garden of Eden. Let me assure my readers that the doctrine of original sin is not intrinsically connected to a literal interpretation of the Adam and Eve narrative.

As is well known, the Scriptural basis for the doctrine of original sin was elaborated by St. Paul, principally in his Letter to The Romans, and in that letter chapter 5 has the most succinct account of it. It is also to be seen I Corinthians, 15: 20 ff, and alluded to in Galatians I: 4. Other New Testament writers share Paul's outlook, as for example II Peter 1: 4. It is important to remember that St. Paul's censures on human conduct are always accompanied by the positive remedy, namely Christ's role as the unique, and comprehensive, redeemer of the human race.

The phenomenology of original sin can be presented in a simple scheme. Owing to the influence of original sin, all human beings have an innate tendency to seek far more than our fair share of this world's good things. This comprises not merely material possessions, and sensuous pleasures, but also the pursuit of power, so that we can control the lives of other human beings. If these selfish urges are thwarted we resort to violence to gain our objectives by force. Finally we resort to lies in order to conceal the wickedness to which we have resorted.

The above paragraph explains only the effects of original sin, not its nature. This is complex. One could perhaps suggest that it is rooted in the God given destiny of human beings. That is to say, when this earthly life comes to an end, we are destined for the contemplation of the infinitely good God in heaven, which is the life outside time. I use that choice of words deliberately. Eternity is not a very long time, but a stable present life of constant happiness, which does not diminish, change or come to an end. That is the meaning of being outside time, which is frequently misunderstood. People who have no knowledge of this reward of unlimited satisfaction, which can be anticipated confidently in this present life through prayer, may well seek unlimited satisfaction in less worthy pleasures. Some of these are relatively harmless, like trying to break the land speed record in racing cars. Needless to say, when a given speed record has been broken, the engineers and designers go back to the drawing board to design a yet faster car. St. Augustine epitomised the tendency perfectly in his famous dictum "Thou hast made us for Thyself, O Lord, and our heart is restless until it repose in Thee".[13]

Other substitutes for that restlessness are not so harmless, such as the quest for virtually unlimited wealth, or the pursuit aggressive political power, leading to warfare. Napoleon's career is instructive. How did a junior officer in the army of post-revolutionary France rise to the position of military dictator of the nation, then self-proclaimed emperor, finally as conqueror of most of Europe, culminating in the invasion of Russia. But for what intelligible purpose?

Warfare, discussed above, is a classic example of this descent into violence and deception. Archaeology shows that warfare was endemic to human societies even before written records existed. It has been so constant in our history that some people treat it as a normal expression of human behaviour. The 19th century German military theoretician, von Clausewitz regarded it as an extension of diplomacy. Not everyone evaluates it as a fundamental aberration; such is the power of original sin!

As to the practical relevance of the doctrine of original sin, the well- known Czech theologian, Tomás Halik, has stated: "I consider this doctrine one of Christianity's most realistic and valuable contributions to the philosophy of anthropology, the study of human beings and their nature".[14]

A similar evaluation of human behaviour was expressed by an American historian, of German origin, Fritz Stern. To quote his own words: "Though I lived in National Socialist Germany for only five years,-I have spent the rest of my professional life trying to answer: why and how did the *universal potential for evil* (italics, mine) become an actuality in Germany?"[15]

As the central elements of this doctrine are agreed by all Christian theologians, and the literature on the subject is immense, I will not pursue the matter further, except to remark how perfectly it explains the terrible moral lapses of intelligent human beings.

Another significant indicator of the prevalence of Original Sin, is the modern awareness of climate change and global warming, which is combined with the reluctance of many politicians and business leaders to face up to the realities. Clearly, they fear the wrecking of their political or commercial careers if they adopt realistic measures to curtail the heating of the planet.

During the latter part of the twentieth century, a widespread consensus developed among scientists of all nations about climate change. It is a crisis which may dwarf all the others that I have discussed in this chapter. Namely that our ever-increasing use of fossil fuels to generate energy, was over-heating the planet, on account of the carbon dioxide emissions, which were produced. Early in the twenty first century, a scientist, Jonathan Franzen wrote about it, and the Guardian's reviewer of the book, epitomised its message as, living with despair. I quote "How is it possible to live with despair? If in the wake of last month's horrifying UN report on global warming, you've been asking your-self this question, take some solace (or at least solidarity) from the knowledge that you're not alone". Jonathan Franzen has been grappling with the problem for years, and as the title of his new volume of essays suggests, (*The End of the End of the Earth*), his despair at the state of the planet and our absolute inability (political, psychological, ethical, economic) to save it is, if anything deepening. "I don't have any hope that we can stop the change from coming," he says bluntly at the conclusion of his opening essay, and nothing in the following pages suggests he is anywhere close to changing his mind.[16]

Franzen is not alone. At the time of writing in 2020, other scientists have suggested that the tipping point has already been reached, and that we are now beyond the possibility of reversing it. For example, an article by Prof. Tim

Lenton in the November (2019) issue of the journal *Nature,* raises the possibility that the irreversible tipping point might already have been reached. The warming of the planet in the recent past has produced a thaw in the permafrost in parts of Siberia close to the arctic. The release of vast quantities of methane may fuel other such releases, leading to a cascade.[17]

How can human beings act with such selfishness, short-sightedness and irresponsibility? One concrete example is air travel. It has been calculated that in any one period of 24 hours, globally 100,000 aircraft will have flown journeys of varying distances. In future, air travel will have to be rationed, limiting it strictly to essential government and urgent commercial business. Holiday flights must be abolished. The job losses in the production of aircraft will have to be planned carefully. But holiday makers will have to find other ways of reaching their destinations. In reality, the politicians simply do not have the moral courage to face the rage of their frustrated electors, who would never forgive them. Their political careers would be at an end.

In addition to global warming, there is a parallel problem, not always taken into account by writers are about global warming, namely the exponential increase of the world's population. In the latter part of the 20th century, it became clear to demographers, that the world's population was doubling roughly every thirty years. Theoretically this increase could be limited by smaller families. China achieved this by a draconian policy of commanding merely one child per family.

In the developing world, such as most nations in Africa, families of five or six children are still common. We must not judge them too harshly. In the absence of old age pensions paid out by the State, their large families have traditionally been their only safeguard for security in old age. Allowing for the deaths of infants and adults, before the advent of scientific medicine, it was a reasonable pattern of conduct. Until their own economies are wealthy enough to provide State retirement pensions, it is difficult to see what other course is open to them. Of course, one solution is possible, namely that the richer nations of Europe and North America could pay pensions to people over seventy in those countries. Yet, to be realistic, it is unlikely that the electorates and politicians of the richer countries could rise to that ideal of generosity!

Granted then, that it is a moral problem, similar to slavery, warfare and colonialism, studied earlier in this chapter, it should not surprise us if the remedy should be found in the realm of religion. This is confirmed by the failure of purely humanistic solutions to these very same problems.

These humanistic solutions can be classified roughly into three categories. The first is the hope that education and the progress of science can cure all humanity's problems. Secondly the values of the Enlightenment are put forward: that is to say, the values which have given rise, in the modern world, to such concepts as the equality of all people before the law, equality of the sexes, free speech and democracy in politics. This set of values chimes in with a great deal of common sense and ordinary decency. Thirdly there is Marxism, which has its own perspective and programme for the establishment of a better society.

A brief analysis will indicate the limitation of all these classes of remedies, which claim to have the solution to the evils which have beset the human race, from antiquity up to the present day.

Although education and science have eradicated many diseases and improved the comfort of our lives in many countries, their benefits have not been enjoyed world-wide. Moreover the same processes have made warfare incomparably more cruel, and have paved the way for economic exploitation of poorer people, on a scale that sixteenth century merchant-adventurers could never have dreamed of.

The values of the Enlightenment have indeed yielded great benefits in such areas as the concept of human rights, enshrined in documents like the United Nations Charter, and its Universal Declaration on Human Rights. It does not belittle those achievements if I point out two caveats. Firstly, the majority of the human race do not possess the intellectual capacity or the education, to plan their lives on those laudable principles. It remains something of a theoretical programme. Secondly, we should bear in mind how much it owes to Christianity. Although the leaders of that movement like Voltaire, Rousseau, Diderot, and others were atheists or deists, like many revolutionaries they retained more than they realised of the values of the older regime which they attacked. This can be seen by reference to seventeenth century England. During a lull in the civil war, Cromwell's soldiers were discussing basically the same issues, in their famous debates in Putney parish church. In a thoroughly democratic manner, they were disputing fundamental issues such as the authentic source of political authority, and the practical consequences of acknowledging the basic equality of all men. (Yes, it was about men. Sadly, the equality of women had to wait another two centuries). The only difference between the Parliamentarians' soldiers and the French and German philosophers was that the English Puritans sought the authority for their innovative principles in the New Testament. This connection between Christianity and political thinking in England has been largely ignored, and merits much more research.

Finally, Marxism as a cure for human suffering, has an in-built limitation in practice. That is to say, it deals almost exclusively with economic considerations at the national and international level. It has little to say about personal morality and fulfilment. It is also paradoxical that the first published writings of Karl Marx (when he was a journalist writing for the *Deutsche Jahrbücher* and the *Rheinische Zeitung*) were essays attacking the evils of press censorship.[18] Wherever Marxism has gained power, the press has been censored totally, even in such relatively benign regimes as Cuba. At the risk of some over-simplification, one can say that Marx considered that private possession of land, or the means of production were the sources of social injustice, because it gave too much power to those who were the possessors of land, mines, factories and the like. From this followed the forcible abolition of private property, and its replacement by the State as the universal owner. The intrinsic inefficiency of such a system was demonstrated in the Soviet Union in the 1930's after the nationalisation of all agricultural land. Quite simply it resulted in famine, in the course of which millions of people starved to death. Orlando Figes has commented, "Nobody knows the full human cost of the revolution. By any calculation it was catastrophic. Counting only the deaths from civil war, the terror, famine and disease, it was something in the region of 10 million people".[19]

After the Second World War, the victory of the communists in the Chinese civil war, was followed by just the same pattern. Namely the nationalisation of all farm-land, even the small-holdings of peasant farmers, followed by famines in which millions of people died, until the government reluctantly abandoned the policy. When communism triumphed in North Korea, nationalisation of farm-land was compelled upon the nation, with the same predictable results. In other words, Marxism as a remedy for humanity's ills, has its own built-in weakness.

Significantly it was scrapped as soon as the subjected peoples could throw off the terrifying constraints of the secret police and the gulags, as could be seen all across Eastern Europe and the Soviet Union. It is also worth noting, that in the final period of communist control in the Soviet Union, bitter experience brought about some mitigation. Namely the peasants were allowed to cultivate their own gardens for food. Significantly those small holdings produced approximately one third of the food for the whole nation. They were intrinsically more efficient than the large, state-controlled farms, organised and managed by the central government. The practical lesson which has emerged, is that private property must be controlled, rather than abolished.

So, at this point one must evaluate the claim of religion to be the best remedy for humanity's moral and economic problems. It will not have escaped the readers' notice that the major injustices and cruelties perpetrated within the human race, have been created by bad moral decisions.

The remedies for large scale exploitation in its different forms, sometimes culminating in warfare, cannot be cured by better organisation. Their causes are quite simply moral choices of powerful people, and those among their supporters who hope to benefit from the bad decisions. This points quite naturally to religion as the most likely source of remedies. To keep this book within practicable limits of space, I must confine myself to Christianity, and more particularly to the Catholic Church of which I have been a member for the whole of my life. Writing in the year 2020, I am painfully aware of the disgraceful scandals of the sexual abuse of children by the clergy, and the equally reprehensible attempts of bishops and other superiors to conceal them. My confidence and trust in the ideals of the Church remain unshaken, and I would invite any fair-minded reader to study the New Testament and the documents of the Second Vatican Council. Those are the most ancient and most recent mission statements of the Church, within whose pages are to be found the fundamental principles which can cure all humanity's moral weaknesses. I realise that this is a gigantic claim, but I present it with complete confidence.

I will deal with the above abuses later in the book, in total frankness, without excuses or concealment. But, let it be remembered, all institutions deserve to be judged by their normal performance and not by their abuses.

The capacity of Catholicism to assist in the establishment of morally just societies received a great boost as a result of the Second Vatican Council. Its documents contained such positive and creative insights that they have given rise to other movements, inspired by the Council. One such initiative is generally described as Liberation Theology, but it was not a totally new innovation. The New Testament had prepared the ground hundreds of years ago. In the first part of St. Luke's gospel, we read the well-known prayer *The Benedictus,* which contains the statement, "He swore to Abraham our father to grant us, that free from fear, and saved from the hands of our foes we might serve him in holiness and justice." (Luke 1: 73 – 75).

The basic theological orientation for this movement was set by Jürgen Moltmann. In his *Theology of Hope,* he advanced the crucial insights that grace must not be confined within the soul, but extend to every-day life too. He also declared that theology must not be content solely with interpreting the past, but must concern itself with transforming the present world. Readers will doubtless observe the resemblance to Marx's famous dictum, that philosophers have endeavoured to understand the world, but the important point is to change it. Transforming the world on the basis of Christian principles was the start of Liberation Theology. What made it different from all other branches of theology was that its pioneers set out deliberately to bring their principles into the political arena, by canvassing in elections for candidates who championed Christian principles, for example. The pioneers of that movement were authors such as Gustavo Guttiérez, Leonardo Boff, Paulo Frière, Juan Luis Secundo, and others. Many of their books have been translated into English and they are available in this country, so I will not analyse them here.

With the passing of the years, and as the memory of the Second Vatican Council began to recede, there was a growing hostility to Liberation Theology in the Vatican, who were alarmed by a superficial resemblance to Marxism. They would have done well to recall that in previous successful epochs of the Church's theology, as in patristic times and the high scholasticism of the middle ages, really great theologians had no hesitation in utilising the classical philosophy of Greek pagan culture to elucidate their theology.

However to demonstrate the effectiveness of Liberation theology, it is more relevant to say a few words about the heroic martyrs which the movement engendered. The best known is Oscar Romero, because he was an archbishop, and he was canonised in 2018. After years of delay because of opposition within the Vatican, the process was expedited and completed by the influence of Pope Francis. Oscar Romero was born and bred in the central American republic of El Salvador. It is one of the poorest nations in the world, governed but not served, by a succession of military dictatorships in the latter part of the 20th century. These regimes had the backing of the United States, in spite of the fact that 75,000 of the population were killed by the security forces between 1978 and 1993. When Romero was first appointed as archbishop of the capital city, San Salvador, he was not particularly progressive on social and political matters. However his attitude changed rapidly as he became aware of the cruelties which the government inflicted on the poorest of the population, and upon those whose lives were dedicated to trying to help them, in the political arena. The victims of the government's repression were not arrested and tried in court, they were simply assassinated by the security forces. Such deaths were numerous, and the detailed list can be read on the Oscar Romero web-site. I will mention some high-profile examples. In the 1970's a group of four nuns from the USA were raped and killed. At about the same time a group of six Spanish Jesuits, who taught at the university in San Salvador were shot in their house, together with the woman who was their cook, and the cook's daughter. The fact that foreigners working in the country were targeted is significant of the arrogance of the persecutors. That pattern of government led to indiscriminate violence against their political opponents. It was typical of the regime's cruelty, and it was that which converted Romero to openly public opposition.

One of his last sermons, preached to a packed cathedral, contained an explicit exhortation to the security forces not to shoot their fellow citizens, even if ordered to do so by their superior officers. Shortly after that Romero himself was killed. He was shot on March 24th 1980, while celebrating mass in the chapel of the Divine Providence cancer hospital. Within 20 years, the Anglicans placed his statue among the group of modern martyrs above the main entrance to Westminster Abbey. But canonisation by his own Church had to wait until 2018, on account of opposition to his cause within the Vatican.

Elsewhere in Latin America, similar political/economic policies were pursued by dictatorial governments, and once again the Church was in the forefront of political opposition, based firmly on religious principles. I will describe the work of another American nun, sister Dorothy Stang. In 1966 her congregation had sent her to work as a missionary in a remote part of Brazil. She soon realised that it was pointless to offer the people Christianity as a spiritual enrichment, without working to liberate them from the economic injustices which afflicted them. This took her straight into the political sphere, defending the peasants from the rich landowners who were trying to seize their small farms to make their own large estates even bigger. They employed unscrupulous gun-men to threaten or kill the occupants of those small-holdings.

In 2004 Sister Dorothy travelled to the capital to give evidence to the congressional committee of enquiry, into illegal deforestation of the Amazon region. She knew that she was putting her life at risk, since it was estimated that 90% of the timber from that region had been cut down illegally. In spite of the danger to herself, she returned to her missionary base, after presenting evidence to commission. From that time onwards she began to receive death threats, but she refused to abandon the people and leave for the safety of her home country. On the 14th of February in 2004, she was walking alone to a meeting of local peasant farmers, when two gunmen approached her. She must have known what they intended. She opened the bible which she was carrying and started reading it to them. They shot her six times. Her assassination caused indignation throughout the whole of Brazil. It was a classical, and heroic example of authentic Christian witness.

The next two heroes of Liberation Theology would never have been known to the public, but for the fact that their lives and work were described by a journalist, who had no particular religious axe to grind. George Monbiot described his encounters with them in the following words:- "The only two heroes I have met are both Catholic missionaries. Frei Adolpho, the German I met in the savannahs of north-eastern Brazil, thought when I first knocked on his door that I was a gunman the ranchers had sent for him. Yet he still opened it. With other liberation theologists (sic) in the Catholic Church, he offered the only consistent support to the peasants being attacked by landowners and the government. Joe Haas with whom I stayed, in the forests of West Papua, had spent his life acting as a human shield for the indigenous people of Indonesia, every few months the soldiers threatened to kill him when he prevented them, from murdering his parishioners and grabbing their land. If they did not believe in God, these men would never have undertaken such risks for other people".[20]

Where political and social injustices are so serious that the situation produces martyrs, this surely indicates the importance of religion being involved, as potentially the most effective force for good.

Where the political situation is not quite so brutal, but with a government that is callously indifferent to the plight of poor people, religion still has a role. The English scene since 2010 is just such a situation, and the relative independence of the Churches is a powerful force for change. Justin Welby, the archbishop of Canterbury, discharges this duty admirably, by publicly criticising the government for such policies as universal credit, which actually harms poor people.[21]

Another edifying representative of this attitude was the Anglican priest, Paul Nicholson, (who died in April 2020), who founded the pressure group "Taxpayers against Poverty". Like Welby, he too was able to draw on his experience of a previous career in business. He has been immensely successful in publicly exposing the unjust policies of the Borough of Hackney in London. They had planned to sell off council flats in order to "clear the ground", so that the sites could be sold for spectacular profits to developers who would replace them by luxury flats for wealthy tenants. As a result of his publicity and faultless argumentation, the council were forced to abandon their plans, which would have left hundreds of poor people without homes.

In the twenty first century, in nations that enjoy universal education, free speech, and universal adult suffrage, it is imperative for Churches to involve their communities in the political struggle for social justice. With the passage of time, the main outlines of this struggle have become clear. Human selfishness has found its expression and unifying philosophy in capitalism, and especially capitalism's attitude to profit. It is obvious that all business ventures have to make a profit, or they will collapse. What is uniquely characteristic of capitalism is the desire to *maximise the profit of an enterprise without any restrictions at all.* Its supporters have never formulated it as a conscious element of policy, but it pervades every area of big business. It is justified, sometimes, by vague appeals to "freedom" in democratic societies. However nothing can conceal its true nature when the results are examined. For example, in 2017 in Brazil, just six multimillionaires owned as much wealth as the poorest 100 million people in that country.[22]

Let me repeat once again the explicit and implied message of this chapter. If the Catholic Church is to command any respect in the 21st century it is imperative for its leaders to engage in politics, as I noted earlier in this chapter. This also means that the laity and parochial clergy do the same.

This means party politics. Needless to say, simple common sense will indicate to laity and clergy alike, what issues have a moral dimension, and which of them do not, such as what kind of electric bulbs to install in the streetlights. On the larger issues, such as taxation, and how to distribute that burden, very real moral issues are at stake. In Britain since 2010, when universal credit has increased the hardship for poor people, the really rich have been benefitting from tax breaks.

Similar to the active involvement in politics to ensure that justice is pursued by local and central government, there is also the question of protest where justice is blocked. Like the prophets of the Old Testament, Christians must bear witness to the truth, in public, not just at home. This field entails collaboration with other organisations, like the CND, which organise protests against the real dangers that threaten society at large. At this point I cannot refrain from observing that I have never seen a Catholic bishop at any of the large peace demonstrations in London in the past half-century.

To give another example drawn from the sphere of economics, and relevant to many nations, is the importance of opposing capitalism. This will entail refusing financial support from that quarter, and to pursue policies which will limit its power and influence. Our leaders must also condemn political parties which support capitalism, and which in turn are supported by the money generated by that system. (In Great Britain, at the time of writing, that means the Conservative Party). Otherwise it cannot hope to expect loyalty from conscientious and serious minded people, as well as from exploited workers.

As something of a post-script to this chapter, I feel that it is necessary to add a few words, not to the Church's lost opportunities, but to its own self-inflicted wound. I refer to the fiasco of the birth control encyclical, *Humanae Vitae* promulgated in July 1968. The message was that all forms of artificial birth control were morally wrong. Unfortunately for the authors, (nominally Pope Paul VI), Pope Pius XII had explicitly approved the spacing of pregnancies, making use of the safe period. That is to say, it became apparent in the 1930's that women were fertile for a limited period in each monthly cycle. Confining sex to the infertile periods was a fairly reliable method of limiting a family to a planned number of children. After that was made clear by Pope Pius XII, the logical conclusion was that artificial methods were also morally acceptable, because the artificiality is a morally neutral factor. Within the Church uproar followed, free speech within the Church found its voice, and over the years the ill-fated encyclical was ignored. On the fiftieth anniversary in July 2018, there were no respectful commemorations, just a dignified silence from the Vatican, which said it all.

CHAPTER THREE

DE-CLERICALISING THE CLERGY

The Slow Emergence of Clerical Privilege

The title of this chapter means removing all the elements of a privileged way of life, from those in Holy Orders, which are harmful to the effectiveness of their mission. The very title "Holy Orders" should alert us something suspicious. The Free Churches always refer to that group of full-time professionals as "ministers", which chimes in with the New Testament much more suitably. The word "Order" came straight out of the politico-legal system of the Roman Empire. The most prominent order was that of the Senators. The equestrian ordo was another branch, and the title was bestowed on the Christian ministers during Constantine's reign. Its use in an official document is first attested in the year 395.[1]

It is worth noting that the word "clergy" is already an ominous departure from its original New Testament meaning. The word comes from the Greek word *klerus* signifying the vocation to become a Christian, and not the minority group whose role is to be their leaders, or better, their minsters (in the sense of servants). The change occurred when the original of the First epistle of St. Peter, in chapter 5 verse 3, was put into Latin. The Greek *kleron* was not translated (using perhaps *vocatis),* but transliterated into *cleris,* which became the "clergy" of later centuries. Hence the author's original intention that the elders should not dominate over the laity, was understood at a later period as an injunction that the bishops should not dominate over the clergy, in the Latin writings of the western Church.

After the title of "ordo" had been bestowed upon the Christian bishops and elders, it was almost predictable that special privileges would begin to enter the lives and behaviour of the erstwhile ministers. In the latter days of the Roman Empire they were being, in effect, absorbed into the imperial bureaucracy. The bishops principally, were accorded various honorific titles such as *clarissime, illustre, gloriosissime,* which scarcely need translation! They were also allowed to wear clothing and other items of dress indicating their rank, such as the pallium, stole, sandals, and probably the maniple too.[2] It is reassuring to learn that there was official opposition to these innovations. For example in 428 Pope Celestine reproved Honorius, the bishop of Arles, because he had introduced for his clergy the wearing of the monastic habit, consisting of tunic and belt. He justified his reproof with the words: "We should be distinguished from other people not by our dress, but by our knowledge, our outlook on life, not by our style of life".[3]

It is reassuring to realise that the clergy as a whole did not quickly become a privileged class. After the collapse of the Roman Empire in the West, a series of provincial councils in France and Spain provide valuable evidence, as to how the clergy supported themselves and their families by a variety of ordinary occupations. The first piece of evidence is conjectural. In the twentieth century archaeologists discovered the oldest known church building, at Dura-Europos in modern Iraq. It is so small

that it could not have held more than about 60 people.
Clearly a community of that size would not have needed
a full-time salaried priest. In the same century as that small
church was in use, there are indications in the
correspondence of St. Cyprian, that priests who were
supported by donations from the laity, were forbidden to
pursue secular business.[4]

However it is the records of the provincial councils which
provide the clearest evidence of their occupations. The
fact that they provided detailed rules for clerical
employment indicates how widespread the practice was.
Canon 18 of the Council of Elvira in Spain, shortly after
the year 300, states: 'Bishops, priests, and deacons shall
not depart from their districts for the sake of business, nor
shall they follow up profitable business deals going around
the provinces. In the course of earning their living, let
them send a son, a freed man, a servant, or a friend, or
anyone: and if they wish to negotiate business, let them do
so within the province'. Canon 20 of the same council also
speaks about usury: 'If any cleric shall be detected of
accepting interest on a loan, it is our decision that he shall
be degraded and excommunicated'.[5]

A similar picture emerges from a document known as the
Statuta Ecclesiae Antiquae, which was thought to have
been a collection of regulations of several councils at
Carthage at the end of the fourth century. However it is
more likely that it originated in the south of France, in the
second half of the fifth century. Canon 51 reads, 'Even
the learned clergy shall earn their living by a trade
(*artificium*). Canon 52, 'The clerics shall earn their food
and clothing by a trade, or by agriculture, without
prejudice to their office'. Canon 53, 'All clerics who are

capable of work shall learn a trade, besides their regular duties'.[6]

The moral character of their work was taken seriously. The general tone of the regulations was that the cleric should adopt work which would support him and his family, but not open the door to enrichment. The management of large estates was considered reprehensible, since it was not compatible with the New Testament ideal of repudiating wealth.

Towards the end of the fifth century, Pope Gelasius wrote the bishops of Luciania concerning clerical involvement in commerce. His letter implies that it was normal, and he is anxious to ensure that they should not give way to greed. His own words deserve to be quoted verbatim:- "Many clerics are involved in business which is dishonest and reprehensible... Thence they must learn to desist from this unworthy commerce, and must refrain from all astuteness and cupidity in business, otherwise they will be forbidden to take part in the liturgical offices, no matter what rank they may occupy".[7]

So the custom of clerics working in ordinary occupations unconsciously served a double purpose. It provided a simple solution to the practical problem of their paying for the basic necessities of life, such as food, clothing and a house, and quite unconsciously it kept them in contact with ordinary life, acted as a brake on the tendency for them to assume the status of a privileged class.

However, with the passage of the centuries, and the conversion of the erstwhile pagans of northern Europe, the Christian priests, especially in rural areas replaced the pagan priests theologically, and in their social position too. During the collapse of the Roman Empire in western Europe, Christianity was sufficiently well established in Italy, France, and Spain, for it to survive intact into the new political realities which replaced the Empire. Further north, the nations required conversion by missionaries. The situation in England seems to have been unique. There is strong evidence that Christianity was well established when the Empire was still intact. The firmest evidence is found in the records of the provincial council at Arles in 314. The list of bishops who attended the Council contains unexpectedly, the names of the bishops of London, Lincoln, and York. Since it is unlikely that all the bishops left England to attend the council, one may assume that other major cities had bishops too. This piece of evidence is confirmed by archaeology, which has discovered numerous Christian artefacts, including house churches. In addition to those domestic churches, the remains of what could be termed as a 'normal' church building, were discovered by archaeologists in the early 21st century at Colchester. Despite all this evidence of the establishment of Christianity in Britain, it did not survive the invasion of the pagan Saxons. Along with Ireland, and what are now Belgium the Netherlands, Denmark and Germany, missionaries came to start the evangelisation from zero, so to speak.

I described the actual evangelization of England in Chapter One, in this chapter I am dealing with the narrower issue of the establishment of the clergy and their social position in the nation.

During the period of evangelisation, the monks were based upon community houses known as minsters. When the small kingdoms had been converted a different deployment of the clergy took place. The monks adopted the stable way of life, which had been established in mainland Europe during the latter years of the Empire, following the example of the pioneers in Egypt, and they lived permanently in the minsters. The local clergy adopted the pattern of life which the Germanic tribes had brought with them. Quite simply it had been incumbent on the local land-owner to provide a sanctuary dedicated to the pagan gods, and to provide the material support for a priest who would conduct the worship in the sanctuary. This simple pattern easily lent itself to Christian adaptation, with a Christian priest providing the worship of the true God, in mass the sacraments and other services. The financial provision consisted in a steady income derived from a grant of land from whose produce would support the priest and his family.[8]

That was the origin of the parish structure which eventually spread across the whole of Europe, it gave the incumbent a recognised place in the structure of mediaeval society. That society was relatively static, one writer of the period classified the men(!) into three categories, the upper-class landowners who were at the same time the soldiers who fought, the clergy who prayed, and thirdly the peasants who worked on the land. In that context it was almost inevitable that the clergy would become a privileged class.

During the latter part of the first millennium, Christianity was becoming the sole religion of the civilized nations (for want of a better description). Far sighted rulers like King Alfred in England and Charlemagne in central Europe, realised that a partnership with the Church was essential.

Gradually the two organisations (Christianity and the State) became inseparable. Religion provided the basis of their legal systems and the rule of law, the monks were the educators of the nations, its worship inspired all the arts from architecture to music, painting and sculpture. Eventually this partnership between Church and State produced the immensely sophisticated culture of mediaeval Europe, and its intellectual achievements. Religious orders also created and performed the day to day running of hospitals, providing free treatment for poor people.

Regrettably it had its down-side as well. A sort of mutual osmosis was taking place. The kings and their various councils of advisors were adopting Christian principles, to shape the administration of their kingdoms. For example, their legal systems absorbed a Christian ethos. For their part, the rulers of the Church, began to adopt secular institutions and methods to further the advance and consolidation of Christianity. As early as the missions in Saxon England, warfare accompanied and promoted the acceptance of the Christian religion. Charlemagne's expansion of his empire relied on military force to impose Christianity, in which process the violence was sometimes completely out of control, as in his treatment of the pagan Saxons. The scholars and clerics at his court seem to have been too embarrassed to protest.

Violence became one of the tools of Church policy. Over the centuries the method of dealing with heresy, came to resemble the secular authorities' methods of dealing with crime. The arrest, trial and execution, of heretics (burnt to death), became the norm, although it was totally at variance with the values of the New Testament.

The crusades were the largest co-ordinated military operation of the middle ages, although with the wisdom of hindsight, we can see that both the objective and the means were contrary to Christian principles. The Church seemed to regard warfare as normal (or inevitable), and the theory of a just war, dating back to St. Augustine of Hippo, seems never to have been applied in practice

One unforeseeable factor entered the picture. It was the creation of separate law courts for the clergy. It meant in practice that if the clergy had been accused of criminal offences, their penalties would be more lenient, as was then judged to be fitting for the privileged class! Unfortunately, something close to the ancient concept of a separate legal system was re-created by Pius XI in 20th century. Basically, he decided that if priests were accused of sexual misdemeanours, the matter was to be dealt with in secret by the bishop, and the priest was not to be handed over to the police. Sadly, this paved the way for an unnecessary complication to the Church's dealing with child sexual abuse cases in the latter part of the 20th century. (See Excursus One at the end of this chapter).

The structures of parishes and monasteries, and later the friaries, all became enshrined in mediaeval Canon Law, and survived intact in the codification of Canon Law in 1918 and in its post- Conciliar revision in 1983. The most insidious element in this legislation was the right of tenure which was bestowed on the parish priests. In the middle ages, the concept of human rights had not appeared in the scheme of rights. At that time rights derived from property, and the owner of land or buildings enjoyed great security in the possession of his property (I used the pronoun "his" advisedly, because in the middle ages, and long afterwards, women could not possess property, nor the rights which were connected with such possession). In practice, this meant that the parish priest had effectively dictatorial powers over everything that took place in his parish.

Thus, we see the mediaeval parish priest, totally integrated into the structures of that homogeneous form of society. Thanks to his having a benefice, which comprised life-long tenancy of the house attached to the church, and access to the ecclesiastical courts of Canon Law, he had a privileged position in society, and thus enjoyed more material security than any other class of people. Within his own department he had more of less absolute control subject, of course, to the general oversight of the bishop. Paradoxically, and regrettably it is this image of the parish priest which is implied in the definition of a parish in the 1983 revision of the Code of Canon Law. Canon 515 §1 defines it thus: "The parish is a determinate community of Christians, permanently established within a diocese (Ecclesia particulari), whose pastoral care, under the authority of the diocesan bishop, is entrusted to the parish priest as their own pastor." Despite what Vatican II stated about the laity's position in the Church, Canon 515 gives no hint of a partnership. The paternalistic, all controlling image of the priest is still firmly in place.

The dangers of such power were exposed in the period after Vatican II. For example, after that Council a significant number of parishes had parish councils, whose members were elected. Yet a new parish priest was within his rights if he should decide to abolish the council, which his predecessor had set up. Similarly, in the liturgy, an incoming parish priest could ban the giving of the chalice to the laity during mass. These examples are not fictitious; I have known of such incidents from personal experience. They epitomise the very worst aspects of the clergy's privileged position in the Church.

What is needed in the secularised societies of the 21st century, is a far more flexible clergy. It is important that the bishops should have more power to move the clergy, rather like commercial organisations, where the deployment of personnel is governed by their ability to make the overall organisation more efficient, in achieving its objectives, whether that organisation might be a factory, a shop, a school or a political party.

It goes without saying that some structures of government and administration will always be necessary on account of the theology of the Church's nature, as a world-wide united community. But the important thing in reforming their effectiveness is to remove the status of privilege from the personnel working within those structures. It is genuinely difficult to understand how the clear teaching of Jesus on the matter, had been completely ignored at various times in the Church's history. For example the 23rd chapter of Matthew is unambiguously clear:- "The scribes and Pharisees sit on Moses' seat; so practise and observe whatever they tell you , but not what they do; for they preach, but do not practise... They do all their deeds to be seen by men; for they make their phylacteries broad and their fringes long, and they love the place of honour at feasts and the best seats in the synagogues, and salutations in the market places and being called rabbi by men. But you are not to be called rabbi, for you have one teacher, and you are all brethren. And call no man your father on earth, for you have one Father who is in heaven.

Neither be called masters, for you have one master, the Christ". (Matthew, 23: 2-10).

In order to attract the right sort of candidates to the clergy, and increase the effectiveness of those already ordained, the removal of the status of privilege is essential.

Priority in this operation is the removal of titles, because of the psychological power on the recipient of his being endlessly addressed thus and reinforcing daily the sense of his imagined importance. The most pernicious is the custom of addressing priests as "Father". It is one of the very few practices that Jesus forbad clearly and explicitly, as the quotation above, from St. Matthew demonstrates. Paradoxically the habit is not so widespread, nor so ancient, as some people would assume. The word abbot means 'father' in Semitic languages and was unaccountably bestowed on the superior of communities of monks. Other religious orders did not follow the custom. The head of a Franciscan house is known as the Guardian, the Dominicans designate their leader as the Prior, which is also the custom of other religious orders.

At a later period, the parochial clergy in many nations adopted the word Father, but the French form of it betrays a hybrid provenance. 'Monsieur l'Abbé' could literally and clumsily be translated as 'Mister Father'! In England the title 'father' was enjoined on the parochial clergy as late as the 19th century, when Cardinal Manning wanted to secure for the secular priests the same social standing as the religious orders enjoyed. Hitherto they had been addressed in speech and in correspondence as "Mr. Morgan", for example.

Other titles, such as 'Monsignor' are more easily disposed of, because they do not denote rank, or special responsibility. It is rather like civil servants being awarded the C.B.E. as a reward for good work, as when Fr. Northcote, for example, became Monsignor Northcote without any augmentation of his responsibilities for the parish which he served. Even more childish is the pattern of gradations of being a Monsignor. Some are designated as papal chamberlains, others are domestic prelates, and protonotaries apostolic claim that they should be addressed as 'Your Excellency'. Nothing in this childish pantomime could be further from the letter and spirit of the New Testament. The system must be abolished entirely. Actually, shortly after Vatican II, there was some suggestion that all grades of "monsignor" should be suppressed, since they represented no function in the organisational structure of the Church. It was clear that it was merely an acknowledgement of faithful service in the past, and an excuse to wear small items of distinctive clothing, like red buttons on the cassock. Sadly the initiative petered out and came to nothing,

The next element of privilege is distinctive clothing. Originally the monks all wore a simple uniform of a tunic of the same colour and a belt. It symbolised their equality and collective poverty in their daily life. In mediaeval Europe with the proliferation of new religious orders, they devised variations on the monastic habit, to display their own particular self- identity and way of life. In the middle ages this was not unusual. Students at universities wore distinctive gowns, and this was not an implicit claim to privilege. The parochial clergy adopted something like the habits of the religious orders, namely the simple black tunic. However, taken together with the steady source of income, and the titles, this garment did become part and parcel of the proclamation of a privileged class. Its survival into the modern period reinforced the message even more clearly. After the French Revolution, there was a tendency all over Europe to make clothing simpler, less colourful (particularly mens' clothing) and more egalitarian. It was a sign of the spirit of the times, when people were deliberately giving expression to equality and fraternity, as opposed to manifestations of superiority. It is no coincidence that in France, in the 19th and early 20th centuries, laws were enacted specifically forbidding monks, and members of other religious orders, from wearing their religious habits outside their houses, i.e. not in the streets.

In England the issue of clerical dress was not a major problem. Since the time of Elizabeth I, the Catholic priests who served the recusant minority, lived in hiding and did their best to make themselves invisible in public. Even after the cessation of the active persecution of Catholics, the practice was firmly ingrained of avoiding the limelight. After the Catholic Emancipation Act of 1829, the Catholic clergy wore the same style of suits as laymen, but always in black, and with the discreet white clerical collar, to remind people of the difference.

The final component of the privileged life of priests is the matter of payment. In countries which retained Catholicism as the national Church during the Reformation, like the Hapsburg Empire, the priests are paid a salary by the government, which raises the money through the Kirchensteuer (Church Tax), which I discussed in greater detail, in the Introduction. In modern Germany the same system applies to the Protestant clergy too. That is to say, the governments collect the money, and hand it over to the Church authorities, in strict proportion to the number of citizens who have declared their membership of the different Churches. Then the Church authorities distribute it to their own clergy. In those nations it is a very powerful indicator of a privileged class.

Elsewhere in countries where Catholics are a minority group in the population, such as the United States, Great Britain, Australia, the money comes from voluntary donations by the laity. In both systems the atmosphere of privilege is clear, since there is no direct connection between work done and money paid. For example, a family business like an independent baker's shop, there is an absolutely clear connection between the number of loaves that they bake, and the money which they receive when they sell them. Other occupations are less clear, such as teaching, but even so, elements like time spent per week in the class-room are fixed in their contracts. Only the clergy are exempt from that direct connection between work performed and money received.

It will not have escaped the reader's notice that the survival of this pre-mediaeval structure is an anomaly in the modern world. The first serious harbinger of change occurred during the Second World War, with the establishment of 'worker-priests'. The Nazi regime decided to conscript able bodied civilians from the countries which they had occupied, for factory work in Germany, so that all young men in their own country could be called up for the armed forces. The French bishops reacted in a very original way, by asking for volunteers among the clergy to go to Germany as workers to ensure that the French workers would not be totally deprived of mass and the sacraments. The priests who volunteered found it an extremely effective form of pastoral work, precisely because they shared the life of the workers in every respect. With the termination of hostilities, the French workers and their priests returned home. The priests decided to continue working in factories, and the scheme had the support of the French bishops.

However in the latter years of the pontificate of Pius XII the role of worker priests was suppressed. One wonders if he was pressurised by conservative cardinals in the Roman Curia. The suppression received widespread publicity in the press. Fortunately, the Second Vatican Council restored that style of ministry in a well-balanced statement. "All priests are sent forth as co-workers in the same undertaking in a parochial or supra-parochial ministry, whether they devoted their efforts to scientific research or teaching, whether by manual labour they share the lot of the workers themselves-if there seems to be a need for this and competent authority approves-or whether they fulfil any other apostolic tasks or labours related to the apostolate. All indeed are united in the single goal of building up Christ's Body, a work requiring manifold roles and new adjustments, especially nowadays."[9] This re-instatement of the role of worker priests received virtually no coverage in the secular press.

One final remark is relevant, concerning the clergy's clothing, namely the purpose of liturgical vestments. Personally I am convinced that they have a valid place in the Church's life, precisely because they are not the garments of everyday work and recreation. As they are worn only for the celebration of mass and the sacraments, they carry an important symbolic message. It reminds the congregation that the spiritual gifts emanating from the ceremonies of mass and the sacraments, are from God's free benevolence, and not from the celebrant's cleverness, or dramatic abilities, as a theatrically gifted preacher for example.

After the consolidation of Christianity as the religion of virtually the whole of Europe, which was achieved roughly by the end of the first millennium, the clergy's position as a privileged class was similarly stable, as an integral part of that vast and complex socio-political reality.

The next factor to introduce significant changes to priests' way of life was the Council of Trent in the 16th century. The relevant contribution of that Council to the clerical pattern of life was the establishment of seminaries.

At one level their creation can be regarded as a far-sighted original idea, namely that the parochial clergy should henceforth have a proper professional training. In that context the Catholic Church was an authentic pioneer, enshrining a principle that most other occupations had not yet made provision for. Admittedly theology was taught at virtually all universities, yet the academic acquisition of theology is not the only important element in preparing a man to be an effective pastoral priest. Moreover it opened up the role of parish priest to a class of admirable men who did not have the intellectual ability to master the academic study of theology at university level, or whose families could not have afforded the universities' fees. Moreover, the seminary could provide the opportunity to acquire the other skills needed to build up a Christian community, so that the laity could appreciate and live out their faith.

This admirable innovation inevitably brought with it some complications about vocations, and their discernment, which were not insoluble, and merely required some imaginative adjustments by the bishops, in how they made use of the seminaries' programmes. Trent stated that boys could be admitted to the seminary only if they knew how to read and write. What would now be described as the programme of primary and secondary education, could be acquired at the seminary, as a pre-requisite for the study of theology, and biblical studies. However it might entail that a 12 year old boy, for example, was effectively putting himself forward for training, implicitly claiming to have a vocation to the priesthood. From that time onwards, it was possible that the programme at the seminary could propel him forwards, like a theological escalator bringing him automatically to the ceremony of ordination.

Much the same path to the priesthood has been chosen by young men from impoverished families, who wanted to improve their social position in life. If for lack of intellectual potential, or for financial reasons, university was not an option, the seminary provided a path out of poverty. Its academic requirements were not daunting, and the cost of the course would be met by the diocese. That situation has been a very serious problem for the secular clergy. All that was required of a young man with that desire, was to endure the boredom of the seminary's regime for six years, and after that he was set up for a life of middle-class comfort, and prestige too.

That was the danger, but the authorities in the seminary and diocese did make some attempt to work out systems for discernment, as to whether the young man was deceiving himself on account of aspects of the priestly life, which he himself found attractive. In the modern period the teaching staff in the seminaries would hold regular consultative meetings before the bestowal of minor orders, which provided a series of intermediary steps, before the actual conferring of priesthood. Yet it must be remembered that such decisions were basically whether the candidate adjusted well to the seminary's pattern of life, and not to that of a parish where he would live only after ordination. Parish placements were grossly artificial, because the seminarians were largely guest/spectators in those presbyteries. There was no realistic work that they could discharge.

For most of the 20th century, the hidden agenda of discernment was, can this young man endure lifelong celibacy? The guideline was, that if between the ages of, say 18 and 24, he was able to survive without marriage, then it could be presumed for the rest of his life. At one period of my life I taught in an Anglican Theological College, which was their equivalent of a seminary. It was a valuable experience. The first lesson which I learnt was that in three years, that college covered as much ground academically as a Catholic seminary did in six. The next enlightening experience for me was the realisation that the students had chosen to study at that particular college, in preference to at least half a dozen others which provided much the same general formation. In other words, the rector and staff had to keep their programme under constant review, to attract the students to come there. Otherwise the college would simply have had to close, for lack of students. That situation was a very healthy interaction with reality.

By contrast, the Catholic seminaries can become unbelievably lackadaisical, knowing that students will keep coming because they are directed to the local seminary by the command of the bishop, who must be obeyed. The reliance on obedience produces the most debilitating consequences. The competence of the teaching staff is the first casualty. At the seminary where I was a student in the 1950's, the whole programme was mediocre both intellectually and in practical training.

The students could not choose to study elsewhere, when they perceived the shortcomings of the seminary to which they had been sent. In other words, the dead hand of obedience was used to justify serious dereliction of duty by the bishop.

Perhaps the worst of the shortcomings of that seminary was the absence of any provision for practical charity. It so happened that about four miles from the seminary, there was a Cheshire Home for incurable invalids. Senior pupils from a local non-Catholic boarding school, were encouraged by their teachers, to go to that home once a week to help with the domestic work, and other practical tasks. The seminary students were actually forbidden to do any such activity!

In short, the far-sighted plan of the Council of Trent, to provide a specialist training for the parochial clergy, and become seriously disfunctional by the 20th century, largely because the authorities relied on nothing more constructive than obedience. The priests who went through that system, emerged with the expectations of living as members of a privileged class. If they did "survive" the process for six years, few of them showed any spiritual profit from that negative experience. Many of them moved from being self-centred, (related to compulsory celibacy), to loneliness, and in old age many were deeply unhappy old men.

For the future, a completely different pattern must be adopted, namely Non- Stipendiary clergy. This system means that ordination will be conferred on a married man with a career and family (just as the epistles to Titus and Timothy enjoined). At the weekends he will hear confessions, christen babies, officiate at marriages and celebrate mass. It is a pattern which has been tried and tested successfully by the Anglicans for about 20 years.

Origin and Theological Demise of Obligatory Celibacy

Having stated the desirability of a form of priestly ministry which employs married men, the time has now come to examine the origin and present theological legitimacy of compulsory celibacy for secular priests.

That absence of a satisfactory rationale for the exclusion of married men, was made clear to me in a memorable conversation, that I had about 40 years ago with a bishop who is no longer alive. I said to him "If the life of celibacy is presented as bestowing rich spiritual benefits, would it not be reasonable for priests to adopt it freely, if they feel that they have the vocation to the single life?" To that the bishop replied: "Unless it were compulsory, those of us who adopted it freely would be considered as queers". (*his word, not mine*). By an extraordinary coincidence, in recent years my wife was talking with a bishop in the informal gathering after a Confirmation service. In the course of the conversation she said to him: "As there is such a shortage of priests, why do you not remove the obligation of celibacy?" To which he replied: "Unless the celibacy were obligatory, those of us who chose it voluntarily would be regarded as odd." A sense of good manners inhibited my wife from saying: By odd, do you mean gay? The Episcopal attitudes have not changed very much over the years!

The desirability of ordaining married men has been written about extensively during the last forty years. A clear consensus has emerged, so there is no point in repeating the in detail, what is now agreed among enlightened Catholics.[10] However a few key principles can profitably be repeated in this narrative.

The starting point is the New Testament, in which it is significant that Jesus said so little about the matter. Only once is he recorded as having said anything connected with the unmarried life, in the wider context of a conversation about divorce. (Matthew 19: 10-12) "The disciples said to him, if such is the case of a man with his wife, it is not expedient to marry. But he said to them, "Not all men can receive this precept, *but only those to whom it is given.* For there are eunuchs who have been so from birth, and there are eunuchs who have been made eunuchs by men, and there are eunuchs who have made themselves eunuchs for the sake of the kingdom of heaven. He who is able to receive this, let him receive it". This is far short of a ringing endorsement of the compulsory celibate life, but the essential element that it is a gift given by God was stated.

The Epistles contain two explicit directives that the leaders who are now described as bishops and priests, should be chosen from among mature married men with children. The First Epistle to Timothy states (3: 1-5) "If anyone aspires to the office of bishop, he desires a noble task. Now a bishop must be above reproach, the husband of one wife, temperate, sensible, dignified, hospitable, an apt teacher, no drunkard, not violent but gentle, not quarrelsome and no lover of money. He must manage his own household well, keeping his children submissive and respectful in every way; for if a man does not know how to manage his own household, how can he care for God's Church?" The Epistle to Titus (1: 5-9) contains the same directive in almost the same terms, namely a married man with children.

Finally the First Epistle to Timothy (4: 1-3), contains an emphatic repudiation of those who condemn marriage "Now the Spirit expressly says that in latter times some will depart from the faith by giving heed to deceitful spirits and doctrines of demons, through the pretensions of liars whose consciences are seared, who forbid marriage."

It is almost impossible to understand how the Church authorities could have defied the plain message of the New Testament for almost a millennium.

The influence which was militating against this simple idea of married men as spiritual leaders, was the pagan concept of cultic purity. Namely that those men who offer sacrifices to a deity must be free from the alleged contamination of sex, at least temporarily during the time of their sacred functions. Presumably it has something to do with the awe, which was inspired by the mysterious origin of a new life. For reasons which need not detain us in this narrative, it features from time to time in the Old Testament, as for example in the sacrifices which accompanied the inauguration of the Covenant at Mount Sinai (Exodus: 19, 15). Another instance was the request by David, fleeing from Saul's wrath, to Achimelech the priest at Nob, to give him bread. The priest gave him five loaves of the holy bread, on condition that he and his companions had kept themselves from women (I Samuel, 1-6). Instances like these are puzzling, because they are clearly alien to the fundamental insight of the creation narrative in the first chapter of Genesis, which insists repeatedly that the material world is good, and indeed, very good.

The concept of cultic purity first appeared in Christian history in the period after Constantine's conversion, when exceptionally large numbers of former pagans became Christians. One example in a directive from a fourth century pope, will illustrate the matter clearly. The author is Pope St. Damasus, whose words are: "This is established in the first place concerning bishops, priests, and deacons, who of necessity must be present at the divine sacrifices, by whose hands the grace of baptism is conferred and the body of Christ is consecrated, they are compelled to be absolutely chaste,----- If intercourse is a pollution, then indeed a priest must stand ready for the heavenly duty since he is to intercede for the sins of others, lest he should be found unworthy,-----and would the priest or deacon dare to participate, being subject to the behaviour of animals.[11] The three incredible words at the end are the unvarnished expression of the pope, translating quite literally his very own words "animalium more".

To the modern mind such an attitude to sex between spouses is absolutely abhorrent, and not only to the modern mind, but to the spirit of the New Testament. Anyone who employed such an expression about human sexuality, could not have appreciated the clear break from the Israelite principle that some practices were unclean, such as sex when the wife is menstruating. A similar attitude applied to foods, which were deemed to be unclean. A definitive indicator of the new moral outlook is furnished in the Acts of the Apostles, in the vision of St. Peter, prior to his baptising the pagan centurion Cornelius. In the vision, Peter sees a whole variety of legally unclean animals, and to his consternation a voice from heaven commands him to kill them for food. His dilemma is resolved when the voice from heaven spoke again: "What God has cleansed, you must not call common". (Acts 10: 9-16). The immediate relevance was to prepare Peter for entering the house of a pagan, and then baptising him and his family. The overall lesson is that in the Christian dispensation, nothing that God has created is to be treated as unclean, in the religious perspective. In other words, Christians should never have entertained the notion that sex was impure, and incompatible with the worship of God.

Sadly, the notion of cultic purity continued to influence the Church leaders in the centuries after Pope Damasus. At the end of the first millennium the extensive reform of the Church under the inspiration of Pope Gregory VII (1073-85) took place against a background of the prestige of the monastic orders. Their reputation was well deserved in many areas, such as the preservation of the culture of the Roman Empire after its collapse, politically, in Western Europe, as also their being the sole source of education, and the principal inspiration of the arts in general. Other aspects of the monastic life were more questionable. Increasing numbers of monks were also priests, which was contrary to the ancient monastic custom. It might also suggest that the two ways of life should normally be united in one man. Be that as it may, the criticism of married priests was widespread. In 1054 Cardinal Humbert, who had been the papal representative to the Greek Christians at Constantinople, criticised the married priests of the Greeks with these words: "Young husbands, just now exhausted from carnal lust, serve the altar. And immediately afterwards they again embrace their wives, with hands that have been hallowed by the immaculate Body of Christ. That is not the mark of true faith, but an invention of Satan.[12]

A century later, Pope Innocent II, addressing the synod of Clermont in 1130, declared: "Since priests are supposed to be God's temples, vessels of the Lord, and sanctuaries of the Holy Spirit... it offends their dignity to lie in the conjugal bed and live in impurity".[13]

Against such a background, it should cause no surprise that the First and Second Lateran Councils of 1123 and 1139, should enact strict measures against marriages of clergy in major orders. The exact wording of Canon 6 of the Second Lateran Council deserves to be quoted in full: "We decree that those who are in the orders of subdiaconate and above if they should marry wives or have concubines, they shall forfeit their ecclesiastical office and benefice. For they are the people who are named as, and indeed are the temple of God, vessels of the Lord, and the sanctuary of the Holy Spirit, and it is unworthy of them to be subservient to debauchery and licentiousness".[14]

The last few words, in Latin (*non in cubilibus et immunditiis*) are lifted straight from the Latin version of St. Paul's Epistle to the Romans, 13: 13. The wider context of St. Paul's sentence is as follows: "Let us then cast off the works of darkness and put on the armour of light; let us conduct ourselves becomingly as in the day, not in revelling and drunkenness, not in debauchery and licentiousness (*cubilibus et impudicitiis*), not in quarrelling and jealousy." It is puzzling to try to understand why the bishops in Council should have added those bizarre words at the end of Canon 6. After much reflection I came to the conclusion that they wanted to follow an ancient tradition of justifying their Conciliar decisions with words from scripture. However, there is not one verse in the New Testament which could be found, to justify what they had stated about the marriages of priests. Hence the bizarre clutching at straws to insinuate a pseudo biblical warrant!

Canon 7 of the same Council, spells out with more detail the command to separate if clerics in major orders had contracted a marriage. It is also stated that such a union is not a true marriage. This raises an interesting question, as to whether a General Council has the competence to attach a nullifying condition to a sacrament, when Christ had given no warrant for such a rule. But that need not detain us now.

That Council set the pattern which was in force throughout the middle ages, and which Luther, and all the leaders of the Reformation rejected, because they obeyed the New Testament. Needless to say, the Council of Trent upheld the Catholic mediaeval rule, and the obligation of celibacy for the secular clergy continued until the modern period, without being challenged, from within the Catholic Church.

The Second Vatican Council changed everything. In the document about Priesthood, the Council stated that there was no intrinsic connection between priesthood and the celibate life, and drew attention to the edifying lives of the married priests in the Catholic Eastern rites.[15]

In the same section (16) of that document, the Council stated its approval of the current law requiring priests of the Latin rite to observe celibacy. But it was too late. Other Conciliar documents gave a different message. The document *Gaudium et Spes,* meaning Joy and Hope, (usually rendered in English as "The Church in the Modern World"), spoke about sexual intercourse, in § 49. The language is quaint and rather coy, but the meaning is clear: "This love is uniquely expressed and perfected through the marital act. The actions within marriage by which the couples are united intimately and chastely are noble and worthy ones".[16]

In other words, sex is good. This simple statement put an end, once and for all, to any validity of the ancient understanding of ritual impurity, namely that sex was incompatible with the sacred. The ancient prejudice which influenced the pessimistic legislation of the middle ages, was demolished entirely.

The final statement which completed the unravelling of compulsory celibacy was in the treatment devoted to the status of marriage. The document *Gaudium et Spes* § 87 speaks of marriage as a human right. The precise words are as follows, "For in view of the inalienable human right to marry and beget children, the question of how many children should be borne belongs to the honest judgement of the parents".[17] The reference to the inalienable human right to marry, has been a constant affirmation of modern popes. After the Council, Pope John Paul II had stated in his encyclical *Evangelium Vitae*, that no merely human law can invalidate a divine law. (Catholic theologians have always maintained that natural law has its origin in God, whence it derives its authority).

This accords with what Popes Leo XIII and Pius XI had taught about marriage, and how its nature could not be changed by human legislators.[18] Putting all these considerations together, it is clear that ecclesiastical legislators, even in a General Council, simply cannot deny any Christian the right to marry. That was the final consideration which demolished the presumption of the mediaeval legislators, who issued the prohibition on the ordination of married men, or of marriage for priests.

This situation was tacitly recognised in practice, when Cardinal Hume obtained from Pope John Paul II permission to ordain convert married Anglican priests.

The sequel to these conclusions was predictable. Free speech in the Church facilitated the debate about the admission of married men to the priesthood. The first practical result was that literally thousands of secular priests resigned from the clergy in the years immediately following the Second Vatican Council. The next step was widespread agitation for the repeal of the law requiring all secular priests to accept the condition of celibacy.

The reluctance of the Vatican to countenance that step was puzzling. It was particularly baffling in the papal document approving the work of the Synod about the Amazon region, published in February 2020. The question of ordaining married men for that region was simply not mentioned in the final document, although the majority of the participants in the synod had favoured it. Nothing was stated about it, either in favour or against the continued practice of obligatory celibacy.

We must search for an explanation outside the bounds of theology. Apart from the conclusive theological arguments of Vatican II which nullified the rational basis of the law, there is one widely pervasive psychological factor which merits serious reflection. Authorisation for the ordination of married men in a region as large as the Amazon region, which comprises parts of half a dozen different nations, would indicate that the next step would be the universal abolition of compulsory celibacy for secular priests. Such a step would imply unmistakably that for nearly a millennium the Catholic Church "had got it wrong". That is to say, the lonely and sad lives of the parochial clergy had been worthless sacrifices. Worse still, thousands of priests all over the world, alive now and working in parishes, would come to realise that their continuing sacrifice of happiness was irrelevant. It is difficult to fathom the extent that such disillusionment would cause. It might well lead to suicides, possibly widespread alcoholism, and at the very least, a widespread sense of utter despair.

The situation described in the previous paragraph, requires the most careful and sensitive preparation of clerical opinion for such a far-reaching alteration of the law. The obvious agents for such an exercise of collective re-education would be the bishops. At present few national episcopal conferences show any inclination even to consider the question. The German bishops' conference is an honourable exception. For the majority though, time will probably be the agent of change. Since it is the responsibility of bishops to provide priests for their parishes, there will come a time, in a few years, when the annual deaths of priests will so far outnumber the ordinations, that the bishops will be literally forced to face reality. That will be the tipping point for them to seek expert advice on how to prepare the surviving priests to accept a universal alteration of the law of celibacy.

While voluntary celibacy will always on offer to priests who choose it freely, it is clear that in the future the vast majority of parochial clergy will be married, and supporting themselves financially, either from a pensions, or from a salary from their ordinary career. The actual vocation, or calling presents an interesting opportunity to fulfil this element realistically. When a parish priest dies, or retires, the bishop could notify the candidates who have completed the training programme, and invite them to apply for the vacant post. All applicants could then be interviewed by the parish council of the vacant parish. From the candidates' point of view, considerations of distance, for example, would be relevant. That is to say, if the vacant parish was about five miles from his home, the distance would be an inducement. It is an advantage to live a small distance away from the parish which he would serve. As and when necessary he could commute to the parish office, which would be his working base. One of the grave disadvantages of the traditional parish system is that the parish priest, can never "switch off". He is literally living over the shop. It means that the conscientious men never relax, and the lazy ones never "switch on". The final choice of candidate must be reserved to the bishop, and the parish council will act realistically as his advisors. This is reasonable because the bishop has responsibility for all the parishes in the diocese, and he alone can understand the overall picture.

Clearly, the non-stipendiary priest will not be able to give to the parish as much time as the traditional resident priest. But this too is a hidden bonus. The priest will be absolutely dependent upon the parishioners to undertake the manifold activities to keep the parish running as a normally functioning Christian community. In other words, the system of non-stipendiary priests, has benefits in every area. It will have to be the normal system for the future. I will have more to say about this pattern of priestly life in the chapter on the laity. For the purposes of this present chapter, such a way of life will lessen the danger of the priests continuing to live as members of a very privileged class socially.

Although this chapter is concerned with removing clerical privilege for the good of the Church as a community, for the individual priests' lives a parallel history must be noted, namely the damage done to most priests' personalities, emotional life, and psychology by their being compelled to celibacy. Soon after ordination, it is clear that it makes them lonely, then self-centred, which can so often turn into selfishness, and in old age most of them are pathetically sad old men.

Even more serious, is another dimension brought about by their being denied married life, which was noted by the psychiatrist Jack Dominian. Drawing on a wide consensus of research, he concluded: "There are few findings more consistent, less equivocal, more convincing than the sometimes spectacular and always impressive superiority on almost every index-demographic, psychological, or social-of married men over never married men. Despite all the jokes about marriage in which men indulge, all the complaints they lodge against it, it is one of the greatest boons for their sex".[19]

I would like to add another factor to Dominian's list of areas of superiority, namely the experience of parenthood. Over the years it has become more and more clear to me, that men and women do not achieve their true potential as well integrated human beings, until they have become parents. The responsibilities are immense, and so are the rewards of giving and receiving love between parent and child. Both those factors enrich the personality of the normal adult.

Needless to say, Dominian was not writing about the superiority of married men in the context of clerical celibacy, but in a book about the development of the marriage relationship between husband and wife. On reflection, it seems clear to me, that it is all the more convincing when applied to priests', lives precisely because it was not written with them in mind. Surely this is the final tragedy of compulsory celibacy: far from enhancing their spiritual lives and pastoral effectiveness, it is simply damaging their personalities in the areas of normal human qualities.

One important factor in the damage done by obligatory celibacy, is that it rules out the enriching experience of intimacy in the lives of the priests. In previous centuries the experience of intimacy between adults was not known. Fortunately when babies were being breast fed by their mothers, they would have experienced it. As far as adults were concerned, it was absent from their lives. This helps our generation to understand the apparent callousness with which marriages were arranged for young people by their parents. The worst victims of that pattern were royalty. Their marriages were straightforwardly planned for advantageous political alliances.

The identification of intimacy as a psychological reality in the lives of adults, has been one of the most important contributions to human happiness, discovered by the young science of psychology. It consists of the sharing of feelings of joy, sadness, anxiety and trust between husband and wife. It presupposes that they regard each other as equals. They are not ashamed to express to each other their anxieties, and weaknesses. The advantages are obvious. It enhances their sexual relationship, as an expression of very tender love, and also improves their health. Another enrichment of their personalities is a feeling of enhanced self-confidence. The list could be continued. I recommend my readers to study Jack Dominian's book, referred to above.

It should be clear to readers at this point, that compulsory celibacy actually damages the personalities of priests, especially those who live alone in presbyteries. Many years ago in R. I. Classes it was explained to Catholic children that their priests were unmarried so that they could devoted their lives more whole-heartedly to God.

That kind of devotion occurs in the lives of the small minority who experience an authentic calling to that life and receive grace from God. But they are a very small minority of the secular clergy. The majority cope with the privation by self-discipline, which is a form of emotional repression. It is unhealthy and does not result in the re-direction of love to people in need.

I write the next section with great reluctance, but the truth most not be concealed. The thoughts which I will share with my readers, arose from an indirect contact with an organisation started by the Jesuits. It is an admirable agency called "The Jesuit Refugee Service". Recently my wife was in conversation with general secretary of that project. She told my wife that in negotiations with one diocese in the south of England, (which shall be nameless) only one presbytery had taken in a homeless refugee. Moreover, in the same diocese she mentioned that there was a particular parish, which she did not name, where the presbytery had five bedrooms, four of which had en-suite shower rooms, but the parish priest lived there alone. That situation, of excluding the needy from the presbyteries, is at variance with the central message of Christianity, namely love of the neighbour, who might well be a stranger, as the Good Samaritan discovered. In the account of the last judgement in St. Matthew (25: 31-46) the substance of the examination concerns whether people have given food and drink to the hungry, clothes to those who had rags, and welcomed the homeless stranger into their houses. The rule of compulsory celibacy has not liberated the clergy to that pattern of conduct. As I noted above, it drives them into emotional repression in the endeavours to keep clear of marriage, sex and intimacy with women. It is difficult to see whether any advantages at all accrue from obligatory celibacy.

One final element must be considered in stripping the clergy of all elements of privilege, namely it must not be reserved to the male sex. The exclusion of women from the clergy in antiquity was a sociological matter, and not theological. In the discipline proclaimed in the New Testament epistles, it must rank with other sociologically inspired instructions, such as the injunction that slaves must obey their masters. The infant Church had staked a claim to so much that was original, and counter cultural, that they did not want to add further items to their already unpopular image. It was sufficient that they drew people away from the national deities, that were linked to patriotism, and they proclaimed the absolute innovation of an international religion of the one true God, which was open to all nationalities and races on a basis of equality. The originality of that concept was enough to earn them widespread persecution, without stirring up unsettling sociological innovations too.

The eventual acquiring of equality by women in the twentieth century, is a sobering example, of how tenaciously the beneficiaries of power and status hold on to it, trying desperately to exclude the entry of women, with whom they would have to share those benefits. Even the most intelligent societies showed shocking pettiness, as for example the universities of Oxford and Cambridge. The grudging way in which women were finally admitted as students, was a disgrace. So too was the reluctance to confer real degrees on them, when they had passed the exams. At Cambridge they were "deemed to have satisfied the examination system". Real degrees, the same as the men received, were awarded to women at Cambridge only after the Second World War. It showed up the attitudes and prejudices of the masculine governing body of that university, in the worst possible light.

At the theological level, in the Catholic Church, we are still in a similar position to that which confronted the suffragettes in the 19th century. St. Paul had said that women must be silent in the churches. But it is significant that in the reformed liturgy of Vatican II, women have been acting as readers for many years. Originally it had been stipulated that when they were actually reading the scriptures, they should stand outside the sanctuary! Fortunately, common sense and normal courtesies, ensured that such pettiness, has been universally ignored. Nevertheless, it is a disturbing indicator of the limitations of the collective mentality of the Roman Curia.

A vast literature already exists, supporting the case for the ordination of women, so having indicated my own conviction on the matter, I will refer my readers to those excellent books, to deepen their understanding of the issues.

EXCURSUS ONE

THE SEXUAL ABUSE OF CHILDREN BY THE CLERGY

I have decided to attach the examination of this disgraceful series of events, to the chapter on removing clerical privilege, because one powerful factor in enabling the priests to exploit the children, was the authority which accrued to the priests as members of a privileged class. If a priest asked a child to do something unusual, the presumption was present, implicitly, in the child's mind, that there must be a good reason for it, simply because it has been asked for by a priest.

In the course of its long history, the Catholic Church has experienced several widespread manifestations of corruption, such as the crusades, the burning of heretics, widespread concubinage by the parochial clergy, and the accumulations of immense wealth by the higher clergy, such as Cardinal Wolsey. What is really puzzling is why the sexual abuse of children on a wide scale should have appeared for the first time in the Church's history, at the end of the 20th century. Having stated that observation, another possibility must be considered. The abuse of children might well have occurred in the past, but the victims would probably have been totally inhibited from reporting it. Until the establishment of total freedom of speech and criticism in the Church after Vatican II, it is most unlikely that any victims would have had the courage to speak out. They would have been regarded as slanderers of the holy priests, and would have feared being prosecuted for libel, and ostracised by the Catholic community.

Needless to say, child sexual abuse is singularly offensive because it entails the exploitation of those who could not defend themselves against an adult who had power over them, not only by physical strength, but also by spiritual authority which they had been taught to respect and trust. In that sense it is far more repulsive than straightforward practice of concubinage between adults.

In this excursus there are two distinct problems, namely the cases of sexual abuse, and secondly the attempts by the authorities, (in practice, the bishops) to conceal the incidents, and withhold the information, from the police.

The matter has been widely covered in the secular press, but it is important to repeat the numbers in case the matter might ever be swept under the carpet, in the future. In summary one can say that in virtually every nation of the whole world, Catholic priests (and sometimes bishops) have sexually abused children, and other under-age minors such as seminarians, in their hundreds.

In Germany the matter has been examined thoroughly. The Catholic authorities presented the results of cases between 1946 and 2014. During that period 3,677 children were abused, mostly boys, and about 1,670 clerics (mostly priests) were implicated.[1] The Polish Bishops' Conference organised a similar enquiry. The outcome was horrifying. Between 1990 and 2018, 382 priests were accused of abuse, and so far 625 potential victims have been identified.[2] Further research has revealed that similar numbers have been found in other nations. In the U.S.A. 5,948 priests have been accused, in Australia the number is 1,800 (with a staggering 4,444 victims listed) in the Netherlands it is 800 priests, and in Belgium 500.[3] A similar disgraceful incident was reported from the province of Kerala, in South India, where a 44 year old nun accused a 54 year old bishop of raping her, repeatedly.[4] In South Africa, it has been reported that priests, desiring unprotected sex, prefer to do so with nuns, because they are less likely to be infected with Aids.[5]

Before the full extent of the problem was recognised, the Church authorities' method of dealing with the offending priests was so amateurish that it amounted to virtual protection of the guilty clergy. The procedures were also hampered by what was known in canon law as the "pontifical secret". That instruction directed that religious superiors were not to report allegations to the police and public authorities, but they had to keep them "in house". In practice it means moving an offender to another place. In 1987 a monk in a well-known Benedictine boarding school, admitted to having abused a boy in the junior house. He was discretely moved to a parish in Cumbria, for which the same monastery was also responsible.[6] Experience has shown that paedophiles often have a tendency to re-offend. The monk in question was later arrested, and sentenced to four years' imprisonment for the abuse of 10 schoolboys in the 1980's.

One of the factors which inhibited victims from making complaints to the Church authorities, was the suspicion that they would not be believed. This was complicated by the other fear, that they might be prosecuted for libel.

However, once the facts began to leak out, erstwhile victims did pluck up courage and make formal complaints. In the 1990's a famous TV programme covered one such exposure. A teen-age boy accompanied by his father, went to the bishop's office of a diocese in Ireland, and one of the diocesan administrative priests recorded the evidence carefully. However, before the meeting was over, he made the boy and his father swear to secrecy as to any further disclosure to any other authority.

That final detail illustrates the basic dishonesty of the Catholic Church's methods at that time. Universally there was a policy of denial, cover-ups, and simply moving the offenders to other places.

Predictably, when the victims of clerical sexual abuse have discovered the confidence to go public, the crisis sometimes gets worse. In 2019 in the French diocese of Beauvais, a victim actually murdered the priest who had abused him. On 4th November 2019, an elderly priest Fr. Roger Matassoli 91, was found dead in his house. Clearly he had been murdered. A crucifix had been pushed down his throat, and there were signs of multiple blows to his body. The police soon arrested a 19 year old suspect, but he was detained in a hospital because he appeared to be delirious. The suspect's father (whom the newspaper gave the pseudonym Stéphan for reasons of confidentiality) stated that he too had been abused by Fr. Matassoli, when he was younger. When the whole drama unfolded in the press, Stéphan's own father committed suicide, being unable to cope with what that priest had done to his son and grandson. The bishop of Beauvais and his predecessor both received complaints about the behaviour of Fr. Matassoli, but neither of them could give a satisfactory account of why they failed to contact the police.[7]

In February 2019 Pope Francis decided to take the matter in hand once and for all. A special synod was assembled in Rome, consisting of about one hundred bishops from all parts of the Church. The matter was discussed fairly thoroughly. Full collaboration with the public legal authorities was pledged, and all cover- ups were explicitly repudiated.

However the one item which did not feature in their debates, was the basic cause of this widespread failure of the clergy. It would have clarified the whole field admirably, if they had at least discussed whether compulsory celibacy for the clergy of the Latin rite, might be a causal factor. As the Catholic record on this matter is notably worse than that of other Christian Churches, the celibacy factor must be investigated, because it is the only significant variable in the life style of the clergy, where Catholic and Protestant clergy have inherited the mantle of their mediaeval predecessors, if not the full programme of privilege.

To one serious minded observer, at least, the danger had been foreseeable. He was an eminent Catholic psychoanalyst in Germany, (Erwin Ringel) well known for his independence of mind. He was able to warn of the dangers of obligatory celibacy, from the stand-point of neutrality. That is to say, he died on the 28th July in 1994, before the massive crimes of child sex abuse by Catholic clergy had come to the notice of the public at large. Nevertheless, he warned that obligatory celibacy was a danger to the priests' personalities, since it robbed them of an important part of the autonomy of a mature adult personality, and left them with seriously distorted personalities, subject to infantilised and narcissistic tendencies.[8]

In the 20th century, the seminaries, had no realistic process of discernment, as to whether or not, a seminarian had been given the grace of celibacy. The requirement had been enshrined in Canon Law since the 12th century, there seemed to be no prospect of that law's being abrogated. Colloquially it was referred to as a "part of the package deal". The fact that the course lasted for six years was probably connected with an implied test of the students' tenacity. In other words, if these young men in their early twenties could do without an intimate relationship with a woman for six years, then they could probably endure the deprivation until death.

If they did observe it until death, there can be no doubt that it did considerable damage to their personalities. The first consequence was loneliness, then self-centeredness, and in old age one saw a large proportion of deeply sad old men. Charity did not flourish. One clear indicator of this emerged in the 21st. century when the nations of Europe were flooded by thousands of refugees from Africa and the Near East. It is a fact of common experience, that people do not depart from the place of their birth, in massive numbers, unless they are forced to do so by circumstances beyond their own control. That was the plight of the 21st century refugees from Africa and the Near East. Those people were forced out of their homelands by warfare, violence from corrupt governments, indescribable poverty arising from the inefficiency of their rulers, and a host of other factors such as climate change making agriculture impossible. The presbyteries of the celibate priests, and the houses of religious orders, have not been conspicuous in providing shelter for the homeless strangers, as is urged on Christians in the 25th chapter of St. Matthew. I dealt with this matter more fully in the Chapter Three, so I will say no more about it here.

There were several other signs of emotional damage, albeit not dramatic, but debilitating, such as neurotic shyness. In spite of the well-established practice of the clergy visiting their parishioners in their homes, a significant number of priests were so shy, that they could not bring themselves to undertake that straightforward task. One priest whom I knew of, tried to solve the problem of communication by writing letters. To speed up the process, (and perhaps to save on postage) he would get into his car at about midnight, drive from house to house, and quietly put the letters through the letter boxes of the parishioners!

Another fact must also be taken into consideration. As I noted above, other organisations, like sports clubs, and the BBC have unwittingly provided the setting for child abuse, and so have other Churches. In fact situations where children will be in close contact with those who are famous, or in a position of guidance (football coaches, scout masters and others) cases of sexual abuse are known to have taken place. Significantly, and sadly, I have to repeat what I noted above, that in the institutions of the Catholic Church proportionately far larger numbers of abuse have been recorded than in all other comparable organisations.

Quite apart from clergy abusing children, early in the twenty first century information began to leak out concerning other of clerical failures in the realm of celibacy.

In the United States the matter has been investigated scientifically. One researcher was Richard Sipe, a former Benedictine priest, who later became a psychotherapist. Among his many publications, in the book *A Secret World: Sexuality and the Search for Celibacy* 1990, which was based on 1,500 interviews. Sipe suggested that only about half the priests in the United States were at any one time practising celibacy.[9]

Quite apart from what one might describe as heterosexual disregard for the law of obligatory celibacy, more sinister infringements of that law also came to light. A systematic examination of the matter has been carried out in recent years by a theologian, James Alison, who published the results of his researches in two extremely important articles in The Tablet, (*Caught in a Trap of Dishonesty,* and *The Lying Game,* 4th and 11th August 2018).

Matters came to a head in 2018 when the sexual misdemeanours of the former Cardinal Theodore McCarrick, archbishop of Washington, came to light. I will quote the words of James Alison: "The McCarrick shock was not what he was getting up to with seminarians and other adults. This was widely known about. It was that in addition to a standardly furtive, albeit egregiously creepy, clerical gay life, this generally kind and well liked man had also abused at least two minors.------ -In all these cases, in as far as the behaviour was adult related, plenty of people in authority sort-of-knew what was going on, and had been known throughout the clerics' respective careers."[10] Alison cites the Tablet's former Rome correspondent about the prevalence of the gay life among the clergy, who says that he had been aware of this 'elephant in the sacristy' for many years. It is the massively disproportionate number of gay men in the clergy. It is also connected with the Roman authorities' refusal to engage in any kind of publicly accountable, adult discussion about this anomaly. This reinforces collective dishonesty and perpetuates the psycho-sexual immaturity of all gay clergy, whether celibate, partnered, of practitioners of so-called 'serial celibacy'.

Alison continues, "I don't think there is a healthy way to address this without opening up understanding of some of the dimensions of the systemic structural trap that is the clerical closet.------The first is its size. A far, far greater proportion of the clergy, particularly the senior clergy is gay, than anyone has been allowed to understand, even the bishops and cardinals themselves.------ -But the proportion is going to become more and more self-evident, thanks to social media and generalised expectations of gay honesty and visibility in the civil sphere. This despite many years of bishops resisting accurate sociological clergy surveys.[11]

On the very essence of homosexuality, scientific enlightenment and the Vatican's policies became ever more divergent, in the latter part of the 20th century. After the middle of the century, psychologists and other medical specialists agreed that being gay was not a pathological condition. The most obvious consequence of that consensus should have been that it was in no way reprehensible. However the Congregation for the

Doctrine of the Faith published documents in 1975 and 1986, which had not accepted the findings of the scientists. In the latter document, what they described as the 'homosexual tendency' was also judged to be 'objectively disordered'.

Consistent with those assumptions was the conclusion that homosexual acts were 'intrinsically evil'. This placed the gay clerics in an even more difficult position, which motivated many of them to become even more secretive, and determined to conceal their sexual orientation. Paradoxically this did not diminish the number of gay men entering the seminaries. Heterosexual young men had long since been a minority among the entrants to priestly training, on account of the inability of anyone to justify the imposition of celibacy on their lives. Yet the Church still urgently needed priests, so men who were secretly gay, yet did their best to conceal it, were admitted to seminaries. I have secured information from reliable priests who have taught or are teaching at three English seminaries, that from the first decade of the present century gay candidates make up the clear majority of the student body. Moreover many of them display immature personalities whose emotional lives lack healthy integration. Sadly this is probably to be expected in view of the Church's unconvincing position on the priesthood and sexuality in general.

EXCURSUS TWO

THE VATICAN BUREAUCRACY

By far the most privileged class within the clergy is the central administrative staff at the Vatican. Its very existence brings into focus several serious theological problems. Since the definition of papal supremacy at the First Vatican Council in 1870, the administrative staff in Rome has expanded greatly. This is in contradiction to the Principle of Subsidiarity enunciated by Pope Pius XI, in his encyclical *Quadragesimo Anno,* namely that decisions should be made at the lowest feasible administrative level and not at the highest.[1]

At one level this is a consideration of administrative efficiency, and at its worst it is a dangerous element in the power game, whereby the senior administrators in an organisation augment their power, by gathering to themselves more and more control over the organisations' policies. It is a very insidious vice which has a peculiar fascination to certain temperaments.

A complementary theological problem is, of course, that the local bishops have been gradually stripped of all decision-making competence and reduced to administrators of decisions which are made at the Vatican. A relatively recent example illustrating both these shortcomings, was when the English Bishops' Conference wanted to admit women and girls as altar servers at mass. Not even that limited decision was within their competence, and permission had to be sought from Rome.

A further serious theological question, which must be faced by the very existence of this central bureaucracy, is the simple fact that virtually all the functionaries are in holy orders. The vast majority of those who work at the Vatican are priests, bishops and cardinals. Since their work does not entail any sacramental ministry, there is no reason for any of them to be ordained. The standard justification for their all being in holy orders, is that when they are issuing commands to diocesan bishops around the world, they will be listened to more respectfully, if they are themselves clergy, and indeed bishops or cardinals. That attitude to the importance of power is totally at variance with the whole ethos of the New Testament. Something closer to Christ's washing of the apostles' feet, ought to animate the Pope's secretariat, for in truth, that is all that is needed. Since ancient times, the Popes have always required a number of people to write and make copies of their letters. In modern times the need is much greater, simply because the Church has expanded. How that group of secretaries evolved into an organisation of overwhelming power is a very sobering cautionary tale for the Church.

It is quite possible that the existence in Rome of hundreds of cardinals, bishops and priests, with no sacramental ministry, might well have some connection with the worst aspect of their lives, namely rampant irregular homosexuality, which they do their best to conceal.

In antiquity homosexuality was regarded with varying degrees of disfavour, for one simple sociological factor.

Life was precarious in the extreme. Infant mortality was high, and the diseases of adults were incurable. Without any knowledge of scientific medicine, there was always a danger that the clan or tribe might, quite literally die out, or be so reduced in numbers as to be non-viable as a functioning community.

As a result, young women were paired off with young men, as soon as they were biologically capable of producing a child. In that context, it is perhaps not surprising that men and women who were not interested in producing children might become unpopular, or face hostility. Such an attitude has no place in the modern world.

St. Paul's harsh words against the homosexual behaviour of men and women in Romans 1: 26, 27, was the basis of Christian aversion for the practice. The reason for its criminalisation in several nations, including England, in the 19th century is not altogether clear. Possibly it had some connection with the strong revival in that century of evangelical Protestantism, and the tendency to follow a very literal interpretation of Scripture. Public opinion in England, and many other countries too, was strongly against homosexuality especially between men. The repeal of the homophobic laws in the latter part of the 20th century, did not immediately change public attitudes to the lifestyle. It was only the consensus of psychologists and other scientists that the orientation was innate, that enlightened public opinion became favourable to the toleration of homosexuality. The almost universal adoption of the epithet "gay" has been a sign of the change of attitude.

Nevertheless, a minority of gay men still exists who are either ashamed of their innate orientation, or angry about it, so that they do everything possible to conceal it. The most effective means of concealment, for Catholics is to enter the ranks of the clergy, for whom celibacy is still obligatory. (In spite of its being theologically unjustifiable, since the Second Vatican Council).

In 2019 the whole unhealthy network of deviant homosexuality in the Vatican, and the attempts to conceal it, were exposed by the publication of an important book by Frédéric Martel, entitled *In the Closet of the Vatican.*[2] For the remaining pages of this excursus I am greatly indebted to his book, which is my principal source. His researches and the presentation of the evidence are so thorough, that it would be superfluous to repeat it in detail. I will therefore summarise his conclusions and recommend to my readers that they study that book carefully.

In the first place it is probably useful to begin with clothing, and to analyse just how attractive is the Vatican background to immature men who have not come to terms with their homosexuality. They positively enjoy living out its superficial sartorial aspects, and particularly the colourful display. In the first place, the everyday clothing which is normal for them (ankle length cassocks with red buttons), is far more flamboyant than heterosexual men, in ordinary occupations, would feel comfortable in. In addition to this, many of the curial bishops and cardinals spend vast sums of money on their wrist watches, cuff links, pectoral crosses, and their rings of office. Clearly this serves as a substitute for jewellery.

Then for special liturgical occasions the costumes for the bishops are spectacular. The mitre is the most striking because it is solely a sign of rank, and bears no relation to any kind of hat, from which its design could have evolved. (By contrast the chasuble, for example, now worn at mass by all priests, is clearly an evolved and decorated version of the normal cloak/overcoat worn by all men in the period of the Roman Empire).

In such ceremonies the cardinals eclipse all the other participants with their robes, which are by any standard, are absolutely gorgeous. Take for example the cappa magna. This is a garment of scarlet silk, which starts as a sort of cloak around the shoulders and chest of the wearer, it is then lengthened at the back to be like train of a bride, stretching back three or four metres, so that is has to be held above ground by an altar server. In the recent past, various popes have endeavoured to abolish the custom of cardinals wearing such a monstrous garment, which has no liturgical significance whatsoever. Somehow the really desperate *afficionados* have managed to evade the prohibition also they just love to be photographed wearing it.

In addition to the cappa magna, cardinals were entitled to a mediaeval hat, but not actually during a liturgy. This hat, also bright red, is the "soup plate" style of hat, which in black material was common for the clergy in Catholic countries, until the mid-twentieth century. In the cardinals' scarlet form it has two cords at the sides of the hat, which might possibly have been tied under the wearer's chin, to prevent the large brimmed object from being blown away by the wind. However that practical role is now impossible, because each of the cords branches out into a network of tassels, which are badges of rank.

In addition to the extravagant clothing, it is important to bear in mind the sheer magnificence of the palace in which these ecclesiastics live and work. The complex of buildings at the back of St. Peter's basilica were constructed in the renaissance period by the most talented architects in the world. Undeniably, they are magnificent, and confer an unmistakably theatrical atmosphere to the activities which take place within them. Finally, there is the presence of the Swiss Guards whose ceremonial uniform, of red, blue, and yellow, has remained unchanged, since it was designed for them by Michaelangelo in the sixteenth century.

To put all of this in context, it is useful to remember that in the baroque period the kings and queens of Europe wore similar clothes and were surrounded by the same kind of ceremonial. However, after the French Revolution a profound change came over the way in which people dressed. The desire to display signs of rank and privilege disappeared, and in the modern world even the most powerful politicians, like the Russian president, wear the same clothes as other men.

The bearing of this evolution of clothing means that the sartorial customs at the Vatican now have the atmosphere, not of dignified theatre, but of pantomime, rather than anything serious. This factor trivializes their work and life-style, and yet it still has a dangerous attraction to immature and reluctant gay men, who have not integrated their homosexuality into their lives, in a really satisfactory manner.

The final complication in this dangerously artificial situation, is that the Roman Curia holds out the additional attraction of power. In other words it has an added motive for men who are ambitious for the exercise of power, possibly because of their inability to achieve fulfilment in family life. One cannot help reflecting on Lord Acton's famous dictum: "All power has a tendency to corrupt. Absolute power corrupts absolutely".

Frédéric Martel estimated that three out of four of the cardinals at the Vatican are gay.[3] Not all of them are active sexually, but the majority are. Sadly their sex life includes rampantly irresponsible practices, like frequenting gay saunas, cruising for rent boys on the streets of Rome, and dealings with other male prostitutes. At another level, senior archbishops and cardinals adopt gay seminarians, and junior priests, and advance their careers in return for sexual favours.

These irregular sexual practices are not confined to the personnel of the Curia domiciled in the city of Rome. Papal Nuncios and Apostolic Delegates, who are the diplomatic representatives of the Vatican City State to other governments, manifest the same patterns of behaviour when they are abroad in other countries. One particularly disedifying practice, because of its hypocrisy, has been their vocal and vehement opposition to the decriminalising of homosexual practices, which occurred in many nations in the latter part of the 20th century. As if to deflect attention from their private lives, many gay personnel of the Vatican are openly hostile to homosexuals. They are staunch supporters of the notorious judgement in the Catechism of the Catholic

Church, which alleges that such people's sexual inclination is "objectively disordered".

Complaints about the irregular sexual practices of the Curial clergy were brought to the attention of Pope John Paul II, and his advisor archbishop Dziwisz. However he disregarded them, because in Poland, under the communist regime, the secret police used to make similar accusations against the Catholic clergy, in order to try and discredit them. For example, when Cardinal Groër was archbishop of Vienna complaints about his sexual abuse of children and young people, were ignored at the Vatican. That was the time when the secular press (starting with *The Boston Globe*), were exposing the widespread sexual abuse of children and young people by Catholic priests. (The detailed numbers of offending clergy can be found in Excursus One, above).

At the beginning of the new millennium, the disedifying practices of the Vatican's personnel were not widely known to the general public. All that changed in 2012, when the first of what came to be called Vatileaks took place. The essential elements are, that Pope Benedict's butler secretly made his way, presumably at night, into the office of the pope's private secretary. Over an unspecified period of time, he made photocopies of hundreds of confidential documents, comprising thousands of pages. These included hand-written letters which had been sent to the pope, secret notes that had been handed to his secretary (George Gänswein) in person, and even copies of encoded diplomatic cables between the Vatican and Nuncios in foreign countries. What was disastrous for the Curia, was that much of this information found its way into the secular press of Italy, and beyond.

The so-called perpetrator of the crime, the pope's butler, was a happily married 48-year-old man, the father of three children. He was arrested, put on trial and sentenced to 18 months' imprisonment. Clearly this man could not have performed such a massive and time-consuming operation on his own, entailing his having the keys to parts of the Vatican, where he had no right of access. The most likely explanation is that he was the agent of a group of high-ranking Vatican officials (probably cardinals) who had a vendetta against other curial officials, and sought to discredit them by releasing this flood of disedifying information to the whole world. In a subsequent interview on the Italian TV channel *La Sette,* the butler repeated what he had stated at his trial, namely that he had acted out of love for the Church. His own words were "Seeing evil and corruption everywhere in the Church, I reached a point of no return... I was convinced that a shock, even one that happened through the media, would help to put the Church back on the rails". The butler, surrounded by hypocrisy and gay corruption, never accepted full responsibility for the crime, and still refused to express remorse.[4]

What has come to be known as Vatileaks Two, started in Spain in the latter years of Benedict XVI, and exploded in the pontificate of Pope Francis. The central character in this drama was a country priest Lucio Balda, who had been ordained at the age of 26, without any further specialised studies in any field, economics, for example. However he was extremely handsome, and was endowed with boundless self-confidence. He had come to the attention of Cardinal Ruocco Varela, the archbishop of Madrid.

In the latter part of the 20th century, attempts were made to make the Roman Curia more international. The practical steps to achieve this aim were more like tokens to satisfy public opinion, rather than the authentic internationalisation at the decision-making level, which was what the ancient institution really needed. So, when Benedict XVI and Cardinal Bertone asked Cardinal Varela to recommend a reliable priest to look after financial matters, he sent Lucio Balda. Although he lacked any special qualifications or experience in financial matters, Cardinal Varela was glad to have one of his own protégés at the Vatican, within the pope's entourage.

Once in Rome, the glamour of the city seemed to have overwhelmed him with its opportunities for a pleasure-seeking life. Although he did not possess any financial experience or expertise, as noted above, his boundless self-confidence did not desert him. Surprisingly, Lucio Balda was appointed as second in command of the Administration of the Patrimony of the Apostolic See, which looks after the properties and money of the Vatican. Unbelievably, this inexperienced country priest was also put in charge of the Vatican Bank, which meant that he had access to all the financial arrangements of the Roman Curia. Apart from more dangerous consequences, the advancement of such an unqualified man, represents administrative amateurism at the Vatican, at an almost criminal level of irresponsibility. The consequences of such shambolic procedures were not long in coming to light.

The actual explosion occurred, when highly confidential documents about Vatican finances appeared in books published by two Italian journalists, Gianluigi Nuzzi and

Emiliano Fittipaldi. The world was stunned to discover the countless illegal bank accounts, and the unlawful money transfers, which might well have been the money laundering activities of criminals, the Mafia perhaps. Above all there was the all-pervading opacity of the Vatican Bank's way of doing business, and no shortage of evidence to substantiate the allegations.[5]

Pope Benedict was in an extremely difficult position, to put it mildly! He could not deny the revelations, still less could he silence the dissemination of the disedifying information. Moreover, he could hardly protest against the way in which the disclosure was made: to have protested against the breach of secrecy, would simply have drawn even more unwelcome scrutiny, to the intrinsic dishonesty of maintaining it. However he did realise the need to take some action, so he appointed three elderly cardinals whom he trusted, to investigate the whole affair. Their investigations lead to the production of a 300-page report. It has never been published, presumably because the information which it contains, would have been even more damaging to the reputation of the Vatican.

Little has been done to repair the damage of the two Vatileaks, except for the demotion of one cardinal, who was removed from one of the senior positions in the Curia. He has not been named, but he was well known as a homophobe, a felon and ultra-gay. It is clear that he is the link between both of the Vatileaks.[6]

Sadly, it is clear that the Vatican's administrative structures have not been reformed as thoroughly as the scandals would warrant, particularly in view of devastating revelations of the two Vatileaks. This is all the more disappointing, since the authentic solution has been perceived by so many observers, from widely differing backgrounds. Martel quotes one such witness whom he interviewed several times, in 2014 and 2015. He is Carlos Bruce, a member of parliament in Peru, and also one of the leaders of Latin America's LGBT movement. He stated "I think the Church must accept all the consequences of moral failure: it must stop criticizing homosexual relations between consenting adults and authorize marriage; then it must abandon its silence about sexual abuse and completely abandon its general institutionalised cover-up strategy. Finally, *because this is the key to the problem, it must end the celibacy of the priesthood.*"[7] (my italics) In other words, no matter how widely it is ignored by the priests, the fact that obligatory celibacy is still the law, consolidates it as the perfect refuge for gay men, who resent their sexual orientation, and wish to conceal it effectively.

CHAPTER FOUR

THE LAITY

At the start of this chapter, I will devote a few paragraphs to the description of just what form of priestly ministry will best serve the laity, and hence the whole Church, in the 21ˢᵗ century. There will be some repetition of what I have already stated about clergy who should not be a privileged class, but in this chapter it is my intention to describe how the laity and clergy can work together in genuine partnership.

First of all, this form of priestly life must do justice to the Epistles to Timothy and Titus, as well as to the letter and spirit of Second Vatican Council's pronouncements.

It is clear that the Catholic community in Britain could not afford the cost of a salaried clergy, like the Church of England for example. This financial constraint applies to many other nations as well. Far from being a problem, it is a blessing in disguise. The married Catholic priests will have to continue in the ordinary jobs after ordination. They will not have as much time to devote to parochial duties as a full-time salaried priest, so they will be forced by circumstances, to enlist the skills of the laity, who are capable of performing every operation in the parish, except saying mass and administering sacraments. That is to say, lay people are perfectly competent to give catechetical instruction to children, and prepare them for first communion and confirmation, they are the obvious

counsellors for marriage preparation, and its "safety net",
namely advice in situations of marriages breaking down.
They can visit the sick and house-bound to give them
Holy Communion, and generally socialise with them. The
parish finances would be better looked after by a
professional accountant, the material structure of the
church (gutter clearing, and cracks in the brickwork)
should be entrusted to a builder. Coffee after mass (in the
church) should be entrusted to friendly talkative people
who can put shy people at their ease. As to the mass itself,
it needs a cantor to lead the singing. That role in the liturgy
is best performed by a lay person, leaving the celebrating
priest to perform the strictly sacramental parts, and deliver
the sermon. It is worth noting here, that the ancient
custom of the Church has been that when the community
prays together, it is preferable that they should sing. It is
difficult to demonstrate why this should be so, but people
who have had experience of chanting the prayers, find it a
more satisfying expression of community, rather than
simply reciting the prayers. In short, a well organised
parish will not suffer from being led by a non-stipendiary
priest.

In recent years, the Church of England has been obliged,
by financial constraints, to ordain increasing numbers of
such priests. They are described as non-stipendiary clergy,
and the functioning of that form of parish clergy, has
proved to be remarkably successful.

Paradoxically it seems to have been the normal pattern in
European Christianity, after the collapse of the Roman
Empire in the West. The way in which that form of
priestly life functioned, can be gleaned from the
regulations of a significant number of regional councils. I

have already described that pattern of married priests and their wage-earning occupations in Chapter Three, on De-Clericalising the Clergy, so I will simply refer my readers to that earlier chapter, and here I will outline the training programme for such priests.

If a married man in a full-time job is prepared for training as a priest, he is obviously open to the criticism that he might be neglecting his family. The existence of that latent danger is undeniable. However it is reassuring to bear in mind that in other walks of life, many people cope with similar undertakings successfully. Thousands of married people in full time work, devote themselves to serious study, as in the programmes of the Open University. Another role that consumes time and energy, is in politics, especially the role of local councillors. The people who are successful in these scenarios are undeniably, energetic and self-disciplined personalities. That is just the right kind of temperament for candidates aspiring to the priesthood. And that should cause us no surprise!

The theological and spiritual formation of the non-stipendiary priests must necessarily be different from the usual seminary course of six years. They could not leave their families and jobs to study in a residential college. This problem too has been solved already. For more than forty years, the permanent deacons have equipped themselves theologically by a scheme of distance learning, which has been tailored to their requirements over the years. This programme could easily be adapted for the non-stipendiary priests. Similarly their spiritual formation, with a personal director, and occasional residential retreats, as planned for the deacons, could be adopted for the priests as well.

Having identified the sort of priest who is suitable for the Church in the 21st century, we can now turn our attention to the sort of community which will be serviceable for the religious needs of our secularised society. At the risk of stating the obvious, I repeat that it must be a community, and not the sort of group that is attached to a doctor for example, who cures their illnesses. The pattern of expert and clients will not suffice, though in its own sphere, it is perfectly serviceable. Financial advisors perform the same sort of role, in relation to the clients who receive guidance about their investments, and other financial matters.

By contrast, a community can be described as a moral and stable union of a number of people, for the pursuit of a common objective, to be achieved by their combined efforts. The significant difference between this and the client type of association, is that in the community there are no passengers; all are working collaborators. (I noted in Chapter Three, that the description of a parish in Canon Law still implies as its model, the mediaeval parish. Canon 515 § 1 of the 1983 revision of the Code, displays no suggestion of a partnership for mission. What is latent in that text is a maintenance operation, safeguarded by the overriding authority of the parish priest.)

For an authentic community, the first requirement is that they should all be on speaking terms. This can be achieved very simply. At the start of Mass, the celebrant can say to the congregation in front of him, "Please look around at your neighbours in the pews, and when you see an unfamiliar face, go up to that person, say your own name and ask theirs". Then shake hands and return to your original place. Experience has shown that it is a very simple and effective ice-breaker.

Theologically speaking, the kind of community which is needed has four principal characteristics: Worship, Charity, Witness, and Apostolate. For the rest of this chapter, I am drawing extensively on the inspiring course, on the theology of the parish, given by the Professor of Pastoral Theology, at the university of Fribourg in Switzerland in the 1960's. His name was Alois Müller. I have never managed to trace any published version of that course, and it is unlikely that he is still alive. But the memory of the lectures is still etched indelibly in my mind.

The first characteristic: Worship

Worship is the fundamental characteristic of a Christian community. The liturgy is the specifically public form of the wider exercise of prayer. Prayer could be described as communication with God, and more precisely it is the conscious articulation of our commitment to God, following our decisive act of faith. This conscious focussing of our attention on God, lies within the general remit of prayer, which can be of two kinds. The private and personal prayer is basic, and that can take many forms. Some people address God in their own words, rather like a conversation. Others find that thoughtful systematic meditation is more profitable. Yet others find complete satisfaction in wordless contemplation of God in conscious unconditional love. If this should sound so intangible as to be meaningless, let me offer a homely parallel. When children are very young they sleep a great deal, and it is important for their development. Often their parents will stand beside the cot, just looking at the infant. They would love to pick up the tiny child for an affectionate hug or stroke him or her, as a sign of affection. All such contact would be disturbing to the infant whose need at that point is sleep. Consequently the parents derive profound joy and satisfaction as they stand there in adoring silence. Unconditional love is "pouring out" of their eyes and thoughts as they contemplate in silence the object of their devotion. An almost identical attitude of unconditional love can also be directed towards God; the difference being that whereas God does not need to be left sleeping soundly(!) but he cannot be contained within any concepts, definitions, or imaginary pictures, because he is infinite: hence the importance of wordless prayer, which is devoid of any images too.

Whereas private prayer can take numerous forms to suit the temperament and culture of the individual, the communal form (liturgy), must be structured so that it appeals to the temperaments of all members of that community, in order that that all of them find it satisfying, to a greater or lesser degree.

In antiquity the first generations of Christians continued the use of the psalms which they retained from their Jewish background. A couple of centuries later, when the liturgical prayer of the Church was being formalised, it was entirely structured round the Book of Psalms lifted straight out of the Hebrew bible. Shortly after Constantine's official toleration of Christianity, the local communities organised the official public prayer on a weekly cycle. The bishop in each city, accompanied by the clergy, and those lay people who were not at work, met several times a day to sing psalms on a programme which enabled them to complete the whole 150 of them every week. Other prayers were also recited, and passages from the bible were read, but the main substance of that pattern of worship was the Book of Psalms. (At a later stage of the Church's history, when monasteries became more and more numerous, that pattern of communal prayer was adopted integrally. Many people are surprised to learn that it had not been created by the monks!) The Church had no hesitation in adopting what was the official Jewish prayer book. In those poems one can read all the sentiments and attitudes of a believer in dialogue with the one true God. They contain numerous expressions of the love of God, together with dialogues of repentance, earnest petitions for a variety of favours, and expressions of gratitude for benefits received. At times the speaker of the psalm might even reproach God for his apparent neglect or abandonment of the believer. In short, every form of a believer's conscious attitude to the deity finds dignified and beautiful expression in those prayers. The sentiments contained in the Psalms are never sentimental. That is something which cannot be guaranteed in some vernacular hymns and prayers composed in the 19th century!

The structure of that collective prayer was not totally uniform throughout the whole Church, but its principal components were the same, namely readings from the bible, singing a number of psalms at each gathering, and petitionary prayers. At an early stage, homilies were introduced to explain the meaning and relevance of the scriptures which had been read that day. As I noted above, the bishop and the local community met for this activity several times in the course of the day. That was practicable in the early centuries because the cities were so small that the church building was within easy walking distance of all the inhabitants.

What is even more impressive is to realise that in the fourth century, when that pattern of community prayer received its classical form, most of the laity were illiterate. That constituted no problem at all. It was a blessing in disguise, because they would have memorised the psalms effortlessly, by joining in the singing on a regular basis. Illiterate people in antiquity had phenomenal powers of memory, which later literate generations no longer possess.

Despite the vast differences sociologically between the 21st century, and that early period, it is a form of prayer which could easily be introduced in the present day. First of all, we have the text, in the post Conciliar reformed breviary, now aptly entitled "The Prayer of the Church". This prayer book is extremely well planned, based on sound theology, and entirely suitable for use by lay people. It could be used for private prayer at home, or better still, with members of the parish community in church, at least once a day. The final advantage of this prayer book is that it does not need the priest to lead it. Any lay person, man or woman could be the leading voice, so to speak. If this form of prayer were available generally in parish churches, it would be an immense enrichment to the prayer life of the Church.

By contrast, in the recent past, when Catholics gathered in church for a service other than mass, the habitual practice has been to recite the rosary aloud, or pray the stations of the cross under the leadership of the priest. In the 1930's the Sunday evening service was no longer the singing of vespers in Latin, but a more intelligible service, Rosary, Sermon and Benediction. Those services had not been thought through theologically. Stations of the Cross and the Rosary are basically meditations and should more properly be prayed by individuals in silence. Their use in public as a joint prayer was an accident of history, namely that the Tridentine revision of the Roman breviary was never officially translated into modern languages. I suspect that there was resentment in Catholic minds over the beautiful language of Cranmer's Book of Common Prayer, which provided a text with which the laity could take part actively, in the ancient custom of joining the clergy praying the divine office together. There was also a widespread prejudice, after the reformation, that if Luther had initiated it, it must be wrong.

The retention of Latin as the liturgical language of the whole of central Europe is puzzling, and distressing. With the passage of time the Latin language ceased to be understood by the laity. The transition from Latin into the modern romance languages like Spanish and French, was so gradual as to be almost imperceptible to any one generation. The clergy still continued to study Latin, and to use it for their theological studies. When universities emerged into prominence, it was supremely useful for the movement of students and professors across the whole of Europe. It also facilitated the exchange of ideas between individual scholars, as with the friendship between Thomas More and Erasmus for example, neither of whom spoke the other's mother tongue.

The initial appearance of Latin in the liturgy was a simple practical measure. In the fourth century, Latin replaced Greek as the liturgical language in Rome, because the majority of the Christian community no longer understood Greek. Greek had been the daily language of the first generation of Christians there, so it had been quite naturally adopted for their worship. The notion of a sacred language had no place in early Christianity

As Christianity spread through north and western Europe the mass was retained in Latin although the lay people did not understand it. This custom was a deviation of the older missionary practice. When the nations closest to Palestine had been evangelised, such as Greece, Syria, Egypt, Armenia and Georgia, the missionaries translated the liturgy and the bible into their languages, within the first generation of their adopting Christianity. This of course presupposed that those languages were literate and had their own alphabets. At a later stage in the history of the Eastern Church, when the Greeks sent missionaries to the nations who spoke the Slav family of languages, a totally original plan emerged. The two best known missionaries, saints Cyril and Methodius, invented an alphabet for the Russian language. Armed with that instrument, they translated the liturgy and bible into Russian, following the ancient tradition.

Sadly, when the people western and northern Europe were evangelised, from roughly the 6th century onwards, the nations in question were not literate, nor did the missionaries display the sort of originality of saints Cyril and Methodius. St. Bede mentions the matter in his *Ecclesiastical History of the English Nation,* where he points out that in Britain there were five languages, namely English, British, Irish, Pictish, as well as Latin.[1]

Evidently Bede regarded Latin as a useful measure for unity, sparing them the herculean task of translating the bible and liturgy into four languages which lacked alphabets and any secular literature.

Before moving on from the historical accidents which allowed Latin to be retained for so long, it is worth pointing out that the period of the Renaissance could have been the most likely time to make up for lost time and change to a vernacular liturgy. This is because in that epoch literature in the spoken languages of Italian, Spanish, French, and English, to mention only the best known, were experiencing a remarkable literary flowering. This in its turn was favoured by the invention of printing which had facilitated the printing of increasing numbers of ever cheaper books. Luther realised this opportunity, and introduced German into the Churches' public worship, along with his definitive German version of the bible. Sadly it must be acknowledged that since it had been Luther who had made this definitive innovation, many Catholics became automatically antagonistic to the whole concept.

Shortly after the German Lutherans had produced many hymns in the vernacular, French and Swiss Protestants turned their attention to translating the Psalms into a poetic version. Translating poetry from one language to another is notoriously difficult, particularly when the original Hebrew was in a totally different family of languages. The French writers and also the English devised a brilliant solution, by rendering the Psalms in metrical forms. This enabled them to be sung rhythmically, and so easily memorised. In English the most widely used of these translations, was that of N. Tate and N. Brady, entitled *New Version of the Psalms* and published in 1696. At that time the vast majority of the population was illiterate, but like the early Christians, the metric form enabled them to memorise them. Catholics at that period were denied a knowledge of the Psalms for their prayer life, because the authorities' stubborn refusal to allow the spoken languages to be used in the liturgy.

The retention of a Latin liturgy by the Catholics produced another evil, namely the harmful habit of living with institutionalised artificiality. One particularly damaging result was that the many of the clergy did not have a sufficient command of Latin, to enable them to understand the breviary adequately. An extraordinary example of that situation stays in my memory to this day. A fellow student at the seminary had his promotion to the rank of sub-deacon postponed. I never knew why. He told me subsequently that while discussing it with his confessor, he had said that he was not really worried. The reason was astounding. He told that good priest, that for the forthcoming summer vacation, he could still visit the theatre (forbidden to those in major orders), and that he was not obliged to the daily recitation the breviary. In other words, he and many priests, regarded that exercise as a penance. The man in question was ordained priest shortly afterwards, but one cannot help wondering what harm was done to his spiritual life, and to many others of the same outlook, from their failure to derive adequate satisfaction when the praying the breviary.

It is difficult to gauge how much the prayer life of the laity was impoverished in mediaeval Catholicism, by the Mass and Divine Office being available only in Latin. There are other pointers too at that period about the mediocre level of the spiritual life of the average lay person. Although it was understood that everyone should attend Mass on Sundays, they seem to have received Holy Communion rarely. The Fourth Lateran council of 1215 legislated that they should receive the sacrament at least once a year, preferably at Easter time. Unfortunately, what the legislators designated as the minimum eventually became the norm, and generally Catholics received Holy Communion only once a year.

That situation was only rectified in the 20th century when Pope Pius X encouraged frequent communion. However it had to wait for the liturgical studies of the 20th century to make it clear to everyone that it was normal for all participants at Mass to receive holy communion on every occasion. Those same liturgical researches also made it clear that lay people should receive the chalice too. That latter innovation had to wait for the Second Vatican Council to sanction it. Sadly, in spite of explicit conciliar approbation, some parish priests still (in 2020) refuse to allow it in their parishes.

As to the prayer life of lay people, up to the 20th century, I will have to limit my observations to Great Britain. The unsatisfactory form of Mass, and the absence of the Psalms, put them in a situation of spiritual deprivation. It was filled with substitutes of varying value. The reservation of the Blessed Sacrament in the tabernacle, and the fact that churches were open all day, enabled people to pray there meditatively with great profit. Lighting candles before the statues of the saints was another homely form of authentic piety. Exposition of the Blessed Sacrament, Benediction and Corpus Christi processions presented problems, being so obviously unrelated to the Last

Supper. Bishop Challoner's *Garden of the Soul* did not really provide an adequate substitute for the psalm based Divine Office, which had been the laity's staple prayer in antiquity.

Prior to Vatican II, attempts to remedy the situation were very rare. In 1921 some mitigation of the incomprehension of the Mass was provided by the publication the first Latin and English missal, edited by a far-sighted Benedictine liturgist, Fernand Cabrol, abbot of Farnborough. It was widely used among educated people who could afford the book. Poor people who were literate, thanks to universal elementary education, were unlikely to be able to afford the purchase price. In mission territories like Africa, where only a tiny minority were literate, poverty would certainly prevent them buying such a relatively expensive item.

Those of us who live in the aftermath of the Second Vatican Council, should be extremely grateful for the form of Mass which it authorised.

The use of the everyday spoken language of the nation is absolutely essential. It is now difficult understand how the pre-conciliar generations coped with the Latin, particularly as the priest recited most of it in silence, and he had his back to the congregation. The memory of priests turning their backs on the congregations and addressing God silently almost amounts to a deliberate symbol of exclusion of the lay people. It suggests that they were there on sufferance, and that it would be disrespectful to God if they spoke. Any dialogue was restricted to the altar servers, and as they did not understand Latin, the absence of communication was total. As a result, that deformed pattern of Mass was about as far removed from the ancient Tradition as was possible, while just avoiding a sacramentally invalid ceremony.

After the Second World War, attempts were made to introduce what was known as Dialogue Mass, where the whole congregation recited the responses which had been spoken hitherto only by the altar servers, who had been coached in Latin. Its success was patchy, since it depended upon how many people could even pronounce the Latin words, even if they did not understand them. The attitude of the bishops was, at best lukewarm toleration. Early in the 1950's the ultra-conservative bishop of Southwark, declared in a pastoral letter to the diocese "I absolutely forbid dialogue mass". Nevertheless, he was fighting a losing battle. Change was in the air. At that time, in England the laity initiated "The Vernacular Society of Great Britain", whose title says it all. The desire for reform had come to stay.

The reform of the Roman Missal, in the wake of the Second Vatican Council is probably the most successful of the Council's innovations, to date. It embodies the consensus of approximately a century of serious research into the origin and development of liturgy in the early Church. It has been highly successful, in most respects, and has been welcomed by the laity.

Unlike Germany, France, and other nations, there was practically no study of liturgy in Great Britain, and the introduction of the reformed liturgy was presented as an act of obedience to Rome. The bishops realised that such an abrupt innovation might be too much for the laity to cope with. Accordingly it was agreed by the English bishops that on every Sunday, in churches where there was more than one mass, one of the masses must be celebrated in Latin. This was a perfectly reasonable transitional measure. Unfortunately it was not planned sensibly. The Latin form envisaged was the basic universal Latin matrix from which the modern languages for the missal were translated. Had the bishops retained the Tridentine form with which everyone was familiar (whether they found it helpful or not), the plan might have been profitable. In the event, numbers at those Latin masses dwindled so fast, that after a few months all the parishes quietly dropped them. The laity as a whole, retained no fondness for Latin as the language for public worship.

The one problem which still has not been resolved satisfactorily, has been the Vatican's insistence that every translation into a modern vernacular must be the same for all nations using that language. That stipulation might have been practicable in Europe, where for example the German speaking countries were geographically contiguous, namely Germany, Austria and parts of Switzerland. Yet there is no theological basis for that imposition of uniformity. And its impractical nature is most clearly seen in the case of English. In addition to Great Britain, it is spoken all over the world from north America to Australia, New Zealand, and countless small islands all over the world. In these widely separated places, the language has evolved its own distinctive idiomatic forms. The most recent revision of the English version of the mass (in the new millennium) has provoked massive criticism. It has re-introduced technical terms, like 'consubstantial' in the creed (which is understood by very few), and other stilted expressions. The identity of the translator has been kept secret (still a characteristic of how the Vatican operates), but reliable rumours indicated that he was born in India!

Apart from the unsatisfactory English translation, the reformed mass has been a remarkable achievement. The system of a three year-cycle for the biblical readings ensures that lay people who do not read the bible daily at home, will enable them to become familiar with the most important parts of both Old and New Testaments. The fact that lay people are the readers of the scriptures is equally important and emphasises that the mass is indeed an act of community worship. Added to these refinements is the all-important bestowal of Holy Communion with the consecrated wine being given to the laity. Our mass is now substantially in the form, which it acquired in the creative period of the fourth and fifth centuries.

The second characteristic: Charity

The second characteristic of the parish community is Charity. Charity is the love of God and our neighbour, and its practice in varied situations is the most prominent component of the Church's moral programme. In the New Testament countless pages are devoted to urging its practice in widely differing contexts, which are all expressions of the love of the neighbour as a practical expression of our love of God. Basic to this programme is the implied assumption, that it is not the same as liking our neighbour. Possibly the most edifying example of charity as a virtue is the exhortation of Jesus that we should love our enemies.

The basic practical expressions of charity are stated with perfect simplicity in the 25ᵗʰ chapter of St. Matthew. Food and drink for those who are hungry, clothing for those who are cold, and housing for those who are homeless. Moreover, our fulfilment of that programme will be the basis of our being judged by God, after death.

In spite of the simple clarity of the personal needs, their fulfilment can be helped by a measure of organisation, which must not replace the spontaneity of the individual's response. Heroic Christians like Mother Teresa of Calcutta, and Dorothy Day in the U.S.A. have inspired the wider Church by their systematic practices. Mother Teresa and her associates made a point of rescuing terminally ill individuals literally from the gutters of the great cities of India. They were taken to simple clean houses, washed, clothed and given a bed. To use her own words, "Many of died beautiful deaths".

Also, in the 20ᵗʰ century a lay woman, Dorothy Day, organised something similar, initially in the U.S.A. On May 1ˢᵗ 1933, she published the first edition of a weekly newspaper, named *Catholic Worker*. She also began to acquire largish buildings in which she and her collaborators could provide cooked meals for homeless people. One of her earliest collaborators, Peter Maurin, a Canadian lawyer, named the buildings "Houses of Hospitality", which is a more attractive title that "soup kitchens", which is a slight humiliation of the poor people who make use of them. He also put forward the idea that every parish should have such a house, and that it was just as important as the church. In the same buildings such people, who would otherwise have slept on the streets, could also sleep at night in reasonable comfort. That is to say, in security and protected from wind, rain, snow, and being harassed by the police.

Another example is the initiative of a French layman, Antoine Ozanam. Early in the 19th century, while he was still studying law in the University of Paris, he founded the well-known Society of St. Vincent de Paul, whose members (all lay people), would visit poor parishioners in their homes. This society has spread to every part of the Catholic Church. Its ideals are superb, but there is one reservation that must be born on mind. Those lay people who are not members, must not assume that the S.V.P. has taken over their responsibilities for all charity in the parish! Many years ago, I recall hearing a parish priest say to a poor person who had asked for help, "Oh get in touch with the S.V.P., that's their responsibility". No comment needed.

The connection between informal practical charity, such as I have described in the preceding paragraphs, does not exhaust the field of this essential Christian activity. I would like to refer readers to the pages devoted to charity and politics in Chapter 2, *Catholicism's Lost Opportunities* (especially pages 39-52). There I sketched out the total picture, namely that the exercise of charity has four basic methods. They are Amelioration, of which Houses of Hospitality, and the other methods described in the preceding paragraphs of this chapter), are classical examples. Next comes Witness, and in the context of the abolition of slavery, the work of the Dominican, Bartholomé de las Casas, is a classical example. He made several arduous crossings of the Atlantic from the Spanish colonies, to the Royal council in Spain to protest about the colonists' treatment of slaves. The third stage which I described was Enablement, perfectly exemplified when the Quaker community in Philadelphia gave legal freedom to their own slaves and encouraged other communities to do the same. The fourth characteristic is Institutional Change. In the case of the slave trade, that was when the English Parliament passed laws, firstly to outlaw the trade, and then to criminalise the ownership of slaves.

After the Second World War, in Great Britain, and subsequently in most enlightened democracies, National Health Services were set up, together with other social services. This does not take it outside the ambit of charity. It is paid for indirectly by the taxpayers. This development is much to be welcomed by all Christians. It means that the message of Christianity, and of other enlightened people, that the governments should assume responsibility for the needs of their citizens, which individuals cannot afford to pay for from their own salaries or savings. It is not a total innovation. In the latter part of the 19th century the governments of the wealthier European nations provided free elementary education for all the children in their lands. Earlier still publicly funded fire services were also organised. (There may have been an element of self-interest for that measure. In crowded cities, if a poor person's house caught fire, the conflagration could easily spread to the houses of the rich, and even beyond. The great fire of London in 1666 was a devastating lesson of not having a publicly funded fire service).

If anyone should doubt that the NHS is an expression of corporate charity, I would ask them to reflect upon the efforts of some political parties in Britain and the USA, to abolish the NHS in order to reduce the taxes which the citizens pay. Sadly, that ungenerous attitude was so strong in the USA, that President Obama's plan for a nationwide health service, financed from public finances, came to nothing. It was wrecked by the opposition of the insurance industry, the pharmaceutical industry, and sadly, the medical profession too. Those three groups of people, already involved in the nation's health, judged that they could make higher profits if they remained free of the constraints of a national health service. They also foresaw that taxes would be lighter. In Great Britain the Conservative Party has been trying to privatise the N.H.S. for about 30 years, but they have had to move cautiously on account of the immense popularity of the health service. This was made clear at the opening ceremony of the Olympic Games in London in 2012, which included unexpectedly, a pageant in honour of the N.H.S.

The establishment of the National Health Service in the 20th century bears some likeness to the hospitals in the middle ages. They were financed and operated thanks to religious orders, who alone had the resources of money and man-power to run them. They did not replace domestic charity in the care of sick people at home, and alleviation of widespread poverty in mediaeval society. The importance of the hospitals conducted by religious orders became starkly apparent when Henry VIII suppressed all religious houses. At that time the country had approximately 125 hospitals. Only two of them survived, somehow, namely St. Thomas's and St. Bartholomew's hospitals in London. There is some debate about possibly a third hospital which survived in Norwich, thanks to the enlightened generosity of some wealthy citizens.

In a wider context it is clear that the establishment in Britain of the N.H.S. and other social services has not removed all suffering in our society. There are innumerable problems of sadness and hardship in the nation at the time of writing. In 2020 unemployment is relatively low, but the conditions of work for large numbers of workers are literally appalling. Low wages, zero hours, the absence of secure contracts of employment have blighted the lives of countless employees. These situations are compounded by the exclusion of Trades Unions from increasing areas of semi-automated employment, such as purchasing via computers. In many families even if both parents are employed, their combined wages are not sufficient to pay the rent and feed their children properly. This has given rise to the re-introduction of food banks on a massive scale. It is perfectly clear that much of this hardship is the result of policies of the Conservative government dating back to 2010. The re- organisation of the benefit system for unemployed workers has resulted in adding to their problems. This has been made even worse by the housing shortage, and the refusal of the government to build council houses and flats. Private landlords can exploit homeless families, almost with impunity. The list could be continued indefinitely.

One practical course for Christians is to become actively involved in politics and trades union activity, as an expression of Christian charity. Collaboration with other institutions, particularly trades unions, is an expression of the virtue of prudence, as how best to effect the relief of poverty and other social evils. Acting in that fashion should be regarded as a normal responsibility incumbent on citizens in democratic free societies. It is more effective in the elimination of poverty to be active in the political arena, than to hand out cash to beggars on the streets. That kind of generosity may help the symptoms, but it does not cure the causes of poverty.

Even if the public services are functioning properly, the scope for private personal charity is immense. For example, modern scientific medicine is keeping literally millions of old people alive for much longer than in previous generations. An unavoidable result is that serious loneliness is widespread. The remedy for such isolation is quite simply for more active old people to visit them, keep them company, and talk. What could be simpler?

In short, despite the most enlightened and well-funded government initiatives, the scope for individual practical charity is almost limitless.

The third characteristic: Witness

The third characteristic of a parish community, according to Professor Müller's lectures, is Witness. In the English language that word is more commonly associated with the legal sphere when criminals are being tried in court. Witnesses are summoned to state what they saw in order to establish the facts of a case of dangerous driving, for instance.

The wider use of the word in the context of ordinary life, means taking action publicly, to draw attention to injustices which cannot, at the present time, be abolished in practice. Social and political life furnishes countless examples. Perhaps the best known were in the 19th century, when the suffragettes were demonstrating for a whole raft of womens' rights, such as the franchise, entry to universities, entry to the professions and womens' property rights.

In the 20th century the most noteworthy acts of witness were peace protests, such as CND marches against nuclear weapons. This kind of activity is a serious duty for Christians. A few years ago, when it was clear that Prime Minister Blair was likely to follow the Americans by invading Iraq, approximately a million people marched through central London in protest. Their sentiments were made explicit by the messages written on thousands of banners, such as "Not in my name", or "No invasion of Iraq". The government ignored the message, and the long-term consequences of that invasion are still causing violence, cruelty and instability in the region of Iraq and its neighbouring states. It is a matter of moral integrity, and a duty on Christians (and other honest people) to proclaim publicly the right cause that their government should follow.

Similar examples are strikes over pay and conditions of work in industry. Not all strikes result in higher wages, but the disruption to production is justified fully, by publicising widely unjustly low wages, or dangerous conditions of work. As with peace demonstrations, it is a matter of moral integrity that to make clear to all parties, what justice demands. These practical objectives cannot be achieved by private conversations in the comfort of our sitting rooms.

The Church's role in the realm of witness, is precisely because the moral behaviour of all people is part of our religious message, enjoined upon us by Jesus himself. If the Church were fully committed to peace demonstrations and other public protests against injustice, it could convince people of good-will that the message of Christianity is one which could enhance the social welfare of the nation as a whole and deserves to be taken seriously. Sadly, that has not yet been achieved in Great Britain, in the wake of Vatican II. This is due to the psychological imprisonment of the leaders (parish priests and bishops) as members of a privileged class. They do not have to earn their living like other men and it desensitizes them to the laity's anxieties. I have discussed the subject at length in chapter Three, so I will not repeat it here, except to remark, with sadness, that I have never seen a Catholic bishop in any peace demonstration.

Paradoxically in the Church's present state of crisis, the most urgent witness is by lay people to the Church authorities, to make clear to them just what kind of Church policies are currently necessary. One example of this type of initiative can be traced to three people, in the Austrian region of Tyrol on Good Friday in 1995. The immediate cause for their taking action was the scandalous life of the Archbishop of Vienna, Cardinal Groër who was finally dismissed, after having been shielded for too long by Pope John Paul II. Those three pioneers were soon joined by others, and they formulated their aspirations in five simple objectives. These were:

1) The creation of a Church of brotherhood in preference to clericalism and power structures.

2) The admission of women into all ecclesiastical official roles. (i.e. priesthood, and episcopate etc.)

3) Priests should be able to choose their form of life. (i.e. married or celibate).

4) A humanly friendly sexual ethic.

5) To proclaim a gospel of joy, rather than threats.

Within three weeks more than half a million Austrian Catholics had signed up to the programme. The Austrian bishops were instructed by the Vatican to silence the movement. That proved impossible, and before long the initial programme had given birth to the world-wide movement "We are Church International". In 2020 that movement is active in twenty nations in all continents. Most importantly it is firmly within the Church and has not split off as a splinter group. One of Congar's four essential conditions for authentic reform has been maintained, namely the Church's unity.[2]

Witness within the Church to gain the attention of the ecclesiastical authorities is exceptional. Traditionally the quintessential act of witness by Christians in the face of an unsympathetic or hostile society, has been martyrdom. That is when the individual voluntarily undergoes death, rather than renounce Christ and his mission. In the first three centuries after Christ, the missionary activity of the infant Church was mainly within the bounds of the Roman empire. Since the Christians would not honour the pagan gods of the empire, they were soon confronted with the threat of legal penalties if they continued with their refusal. The ultimate penalty was death. So many of the early Christians suffered the death penalty, that it is impossible to give even an approximate number. However, since the authorities wanted to make a public example of the victims, so as to terrorize other citizens not to join them, the executions were frequently carried out in the amphitheatres which existed in practically every city. However, the plan miscarried spectacularly. On a regular basis, thousands of people perceived the outstanding courage of the martyrs, men and women, from every category of society, who were clearly not fanatics. Some detailed records have survived, which indicate that they faced death with calm dignity and confidence. It was undoubtedly the principal cause of recruitment to Christianity for those early centuries.

Martyrs are still being executed in the modern world, though the motive for their being persecuted is usually not by governments wishing to deter them from being Christians, but for the loyalty to Christian principles in everyday life. The possible circumstances cannot be foreseen or planned in advance. But Christian leaders should encourage their followers to lead a life of total commitment to Jesus, so that if a cruel and repressive government should demand that they abandon Christianity, they would be spiritually prepared to make the heroic choice.

The best-known modern martyr is probably Archbishop Oscar Romero of El Salvador. I have discussed the circumstances of his martyrdom in detail in Chapter 3, so I will merely repeat the most significant points here. When he was appointed as archbishop of the city, San Salvador, he was recognised as a conservative. However the blatant injustices and cruelties of the government soon changed his attitude. For example 75,000 citizens were killed by the government's security forces between1978 and 1993. Romero became an active supporter of those who campaigned for political reform. So the government ordered his assassination. He was shot while celebrating Mass.

The adherence to Christian principals was the cause that brought about the execution of several martyrs, during the Second World War. Franz Jägerstatter is the best known. Actually he was an Austrian citizen, but after the union between Austria and Nazi Germany, young men of military age were conscripted into Hitler's army. When he received his call-up papers, Jägerstatter refused to join. His parish priest told him that he should obey the government. The local bishop also joined in the pressure, telling him that it was his duty of obedience to the legitimate(?) government to join the army. Jägerstatter still refused, because he considered that as a Christian he should not kill any other human being at the command of political leaders. He was arrested, tried, found guilty, and executed by guillotine on 9th August 1943.

In the immediate aftermath of the war, his sacrifice was virtually unknown even in Austria. With the devastating revelations about the Nazis' extermination camps for Jews and other categories of "non-conformists", the Austrian people became extremely self-conscious, about the extent of their nation's collaborations with the Nazis during the war. 700,000 citizens had been members of the National Socialist Party, and 1.2 million men served with the German army. With the passage of time Jägerstatter's protests and execution became widely known internationally, and the Bishop of Linz procured his beatification on 26th October 2007. He was canonized as a saint in 2018.

There were other martyrs for the cause of peace in Germany, but very few in comparison with the almost total tacit support of the main Churches for the Nazi government, and their silent acquiescence to all their policies.

A remarkable example of Christian heroism was displayed by a group of about half a dozen students at Munich university, known as The White Rose Movement, all of whose members were committed Christians. In 1943 they realised that the shattering defeat at Stalingrad, had turned the tide against the Germans on the Russian front. They also judged correctly that the entry of the USA into the war against Hitler, had made it impossible for Germany to emerge as the victor in the conflict. They considered that further prolongation of hostilities was a pointless sacrifice, of the lives of thousands of soldiers and civilians. It would have been prudent for the Nazi government to negotiate a peace deal from that time onwards. To make their message known, they printed leaflets and distributed them widely, in the university and the city. Needless to say, the authorities soon traced the source. All the members of the movement were arrested, tried, and executed.

There were other martyrs in the Nazi period. Just a few! Sadly, their numbers were insignificant compared with the massive public acquiescence to the Nazis' total programme, by the Church authorities, and most other organisations. In the spring of 2020, the Catholic Bishops' conference issued a public disavowal of their predecessors' tacit collaboration with the Nazi government's policies during that war.

In the immediate aftermath of the Second World War, serious minded people reflected deeply on its horrors, such as the use of atomic weapons, the indiscriminate bombing of civilian targets, the extermination camps, to name just a few. There was a genuine desire to limit the increasing cruelties of warfare, which were getting worse, on account of the progress of science and engineering, developing machine guns, tanks, submarines, and many other devices to augment cruelty. The problem was also complicated by the consensus among historians and archaeologists, that warfare had been endemic in the history of all nations of the word, even the most primitive societies.

Providentially there was one phenomenon which offered a ray of hope, namely Gandhi's employment of the method of non-violent protest. (Gandhi's fundamental principle was expressed in his famous saying "I am prepared to die for my convictions, but not to kill for them"). This method was limited to dealing with free democratic societies, and it achieved the end of British colonial rule in India, as I have noted earlier in this book.

The principles were adopted and imitated by a variety of peace movements. The most prominent in Britain was the Campaign for Nuclear Disarmament, which staged the annual protest marches, of thousands of people, from London to Aldermaston, which was the location of the national experimental laboratory for nuclear weapons.

The Catholic Church gained some public credibility in that campaign, because a secular priest, Bruce Kent, was for many years general secretary of the CND.

In the very earliest period of Christianity, before Constantine's decree of toleration in 314, Christians refused to join the army, or if they were already soldiers at the time of their conversion, they refused to do any more killing. A considerable number were martyred for that precise reason. A few centuries later, when Christians comprised the majority of the population, they were accused to neglecting their duty, by standing aside and leaving the pagans to defend the nation against invasion. In that context attitudes in the Church changed, and St. Augustine formulated the principles of a just war. In the middle ages, theologians elaborated it. Its conditions were that the cause should be just, that all peaceful methods of diplomacy and negotiations had been exhausted, and that the inevitable damage and carnage should be proportional to the seriousness of the issues at stake. On this basis a defensive war would be more easily justified, than one of aggression. Sadly, over the course of centuries it proved to be largely ineffective. With the wisdom of hindsight, it is clear that it had to await the establishment of democratically elected governments in free societies, if it were to be exercised effectively. Gandhi's strategy of massive non-violent protests, against the British imperial power, fitted into that scenario remarkably well.

Whereas the presence of democratic government in England favoured the ultimate success of Indian independence, the mirror image of that situation is Christianity's potential to give moral strength, and encouragement to the long-term task of the peace movements in free societies. The existence of good will among intelligent citizens is not sufficiently strong to eradicate such a deeply rooted human malady as warfare. Christianity has a more persuasive message than rationalism, and Catholicism best tactical advantage, since it is not a national Church, and has no legal connection with any government. (Unless of course the Vatican should arrange a treaty, known as a concordat. These may bestow short term benefits, but ultimately they undermine the Church's spiritual freedom). To be realistic, we must accept that such a deep- rooted phenomenon as warfare will not be eradicated swiftly. That does not warrant Christians abandoning the task altogether. The virtue of prudence would suggest that we begin with limited objectives. The British CND is a classical example, as its concern is specifically nuclear weapons.

Even smaller objectives are demanding of specific attention. In 1983 the nuclear arms race between the NATO and the Soviet Union was ratcheted up to a further degree of risk, with the invention and deployment of Cruise Missiles. In the eyes of the possessors, these missiles gave them an advantage. Their flight was directed by computerised programmes, and they flew at a very low altitude, literally hugging the contours of the hills and valleys, to as to enable them to fly under the radar detection systems. They had one inbuilt defect, which was spotted by the peace movement, namely that for technical reasons, their flight was relatively slow, about 600 mph. By comparison, the inter-continental ballistic missiles of the enemy could have demolished their home bases before they had completed about three hours flight. That might not even have taken them beyond their own national frontier. Consequently they could only be used to start a war, or carry out a strategically useless revenge, when the "real rockets" had completed the conflict, having delivered their nuclear warheads some hours previously.

The peace movements in England organised large-scale demonstrations which took place in London and other cities on the day that the Cruise Missiles arrived at air bases in this country. Significantly large numbers of the protesters were arrested and detained in police cells. That latter detail is important. If the protesters are to be taken seriously, they must be willing to submit to punishment by the police and public authorities.

Before discussing Professor Müller's fourth characteristic of a parish, it is necessary to describe a practical means of carrying out the first three. It will not have escaped the attention of my readers, that the volume of work which will devolve on the laity, in a parish whose priest is non-stipendiary, is so complex, that careful organisation will be needed. Fortunately the Second Vatican Council has already supplied the answer. There will have to be an elected council in every parish. The Council's statement on the matter, in the document on the Lay Apostolate, is so clear that it deserves to be quoted verbatim: "In dioceses, as far as possible, there should be councils which assist the apostolic work of the Church, either in the field of making the gospel known and [making] men holy, or in the charitable, social, or other spheres. To this end, clergy and religious should appropriately cooperate with the laity. While preserving the proper character and autonomy of each organization, these councils will be able to promote the mutual co-ordination of various lay associations and enterprises. Councils of this type should be established as far as possible also on the parochial, inter-parochial and diocesan level, as well as in the national and international sphere".[3]

A parish pastoral council is relatively easy to organise. Clearly it must be elected democratically, and the voters must be all adult Catholics resident in the parish's territory. The committee should be no more than a dozen, otherwise the meetings will be too diffuse. It would probably be prudent to ensure that there is an equal number of men and women. The parish priest (and curates) should be present at all meetings, but the chair must be elected. Ideally one third of the members should retire each year, and the same number should be elected to keep up the total number. This will guard against the presence of lonely people, who seek committees as a social activity, and do no work.

The plan which I have sketched out for the structure, could be modified somewhat for local conditions. What is more important is to define its area of competence. Quite simply, all important matters which affect the whole parish, must be discussed, and the parish priest has no right to conceal anything important. Within the limitations of space, I cannot enumerate all such eventualities. One example could be, that any expense from the parish account above £ 500 (perhaps), must be discussed with the pastoral council. This means that repairing a broken window, should not occupy the time and energy of the council, but the replacement of all the windows in the presbytery with double glazing, must.

The most important business of all, concerns the clerical personnel. Before a new parish priest is appointed, the bishop should advertise the vacancy in the diocesan newspaper, so that any priest in the diocese can apply for the post. The bishop should draw up a short list of about four or five. This is reasonable, because he has the oversight of the whole diocese, and it might damage his long-term plans if the moving of clergy were to be taken out of his hands altogether. The next stage is that the short-listed candidates would be interviewed by the pastoral council, who would then inform the bishop of their order of preference among those who had applied. The final decision would be made by the bishop.

The appointment of the new priest would be the ideal time to introduce the practice of a time limit. In the past, a parish priest might well stay in a parish until he dies. Psychologically this sets up a situation of lassitude and non-urgent routine. Comparisons with other professions are not helpful. For example many teachers will remain in the same school for many years, until they choose to move, teaching basically the same programme year after year. The leadership of a parish community is a totally different task. It is the responsibility to lead a specific number of people to a more committed relationship with God, and for that task there is no syllabus or blueprint. This imprecise objective could be helped considerably, if a fixed term were included into the parish priest's letter of appointment. It would also discourage the priest from looking on the parish as his perpetual fiefdom until death, which was implied in the mediaeval arrangement.

Clearly in the selection process which I have described, the final decision remains with the bishop. Some readers might think that this is little more than "tokenism". This would be to undervalue the exercise. It is very important for lay people to know that they have a right to be consulted and express their collective consensus to the bishop. It would alter the priest's attitude to the parishioners, as he could no longer assume the role and outlook of an absolute dictator in parish affairs. Sadly the phenomenon of the "dictator parish priest" has not vanished after Vatican II. As recently as September 2019, a letter was published in *The Tablet*, of which the following is an extract: "In the town where I live we are lucky enough to have two Catholic parishes. However the availability of Holy Communion under both kinds is something that we are not permitted as a matter of course.----At Sunday Masses in one parish the chalice is not offered unless there are large numbers, but not at all on weekdays; in the other the chalice is never offered. Having challenged both parish priests about this, I was told by one that it is "because I have decided and that's that", and by the other that "it would be too confusing" for the laity and that it was also "impossible".[4]

In the absence of any such "right of audience", lay people who are enthusiastic to promote the mission of the Church, can be totally demoralised by lack of dialogue. For example, the Movement for Married Clergy has been trying to enter into dialogue with the English hierarchy for more than forty years. Round about the turn of the century two or three enlightened bishops met with the chairman and secretary, but after about 2010, their letters are not even being given a reply. No comment needed.

At the next level, namely the diocesan pastoral council, a more highly organised structure is required. Depending on the size of the diocese in terms of the population, every parish should elect one or two representatives. The regularity of meetings would be less frequent than that of parish councils. Once again the chair should be elected, and the bishop should be present. He does not abandon his responsibility for the diocese, but as with parish councils, it is extremely important for the laity of the diocese to know that they have a right to express their opinions. In the background there is always the unspoken realisation that if the bishop needs a large sum of money for a project, the laity will not be generous if he has not persuaded them of the necessity of the project which he has put before them.

The next stage upwards, envisaged by the Vatican Council, in the extract quoted above, is for a national pastoral council. A good example of a national pastoral council, on a very large scale was the gathering of bishops from every nation of Latin America, at Medellin in Colombia in the year 1968. At the end of their deliberations they published a document entitled "The Preferential Option for the Poor". It was not a detailed plan, but a form of witness to their collective conviction that the Church's mission should be concerned for social justice to the poorer section of society.

England came very close to a similar meeting in 1980 with the gathering of the National Pastoral Congress in Liverpool. The genesis of that meeting was dependent on another organisation which came into existence 21 years earlier, namely The National Conference of Priests. In 1969 the English bishops decided to summon a conference of the secular clergy. The bishops' motive was either to heal the wounds of the birth control crisis of the previous year, or to co-ordinate the response to the message of the second Vatican Council. To keep the numbers within manageable limits, they decided that four priests should be elected by the clergy of each diocese, to represent them at the assembly. The candidates were selected from four age bands. I forget the exact age boundaries, but it was approximately, those ordained with the previous ten years, previous eleven to twenty, then twenty-one to thirty. The senior group comprised all those who had been ordained for thirty-one years or more. It proved to be a remarkably even representation. We met for the inside of a week at Wood Hall in Yorkshire, which was the pastoral centre of the diocese of Leeds. The Episcopal committee which had organised the conference, had also appointed a number of priests to read papers about Vatican II, and lead the discussion. After one day of that programme, the priests became restive. We realised that this was probably a once-only opportunity to create a permanent organisation. The "teachers" were thanked for their efforts and politely informed that further instruction would not be needed. A committee was elected, which soon set out the structure of a permanent organisation of elected priests, and then set about practical suggestions to be addressed to the bishops to implement the letter and spirit of the Second Vatican Council.

One such plan which stays in my memory. It was agreed unanimously that their remuneration of the secular priests, should consist of a properly planned structure for their salaries and pensions. For a long time it has consisted of stole fees, mass stipends, and the special collections for the clergy at Christmas and Easter. It was a completely haphazard arrangement, more like tipping a waiter in a restaurant, than providing a regular income for a highly educated professional man. (At least that was the ideal.) It was also added that long-term resident housekeepers should have something similar. I have forgotten the other decisions, apart from the setting up of a permanent committee which would be renewed regularly, and our announcing our existence to the hierarchy. They acquiesced to our existence. The Vatican Council had enshrined the "right of association".

When the committee of the National Conference of Priests found its feet, one of the first decisions as a long-term objective, was to plan a National Pastoral Congress of the Laity. As events unfolded, the actual organisation of the gathering, was somehow 'taken over' by the bishops, who chose one priest from Wales, and gave him a year of absence from his parish to do the practical organisation. It was a classical example of how difficult it is for an annual gathering of elected representative, to control a permanent central bureaucracy. That was the genesis of the Liverpool congress.

Before going into detail about Liverpool, I should mention that, over the years, all the plans which had been put forward by the priests at the Wood Hall meeting and later, were turned down by the bishops, even such theologically non-threatening suggestion as the salary structure, outlined above. After more than thirty years of stone walling by the bishops, the secular clergy became demoralised, and the National Conference of Priests eventually just dissolved as a result of a widespread feeling of total frustration.

Having set the scene, I will now return the reader to the Liverpool Congress of 1980. The preparation for the event gave every reason to hope for an effective outcome. Every diocese in the country undertook a process of reflection and study. Representatives were elected democratically from every diocese. So that the representatives would not have to be absent from their families and jobs for too long, the duration was arranged for four days, over a weekend. The representatives (hundreds of them) were lodged with Catholic families in Liverpool, who had responded enthusiastically to the invitation to house them. The limitations of time, made it inevitable that the work had to be divided into several areas (actually seven), whose participants met simultaneously in seven large venues in the city. That arrangement had the advantage that a large number of issues could be discussed simultaneously in a limited period of time.

The fatal disadvantage was that no plenary meeting was held, at which all the representatives could have voted on all the decisions of the seven departments. Worse still was the absence of any method of deciding on a follow up meeting to evaluate the implementation of the resolutions agreed in the seven large groups. In other words, accountability had no place in the sequel to the Congress. The aftermath of the event was limited to two documents. The first was entitled *Congress Report*, published by a working party of the representatives, in 1980, few months after the event. It contained a list of all the resolutions and recommendations which had been agreed upon in the seven sections of the Congress. The second document, published in the following year, was the hierarchy's response, entitled *The Easter People.*

In total 40 resolutions were put forward by the Congress. Not one of them was accepted by the hierarchy for implementation. If any reasons were given they were unconvincing, and expressed evasively. As it is all past history, and forty years after the event, I will not devote undue space to repeating the sad tale. I refer my readers to a previous book.[5] However I feel that one typical example ought to be repeated here. The situation of Catholics in a second marriage after divorce was considered carefully by the Congress. Their request was worded thus: The Report asked that the bishops should consider compassionately their desire for the sacraments, meaning of course Holy Communion (C.R. p. 22 n.13). The reply was rather evasive: "The question of the reception of the sacraments in such cases is one which the Bishops' Conference has been considering for some time... we take to heart the sympathy and compassion expressed by the Congress delegates as we continue our deliberations on this very delicate doctrinal and pastoral issue." (Easter People, § 111).

The real intention of the hierarchy was made ominously clear in § 49 of The Easter People: "We do not intend to provide comprehensive legislation or teaching for every area of our Church's life and mission. To attempt to do so would be seriously to misunderstand the enabling and co-ordinating role of a Bishops' Conference and the kind of spiritual leadership required of it: possibly to override the legitimate freedom and responsibility for mission which are the prerogatives of each individual diocese as a local Church under the pastoral guidance of its bishop, or even to appear to encroach upon the allegiance and love which we owe to the Holy Father and the universal Church."

Sadly that says it all. In effect the bishops refused to take the laity seriously in spite of all that Vatican II has said about their role in the Church. The sycophantic tone of the last part of the above quotation is just unbelievable. Within a few years the whole Congress had been so completely side lined that it might as well not have taken place.

Worse was to come. In 1983 The Code of Canon Law was revised, allegedly so that it could include the insights of the Second Vatican Council. In the event, it severely curtailed much of the Council's creative forward-looking vision. It is sadly instructive to compare the Council's statement about pastoral councils, quoted above, and the section in the Revised Code of Canon Law, canons 511 to 514 which are devoted to pastoral councils.

Canon 511 states "In individual dioceses, insofar as the pastoral situation would warrant it (id suadeant), a pastoral council should be established (constituatur), whose task is to investigate, and assess, under the authority of the bishop, those things which pertain to the pastoral work of the diocese, and to propose practical conclusions about them". This is already a significant weakening of the recommendation of the Vatican Council. It has become more or less an optional extra to the bishop's authority.

Canon 512 §1, declares "A pastoral council shall be composed of Christians (christifideles), who are in full communion with the Catholic Church, whether they be clergy, or members of institutes of the consecrated life, then especially lay people, who shall be selected by a method determined by the bishop." The last sentence is so imprecise that the bishop could select them by individual invitation, and he would not be breaking the law.

Canon 512 §3 states "Christians shall not be admitted to the pastoral council unless they are prominent for their reliable faith, good moral conduct, (bonis moribus), and prudence." How the members moral conduct is to be established, is not stated, but it could be important. One of the most urgent problems facing the Church in the post-conciliar years is the pastoral care of divorced and re-married Catholics. In this period, the national divorce rate has risen above 40% of all marriages, and experience suggests that catholic marriages follow closely the overall national trend. The wording of the canon clearly rules out the presence of a Catholic in a second marriage. Yet if the problem is to be considered realistically it is of the utmost importance that one or more Catholics in second marriages should be in the pastoral council, to ensure that the problems should be studied realistically, rather than relying on hearsay.

Canon 514, § 1 states "A pastoral council, which enjoys only a consultative vote, is to be presided over solely by the diocesan bishop, who is competent to convoke it according to the necessities of the apostolate; to whom also belongs the unique competence to decide which items should be made public, among those discussed." The plain meaning of that convoluted language, is that the bishop decides on the agenda, acts as chairman, and determines what shall remain secret, and what can be released to the press.

It is clear from a careful reading of those canons, that lay people do not have the right to take any initiative, and there is nothing to suggest that there is a real partnership between them and the clergy. A more dismal departure from the letter and spirit of the Second Vatican Council, would be hard to envisage. In the new millennium only two of the English dioceses had pastoral councils. The facts speak for themselves!

The fourth characteristic: Apostolate

Professor Müller's fourth characteristic of a parish, namely apostolate is in a sense the most urgent, yet it is equally the most difficult to organise systematically. That is to say, the end purpose is clear: an individual becomes a member of the Church, having made a personal commitment to Christ in faith. Yet how to present the Christian message to an individual, as a practical invitation, in a way that is likely to be accepted, is no simple task. There are no clear rules as to how it should be done.

In the 21st century, the situation of the Church, even in the traditional strongholds of Catholicism, like Italy, Poland and Ireland, is once again that of mission and not maintenance. The reason being that fully committed Catholics are a small minority in those countries.

To set the scene for this gigantic task, it is profitable to look back on the "commissioning" of the early Church for this task. The idea that every nation and culture should share one religion was so original, and counter-cultural, that it almost inevitably invited persecution by the Roman authorities. Religion and patriotism had always been linked, so much so that the subjugated nations of the Roman empire, were obliged to accept the Roman gods, alongside their own original deities.

The initial command from Jesus to his immediate followers is unambiguous. "All authority in heaven and on earth has been given to me. Go therefore and make disciples of all nations," (Matt. 28: 18-19)

In spite of that explicit command, the first clear evidence of the conversion and baptism of a pagan, took place some years later. It was the conversion and baptism of the Roman centurion Cornelius by St. Peter, as recorded in Acts chapter 10. Even that step forward was preceded by a special vision and command from God. The presentation of Christ's message to pagans only received final clarification, some years later, at the Council of Jerusalem (recorded in Acts 15). In other words, pagans could enter the Church simply by accepting baptism, (which presupposed faith). It was not required of them that they should first adopt Judaism, as a sort of "apprenticeship".

Faced with the post-Christian culture of Europe in the 21st century, it may help to clarify the possible methods of presenting the Christian message now, to examine briefly those which were successful in the past, but which cannot be used in the 21st century, on account of cultural and social changes to societies.

Earlier in this book, in connection with St. Augustine's mission in Kent, I described the follow up, where warfare was the first stage. Needless to say, it has no place at all in the 21st century. But let us not judge our ancestors too harshly. King Alfred, whose leadership and wisdom was so important in English history, insisted that the Danes should adopt Christianity, after many battles against them, when they became permanent settlers here.

In the Saxon period, once the king and his subjects had accepted Christianity, they retained it for the indefinite future, passing it on to their children in much the same way that the next generation automatically acquired their family name and nationality. That process of simple cultural inheritance lasted, in one form or another, until the 1960's. In society as a whole, that decade was one of critical scrutiny of the customs and practices of the whole of society. For Catholics, it was intensified by the Second Vatican Council, which reviewed practically every aspect of our religious thought and practice. The Christian Churches have still not worked out an alternative method to transmit the parents' religious convictions to the next generation. In Chapter One I suggested that we should adapt something like the paschal supper of the Jews, enshrining a carefully worded invitation, so I will not repeat it here.

Turning our attention back to the Saxon period, it is clear that preaching did accompany the warrior kings. Earlier in this book I have reproduced St. Bede's account of the sparrow flying through the king's hall on a cold winter night, and the councillor's advice that they should listen carefully to the message of the Christian missionaries. Open air preaching was their method. It is worth remembering that among illiterate people, listening to a well-prepared speech is a genuine pleasure. In the 20th century that situation was mirrored in many parts of rural Africa, where the people were illiterate, and radio, TV and cinemas did not exist. But the Christians genuinely enjoyed a good sermon. Open air preaching has had a long history. The last really great preacher in that tradition was probably John Wesley, who regularly spoke out of doors to audiences of hundreds of people. In Great

Britain, universal primary education was provided, not long after his death. Tracts and pamphlets were printed cheaply and given away free of charge by political parties and Churches. Newspapers were cheap, as were bibles, thanks to the subsidised editions from the British and Foreign Bible Society, and other such charities. The days of open-air preaching were numbered. Yet it is worth remembering that as late as the first half of the 20th century, organisations like the Catholic Evidence Guild were still conducting a "rear-guard action" in that medium, namely soap boxes at street corners!

Somewhat akin to open air preaching is the practice of unsolicited door knocking, like travelling salesmen. Sometimes they offer tracts, or invitations to attend their churches. The likelihood of an individual adopting a life changing way of life, in response to an unexpected invitation from a complete stranger on the doorstep, is minimal.

Another method of propagating Christianity which at one time was very successful was colonialism. Within the lifetime of Columbus, Spanish missionaries were actively propagating Catholicism in the mainland of central America, and the adjacent islands. The process was organised in an extremely thorough manner. Language was the first hurdle which they overcame. All the missionary priests were required to master one or more of the indigenous languages. Thanks to the to the thorough linguistic preparation by the Spanish missionaries, the indigenous peoples knew exactly what the new religion entailed. This may well explain the permanence and cultural influence of Catholicism in the whole of Latin America. I have elaborated somewhat on the linguistic demands required of the missionaries, in order to make clear that evangelisation in the context of colonial expansion was not an automatic concomitant of the military conquest.

In this brief survey of the principal methods that have been employed with greater or lesser success over the centuries, it will have become clear to the reader that none of them would have any chance of success in the de-christianised societies of modern Europe.

In the search for a method which might work in the 21st century, it is profitable to look back at the Roman Empire in the years prior to Constantine's toleration of the new faith. At that period, the Empire, and particularly the city of Rome, were thoroughly cosmopolitan, and also that was the period of Christianity's most prolific expansion. For the next few paragraphs I am deeply indebted to the indispensable study of Peter Lampe, *Christians at Rome in the First Two Centuries.*[6]

That society was highly urbanised, pluralistic, and possessed of many religions and philosophies. To that extent it had more similarity to modern English society, than anything in the middle ages and beyond. Clearly there are great differences too, such as universal franchise in a democratic society, universal literacy, and freedom of speech. Because the Christians could not build churches, they were forced to conduct their meetings in private houses. There is ample evidence for this, as early as the period when the New Testament books were being written. Perhaps the clearest evidence is from Romans 16: 3-5, "Greet Prisca and Aquila, my fellow workers in Christ Jesus, who risked their necks for my life, to whom not only I but all the churches of the Gentiles give thanks; greet also the church in their house". Other equally clear evidence is to be found in Acts 18: 7. Acts 19: 2-7. Acts 20: 7 & 8. Romans 16: 23. I Corinthians 16: 19, and Colossians 4: 15.

Of the various descriptions of the Christians in Rome in the Second Century, that of St. Justin the martyr supplies perhaps the most detailed information about the social composition of that community. Justin was born in Palestine of pagan parents. As an adult he moved first to Ephesus, in search of philosophical teaching, and thence to Rome where he arrived during the reign of Antoninus Pius (138–161), and there he founded a school of philosophy, and became a Christian. Between the years 148 and 161 he wrote two Apologias, the longer comprising 68 chapters, and the shorter consisting of 15 chapters.

Both these apologias contain valuable information about the social composition of the house communities, usually described as house churches. They have been analysed meticulously by Peter Lampe.[7] We begin at the bottom of the social ladder, and Justin informs us that among the community there are some who are illiterate, and speak a simple and unrefined language. Akin to them are cripples and blind people, who also find a place in these communities. In every house church there is cash box for the alleviation of the poverty of the needy members (widows, orphans, and others). The administrator of the charity box adherents to was also the man who presided at the liturgy. The charity box was filled up at every liturgy, which indicates that there were also wealthy members of those communities. About ten years before Justin wrote,

Marcion had given the Christian community in Rome a gift of 200,000 sesterces. When the same Marcion was excommunicated in 144 A D, the same sum was returned to him without any apparent difficulty. The generosity of the Christian community in Rome seems to have been well known. As early as 170 A D, Dionysius of Corinth wrote in his letter to the Romans, of the generosity of the Roman community to other Christian communities in the Mediterranean sphere.[8] The wealthy Christians are described as business men, not only local shop keepers, some of them travelled abroad in pursuit of business. In addition to those who were financially well off, there were also philosophers, scholars, craftsmen, and ordinary workers with no specific skill. The presence of slaves as well as various categories of free people is important.

Similar to the social mix of the Christian community, were their previous religious allegiances, hinting at diversity of nationalities. People gathered round the same table for the liturgy, who but for their Christianity, would have had no occasion or cause to mix socially. Some of the community had been Christians since their youth, but others represented the most diverse pagan religions to which they had been adherents. They comprised the erstwhile followers of Dionysius, Apollo, Asclepius, adherents of the mysteries of Persephone, Aphrodite and others.

How the individual conversions to Christianity took place seems to have depended on geographical proximity (neighbours in the same tenement), and example. There was the dramatic heroism of martyrs who were killed for public entertainment in the amphitheatres, as I noted above. Justin also draws attention to the example of

Christian business-men, whose patience and honesty were transparent, even if it was clear that people were trying to cheat them.

Those house churches of the Roman world bear a strong likeness to the early Methodist institution of "the class", which was a group of about a dozen people, who would meet on week-day evenings to study and discuss the Scriptures. It was also a period in Methodist history when the role of the lay preachers was strong. Among the Tolpuddle martyrs, about ten or a dozen of them were from the same class. The small size of the group was important, because it enabled them all to meet in the house of a poor person.

House groups of the size envisaged above have the essential characteristic, almost thrust upon them, that they cannot avoid becoming communities.

Lonely anonymity is impossible in such a small number. Flexibility is their second advantage. Their basic activities should include, prayer, reflexion on the bible, and some form of socio/political action. From time to time Mass could be celebrated, but not on a regular basis in case clerical leadership were to creep in. Anything like a sermon is definitely out. Anything which would lead to its degenerating into merely a "talking shop" must be avoided. The creative positive influence should be maintained by the realisation that the institutional Church is the instrument for the establishment of the Kingdom of Heaven on earth. This means in simple terms, an unrelenting struggle against injustices to individuals and groups in matters like housing, wages, and discrimination. As to "tools" the self-explanatory See, Judge, and Act method of the Young Christian Workers, could well be taken up again. Collaboration with other altruistic organisation would be wholly appropriate, such as various branches of the Peace Movement, and Trades Unions.

It would not be helpful to map out any more detailed programmes for such groups, as it would threaten the rightful freedom of initiative which lay people enjoy. Groups such as I have sketched out above, would seem to have the best chance of welcoming strangers, and allowing them to see how Christianity has authentic resources improve peoples' conditions in this life. Only then will they be prepared to listen also to our message about the life of eternity. Ideally every committed Catholic who is a member of a parish community, should also be a member of a house group. The well-known Dominican priest, Timothy Radcliffe, came to almost the same conclusion saying "As Christians we can make the hearts of non-believers burn within them if we can communicate the truth that our religion is not just a moral code to keep us in order, but a vibrant way of life".[9s]

In case the reader should gain the impression that I have reduced religion to the level of the pale imitation of a Trades Union, with the worship of God tucked away discreetly in a corner, let me draw attention to an important consideration. From time immemorial religion has always been concerned about the bread and butter issues of everyday life. In antiquity, bad harvests were interpreted as a sign of God's anger, and the appropriate remedy, in ancient Judaism for example, was the offering of compensatory sacrifices. Needless to say, that level of cause and effect gradually disappeared with the advance of science from the sixteenth century onwards in Europe and America.

Paradoxically in the twenty first century, religion is coming into its own again, to motivate and persuade politicians and citizens into saving the planet from climate change, and from humanity's self-destruction. I pointed out in a previous chapter, that with the world's population doubling every 30-40 years, our children will have to grapple with gigantic problems, of a scale which humanity has never before had to face in its long history. The single most urgent problem is to restrict the use of fossil fuels to produce energy, because as we all now know, the exponential rise of CO_2 particles in the atmosphere will soon be heating the planet to a point were global warming will have become unstoppable. The extreme counter measures that will have to be employed, such as the prohibition of all holiday flights, will prove so unpopular with the electorates in all democracies, that the MP's will not have the courage to enforce them. Only Christianity has the moral and spiritual resources, to strengthen the decision makers, to make the right choices, in what looks like political suicide for their careers.

As a post-script to this section, it is perhaps worth pointing out that if every convinced Catholic brought into the Church just one individual in the course of his or her life, it would mean that the Church would double its numbers in every generation. A few minutes reflection, and a little arithmetic, will make it clear that this is the fastest practicable rate at which any society could expand.

CHAPTER FIVE

THE BISHOPS

In the first part of the second century, patterns of Church government were relatively diverse. Charismatic personalities, committees of elders, and the emergence of one bishop per city, assisted by a group of elders (presbyters, much later referred to as priests), and deacons. This latter pattern proved to be the most effective, and it was eventually adopted universally. It seems to be the most efficient way of managing organisations which are constantly expanding, like the branch managers of super-market chains in the modern world. The earliest firm evidence for their existence in what is now south-eastern Turkey, is in the letters of St. Ignatius early in 2nd century.[1]

With the passage of time, those dioceses grouped themselves into larger conglomerates, initially clustered round ancient communities founded by apostles. They met fairly regularly for provincial councils, to discuss matters of mutual concern, such as which books were to be included in the New Testament, and they were competent to make rules for their communities. It is important to bear in mind that they were making rules, and not laws, for the smooth running of their particular society within the Empire. After the adoption of Christianity by the Roman emperors, not even the most devoutly Christian of those rulers would have tolerated the existence of a second law making society within the boundaries of the Empire. The eventual assumption, centuries later by the Church, of the role of a law-making organisation, is another disconcerting indicator of the central administration's desire for power. (The other indicator of this tendency was the conversion of the Pope's secretariat, into a command structure with competence throughout the universal Church, as I noted earlier in this book).

If there was a major crisis like Arianism, international councils were summoned because, matters of belief affected every community and individual in the whole Church. Unity in belief was the essential constituent holding the whole supra-national Church together. Eventually those councils were designated as General Councils, on account of their supreme authority.

After Constantine's edict of toleration, and also after the adoption of Christianity by the newly converted kingdoms of northern Europe, the emperors and kings naturally showed an interest in episcopal appointments. They could hardly refrain from taking an interest in the candidates, since they were the administrators of the nations' source of culture, which was also the moral basis of law, and the immediate directors of hospitals and all charitable institutions. With the passage of time, major disputes arose when the secular rulers attempted to control the episcopal appointments.

In the primitive Church, the bishops were elected by the whole of the community, laity as well as the clergy. This was practicable when the communities were relatively small, and when most of them could be squeezed into the cathedral churches of the small cities spread throughout the Roman Empire. With the passage of time, it became the more usual practice for the canons of the cathedrals to elect the bishop. The kings were principally concerned with the appointment to the principal diocese in the whole nation, and it was over such appointments as those that the most bitter disputes occurred. The murder of Thomas Becket in Canterbury indicates the extreme animosity of those power struggles.

The modern pattern by which the Pope appoints all but a few of the bishops of the universal Church is an innovation which appeared almost by stealth. It is at variance with Pius XI's Principle of Subsidiarity, which states that decisions should be made at the lowest level of competence, not the highest. In the middle of the 19th century there were 646 ordinary diocesan bishops in the universal Church. Of these 555 were appointed by civil governments, kings, noble families, or some other form of lay patronage. 67 were elected by the canons of cathedral chapters, and a mere 24 were appointed directly by the Pope.[2] These remarkable numbers were researched by Fr. Gareth Sweeny.

In the latter half of the 19th century the anti-clerical government in France broke with the established custom of nominating bishops and having no wish to be involved in Church affairs, it literally dumped the appointment of bishops on to the papacy. A similar series of events took place in Italy. The re-unification of Italy had acquired an anti-clerical orientation, on account of the Papal States' resisting the movement, and securing French troops to defend the frontiers. The French army departed in 1870 at the outbreak of the Franco-Prussian war, and the soldiers of the newly reunited kingdom of Italy annexed the Papal States, except for a few acres in the centre of Rome, in which the Pope was allowed independence, like Monaco and a handful of other micro-principalities in Europe. The new Italian government, like the French, handed over to the Papacy the nomination of bishops, which had formerly been exercised by the various small Italian kingdoms, duchies, and republics.

The final stage in this acquisition of episcopal appointments by the Pope came with the codification of Canon Law in 1918. This was the first time in history that the Church's laws had been systematised and codified in one book, (presumably in imitation of Napoleon's having authorised it for French law). It is significant that it was promulgated on the authority of the Pope alone, indicating how his authority was augmenting itself in the wake of the First Vatican Council. In that codification of Canon Law, it is stated, for the first time in the Church's history, that the Pope alone has the power to appoint all but a handful of bishops throughout the whole of the Catholic Church, (Canon 329 §2). There were a small number of exceptions, as in Switzerland where a small number of Cantons retained the right of election by the cathedral canons. In the Catholic Eastern rites, a small number of dioceses retained the traditional custom of local elections. As a result of the pope's promulgating the code, which contained the papal prerogative of appointing all but a handful of the world's bishops, Benedict XVI effectively conferred upon himself, the right to appoint virtually all the bishops of the Catholic Church.

In the first years of the 21st century we are now in a position to examine how effective is this system of appointing bishops. The central problem is just how can the pope cope with the vast number of bishops in the Church? In 2019 there were approximately 2960 diocesan bishops in the universal Church.[3] Weighing up the suitability of possible candidates has been delegated to the Papal Nuncios in each nation. Since they are mostly foreigners to the countries to which they have been accredited, the problem merely becomes worse. The current method is to post questionnaires to priests in the different dioceses. In the course of my years as a parish priest, I received two such enquiries. Their content was more or less predictable. Father XYZ was being considered for promotion to the episcopate, did I (the recipient) consider that he was suitable? The next few questions were merely routine. Did the priest in question uphold integrally the Catholic Faith as defined in the General Councils of the Church? Did he have adequate pastoral experience? Was his health sufficiently robust? Was he known to be totally loyal to the Pope? How could one give meaningful replies to questions couched in such imprecise language? The questions were so bland, that the appropriate replies would be Yes, Yes, Yes!

Among those generalised questions, one of them contained ominous implications, namely the question about loyalty to the Pope. In practice the Roman curia were looking for men who would be slavishly obedient to the Pope, and the Vatican Curia, to the point of subservience. That consideration throws some light on the hierarchy's constant unwillingness, to request from Rome anything, which might cause displeasure in that quarter, such as a request to ordain married men.

However, during the pontificate of Pope John Paul II one surprising innovation was inserted into those questions.

Did Father XYZ adhere fully to the doctrine on birth control as expressed in the encyclical letter *Humanae Vitae* of Pope Paul VI? With the passage of the years, I have forgotten what reply I gave. On reflection, the only honest answer would have been something like this. "If he does not uphold it, but is ambitious to become a bishop, he will have been sure to have concealed his disagreement from everyone". In all seriousness, one must reflect on the possibility that some of the bishops in office today did indeed accept the teaching of *Humanae Vitae*, and in the equally possible opposite scenario, it is possible that others among them did conceal their dissent, for the sake of promotion. In either scenario, intelligence or integrity was lacking. The re-establishment of truth had to wait for that encyclical's 50th anniversary. In the summer of 2018, a petition was signed by approximately 400 conservative minded priests, urging the Bishops Conference of England and Wales to celebrate the promulgation of that encyclical with a declaration of continued support. The result was total silence. A similar gesture came from Rome. The 50th anniversary came and went without any pronouncement from the Vatican. This was a clear indication that the infamous document had become a dead letter.

In other words, those questionnaires were a mere formality, and one can only assume that the Papal Nuncios took most of their advice from the existing bishops, since they were the only group who could supply a manageable quantity of information. Needless to say, organisations which work within so much secrecy usually generate rumours. It was strongly rumoured that Cardinal Hume's promotion from abbot to archbishop was prompted by the then Duke of Norfolk. Both those gentlemen are dead, so I cannot vouch for it, but it seems likely.

So, how should the Church proceed in the future? Election by the whole diocese, priests and laypeople is not practicable, because the numbers of possible electors is too large, and the laity simply do not know all the priests well enough. It would seem that the system best suited to the task would be local election by the canons of the diocese. These priests will have been promoted because they have been successful in running their parishes. Moreover, each of them might well know the vast majority of the priests in their diocese. In addition to that circle of friends and acquaintances, they would probably also know other outstanding priests outside their own diocese. All in all, it would probably be the best process to select the next bishop, when the current incumbent retires or dies.

One further matter needs serious discussion, because it is never raised in public, namely the absence of any special training for bishops. Among the various institutions conducted by the Church, there is nothing like the military college at Sandhurst, set up for the training of the army's future officers. In the middle of the19[th] century it was still possible to buy a commission in the British army and navy. Such amateurism was brutally exposed in the conduct of the army in the Crimean war, in the middle of that century. Public opinion was outraged when the shortcomings of military organisation and planning were laid bare. In the latter part of that century the army's organisation was reformed by Parliament along with similar modernisation of the civil service, and the old universities.

The Church has never contemplated anything like a staff college. The process of selecting bishops is still amateurish, but their specialised training is non-existent. Having mentioned the term "staff college" to set the scene for specialised training, let me point out that the similarity ends after the title. In a nation (England and Wales) where there are 22 dioceses, a permanent college is out of the question. It must be a programme for training the individual designated candidates only after their official nomination. At that point the nominated priest should go to one of the seminaries, where he would receive individual tutorials from the various lecturers. Probably the most necessary would be a refresher course in canon law, which he would receive from the lecturer in that subject at the seminary. Similar intensive courses in theology, and scripture could also be on offer. An important corollary would be to invite a historian from the diocese to which he had been appointed, to come from that diocese to give him a history of that diocese. A Trade Union representative and an economist could also be invited to acquaint the future bishop with the local economy including unemployment.

In short it would be an occasional programme, which would be activated only when it was needed. The duration should probably be about three months. If this should seem too long for the vacant diocese to wait for its new bishop, let it be remembered that due to the inefficiency of the present system of secret consultations going back and forth between Rome and the Papal Nuncios, interregnums of up to a year, are not uncommon.

Another innovation which is never discussed in public is the possibility that bishops might be appointed for a limited period in office. In the English Benedictine Congregation, for example, abbots are elected for a term of nine years. At the end of that period there is another election. This means that a successful abbot can be re-elected, and a less successful occupant of the post can be courteously allowed to stand down, without any drama, crisis, or embarrassment.

Something similar could be organised for bishops. It is commonly said of leadership roles in general (head teachers for example), if those leaders cannot achieve their ambitions for the organisation in ten years, then they never will.

The final consideration for this chapter, is that in the immediate future the most pressing issue concerning bishops is that they must regain their traditional decision-making competence and be liberated from the status of simply being agents, who implement the decisions made by the Roman Curia. Their present situation is completely at variance with the Principle of Subsidiarity, enunciated by Pope Pius XI, and discussed earlier in this narrative, namely that decisions should be made at the lowest feasible level of authority, and not the highest.

CHAPTER SIX

BISHOPS ARE CURRENTLY EVADING THEIR RESPONSIBILITIES IN THE CHURCH

When I employ the word Church I mean primarily the community of baptised Christians, for whose spiritual welfare a clergy exists, to provide leadership which is more comprehensive than just mass, the sacraments, and Christian teaching. It is worth noting that it would be possible to conceive of a Church without clergy (the Quakers have done it successfully), but it is impossible to imagine a Church without laity.

What exactly do the laity require from the clergy? And do they have any sort of entitlement to their services? Ominously the Code of Canon Law (1983) contains only one explicit right for lay people. Canon 213 states that: "It is the right of the laity (christifideles) that they should receive from the spiritual benefits of the Church, by the help of their sacred pastors, principally the Word of God and the sacraments". The term sacraments includes the mass which is also an obligation, and the designation 'sacred pastors' means priests. That description of the services of the clergy could have been written at any time since about the ninth century when the whole of Europe was Christian. To have presented it in the twentieth century, makes no allowance for the fact that in many nations of Europe, committed Catholics are a minority. A whole new missionary situation has arisen, which calls for a new missionary outlook on the part of the bishops. It is significant that the 1983 Code of Canon Law omits any mention of such an orientation. It is a clear sign that the legislators who were responsible for that revision in 1983, were seriously out of touch with the real situation of the Church in practically every nation. It raises the probability that the bishops whom the Vatican appoints would also share the outlook of a "maintenance operation", rather than a missionary vision. In the present situation in Britain, and many other nations too, even the holding operation cannot be maintained properly on account of the serious shortage of priests.

From time immemorial the normal pattern of a Catholic's religious life means firstly attending mass every Sunday, in a community which is not so large as to be an anonymous group, and where the church is accessible by walking. This latter consideration is very important because, to state the obvious, poor people do not own cars.

All of this implies a sufficient number of priests, and the Code of Canon Law also indicates that providing adequate numbers of priests is the responsibility of the bishops. Canon 233, §1, states clearly: "Diocesan bishops who have the primary responsibility for promoting vocations, have the duty of teaching the people committed to their care about the importance of the sacred ministry, and the necessity for the Church of that ministry, and for the encouragement of incipient vocations, they should organise and support organisations for that purpose."

This is a practical measure faithfully echoing what Vatican II declared about it, in the Decree on Bishops (*Christus Dominus*) § 15: "As those who lead others to perfection, bishops should be diligent in fostering holiness among their clerics, religious, and laity according to the special vocations of each------ . For that reason, they should foster priestly and religious vocations as much as possible and take a special interest in missionary vocations".[1] It could hardly have been expressed more clearly. One thing is also implied in those statements, namely, it is not the responsibility of the Vatican to perform the task.

The present situation of Catholicism is one of acute decline in every measurable feature, which is so clear that there is really no purpose in printing accurate statistics here to prove the point. Decline in priestly vocations is no exception. A more significant indicator is the absence adolescents and young adults from Sunday mass, since it is from among them that potential candidates would normally emerge. I have discussed the lack of young people in churches in Chapter One. For the present I will simply make the obvious point that the young men in that age group are the source from which priestly vocations would normally come, for the most part. As a consequence, there is the shortage of entrants into the seminaries, and a consequent serious decline in the number of ordinations. This phenomenon had been observed since the1970's when the seminaries started to receive fewer and fewer candidates, resulting in steadily declining numbers of priests working in the dioceses.

Fifty years ago, the Catholics in England and Wales had nine seminaries, two in Rome, one in Valladolid and another in Lisbon. Back home there were five, Ushaw, near Durham, Upholland near Liverpool, Oscott in Birmingham, Allen Hall (then near Ware, but later moved to London), and Wonersh in Surrey. As candidates became fewer in the 1970's, Upholland, Ushaw, and Lisbon were closed. The authorities wanted to close Valladolid, but its financial basis is strong, and complicated, so even if it were closed and sold, the money could not be withdrawn from Spain. The three survivors in England are running at less than half of their capacity. It is worth noting that the closure of those seminaries was not planned systematically, so as to minimise the harm which it would do to the Church. It would have been less harmful to have retained Ushaw, so as to have one seminary which would retain the interest and loyalty of Catholics in the north of England. Similarly it would have been more sensible to close Wonersh in Surrey. Like Upholland it was one of the newest of the seminaries. Such a pattern would have left a sensible distribution of the three surviving home seminaries, Ushaw for the north, Oscott for the midlands, and Allen Hall (in London) for the south. There is no evidence that the closure of both northern seminaries was the result of any pro-active planning. The bishops merely acquiesced to circumstances. The seminaries were administratively independent, and as they reached the point of financial non-viability, they were simply closed when that point was reached, severally, and with no overall national strategy in existence.

Needless to say, there is a connection between the number of entrants to the seminaries, and the number or ordinations. No statistics are published for the number of entrants to the seminaries at the start of each academic year. What is pertinent to the Church's apostolate is the number of ordinations. One year recently for which statistics were available was 2009, when only eleven priests were ordained for all the dioceses of England and Wales. (Actually, the number might have been thirteen.) Comparison with the Church of England is relevant, because both Churches have roughly the same number of people regularly attending church on Sundays. In the same year, the Church of England ordained 574 priests for England.[2] No comment is necessary.

At this point it is important to identify clearly the cause of such a dramatic decline in vocations. There are a variety of contributory causes, such as the increasing materialism of the collective mentality in Europe and North American nations, but the undeniable practical factor is that after Vatican II, compulsory celibacy for the priests, can no longer be justified theologically. In Chapter Three I presented in detail the theological factors behind the origin of clerical celibacy, and their demolition, thanks to the Second Vatican Council, I will not repeat that argumentation here. At this point it is important to take account of how widespread, was the collective change in the attitude of Catholics, in what could be described as the Western World.

Immediately after the Council, the implications about clerical celibacy had not been widely understood. At that stage of the debate, the whole matter might have stayed within the confines of theological journals, without any influence on the Church's life. However in 1968, the sense of outrage about the birth control encyclical provoked the outpouring of public criticism among clergy as well as lay people. Half a century later it is important to appreciate just how unusual such criticism was. In the

1930's, and indeed until Vatican II, laity and clergy assumed that not only was Catholic doctrine unchangeable, but also pastoral methods and liturgical customs were assumed to be equally fixed. This attitude of security through immovability can be traced back to the Council of Trent in the 16th century. The Catholic Church was then in a state of shock on account of the rapid initial success of Luther's policies. The most obvious among these were vernacular liturgy, the giving of the chalice to the laity at the eucharist, and married clergy. He justified these because they were taught in the New Testament and the practice of the first generation of Christians. An unhealthy attitude developed among Catholics of opposing any innovations advocated by Luther, as a first line of defence for the whole Catholic edifice.

The defensive mentality became even more entrenched over the succeeding centuries, when other modern cultural developments emerged in Europe. Movements like the Enlightenment, the rise of democratic governments, and the seizure of the Papal States in the re-unification of Italy, were all met with hostility by the Catholic authorities. Quite simply they lacked the self-confidence to embrace what was good in them. Even the French revolution, for all its violence, offered to the world the concept of Human Rights.

However in the aftermath of the Napoleonic wars, and the re-building of Europe's societies, the Catholic Church began to modernise itself cautiously. In the latter half of the 19th century a renewal of theology began, when some outstanding individual scholars started to apply the results of modern critical scholarship to the history of the Church and a new approach to the study of the bible. After the

Second World War, this intellectual movement provided the theology and the psychological momentum for the Second Vatican Council, whose decisions provided the theological basis for modernising the Church's apostolate.

Among those innovations was the principle of freedom of speech within the Church. Pius XII was the innovator in 1950 when he enunciated it in an address to an international conference of journalists. The matter was taken up and developed in more detail by Vatican II, in the documents *Lumen Gentium* § 37, and *Gaudium et Spes* § 62.[3]

Ironically, although that right for the laity had been stated clearly in the Conciliar Documents, it was such a novelty, that no one made use of it effectively. The anger stirred up by the theological falsity of *Humanae Vitae's* condemnation of artificial birth control, emboldened lay people to protest openly and vociferously. The enraged feelings of the birth control dispute had literally kick-started the dormant right of free speech in the Church into action. Once activated, that newly found liberty looked around for other avenues of legitimate expression, and clerical celibacy was an obvious target.

It was not just an ephemeral grumble about priests being forbidden to marry, but a whole theological dialogue commenced which has continued to this day. It is also worth noting that practical steps were taken with a view to getting the law changed. In England in 1976, following in the tradition of the suffragette movement to extend parliamentary votes to women, a pressure group was created by a group of secular priests, to work for the changing of the law of celibacy. The two priests who conceived of the idea initially decided to spread the idea among their friends in the clergy, asking the priests whom they contacted to do the same among their friends and acquaintances.

The next stage was to summon a meeting in London to discuss the feasibility of setting up a permanent organisation. To the gratifying surprise of the organisers, about forty priests arrived. What was significant was the age and experience of the men who came forward. A couple of examples will indicate the calibre of those priests who felt strongly about it (at the time of writing both of them are dead). One was Fr. Leo Targett of Portsmouth diocese. At the outbreak of war, he has been earning his living as professional conjuror, in which profession he was a member of the Magic Circle. During the war he was taken prisoner in north Africa when the Germans captured Torbruk. Detention for him was in a prisoner of war camp in Italy, from which he escaped with two other men. After a journey of incredible danger and difficulty they entered Switzerland, obviously not by the roads through the passes, which were guarded, but by climbing the Alps. Their detention was not arduous. The Swiss authorities billeted them with families who received payment for the service, and they had to report to the local police station every day. Leo was lodged with an elderly widow who lived alone. Each day he accompanied her to the shops and carried the shopping for her on the way home. The homeward journey was interrupted by her daily visit to the church to pray before the Blessed Sacrament. That took about an hour! Leo went through a profound spiritual conversion, which motivated him to become a priest.

The other remarkable priest at that gathering was Cyril Scarborough of the Southwark diocese. He had been ordained in the 1930's and was already an army chaplain when the war started in September 1939. He was with the first of the British troops to embark for France in the autumn of that year. He was also with them on the beaches of Dunkirk the following summer when the remnants of that army were being evacuated by sea. Cyril was offered a place on a boat returning to England, but he refused to go, considering that it was his duty as a priest to remain with those men who could not be evacuated. He spent the next five years in a variety of prisoner of war camps in Germany. His decision not to return to England is the only example that I can think of, in the course of my very long life, when his being unmarried probably helped him to make the heroic decision. (I am 90 years old at the time of writing this.)

To return to the description of the first gathering. Needless to say, it followed the conventional path of electing a committee, discussing a draft constitution, and planning our working relationship with the bishops. Cyril Scarborough was elected as the first chairman, which ensured that our movement would be taken seriously. We then informed Cardinal Hume of our existence. We had not sought his permission to initiate the movement, but we took advantage of what one could call the "right of association", which had also been approved by Vatican II, in *Lumen Gentium*, § 37.[4] We informed the Cardinal that he or any of his fellow bishops would be welcome at any of our meetings, we also informed him that we would send him and the other bishops, copies of all the documents, pamphlets, and newsletters which we intended to publish.

Shortly after the establishment of the Movement for Married Clergy, Cardinal Hume gave our cause an unexpected boost. During the 1980's he obtained permission from Pope John Paul II to ordain convert Anglican married priests who sought full communion with the Catholic Church. Individual applications for a dispensation, were applied for by individual bishops, and they were always granted by Rome. This practical measure destroyed the last hope of a pragmatic justification of obligatory celibacy. By pragmatic I mean something like this, "Thousands of good priests who endured celibacy because they saw no other way of serving the Church as priests, would feel completely betrayed, if the law were changed". It would be threadbare theologically, but human beings conduct their lives by motivations which are not always totally rational.

During the next forty or so years, the criticism of obligatory celibacy proceeded steadily, until the majority of committed Catholics favoured a married clergy. This was true of most countries in Europe and America. In Asia and Africa, the sociological conditions are so different, that no discernible consensus for or against can be established. For reasons of space, I must confine my account to the situation in Great Britain. In spite of the overwhelming desire of the laity for married priests, the ever-dwindling number of active priests, and the impossibility of providing a theological justification for compulsory celibacy, the hierarchy would not budge. Clearly it is their plain duty to petition the Pope, collectively to put an end to compulsory celibacy. They need not fear that Pope Francis would dismiss them from their posts, on account of insubordination!

One predictable result of the general realisation that obligatory celibacy could not be justified theologically, was the impossible task which confronted diocesan vocations directors. That problem was seen at its most acute in the difficulty of finding a national director. Abbot Christopher Jamieson struggled manfully in that role until he was elected as Abbot President of the English Benedictine Congregation. After that the post was vacant for a considerable time, until the hierarchy found a secular priest who agreed to take on the task in June 2018. However he did not stay in the post for very long: not surprisingly! After his departure there was an even longer inter-regnum, until in May 2019 a replacement was found, and that person was a religious Sister. Her task is literally a poisoned chalice. I speak with all sympathy for her predicament. In any context it would be difficult for a woman to invite young men into a way of life of which she has no personal experience. As the way of life is now theologically unjustifiable, her task is impossible. Significantly it also underlies the fact that no priest, who has had intimate experience of that way of life, could be found to take on the task of promoting it. What more will it take for the bishops to pluck up their courage and ask the Pope for permission to ordain married men? Possibly in the pontificate of Pope John Paul II they might have been dismissed for taking such an initiative, but no such fate threatens them under the leadership of Pope Francis.

As a result, two unexpected tendencies emerged, disregard of the law and the exposure of the unspoken motivation for the bishops' stonewalling. The disregard of the prohibition is not exactly edifying but was probably inevitable. In secular matters, if a government cannot persuade the public of the reasonableness of the law, then even honest citizens quietly ignore it. The classical example was the Prohibition Legislation in the U. S. A. in the 1920's. The motive which prompted the legislation in Congress, had been the desire to control the evils of alcoholic excesses. However the remedy of totally outlawing of the production or sale of all alcoholic drinks was itself excessive. The population were not convinced that all consumption of alcohol was wicked and socially harmful. This gave rise to the illegal trade in secretly produced alcohol, known as "bootlegging", in which millions of honest citizens participated. Sadly, it also gave a great boost to secret societies like the Mafia, which continued to flourish in other areas, when the prohibition legislation was eventually repealed.

Something similar has taken place among the parochial clergy in Great Britain and elsewhere, and it was predictable. It has never been investigated systematically in this country, but the anecdotal evidence is persistent, that an increasing number of priests have simply ignored the ban on having a sexual partner. And it is not just occasional casual sex.

At this point I feel that it is important for me to state my own evaluation of homosexuality. (I am happily married, the father of two sons now adults, who are the joy of our lives, and I am also a grandfather.) I accept without any complications that homosexuality is innate and must be respected as such. There should be no legal or social penalties against gay people. Some of the most effective pastoral priests that I have known were gay, and their emotional sensitivity in dealing with their parishioners' problems undoubtedly enhanced their work. Socially, I am happy to have a number of gay people among my friends and acquaintances, including two couples whose work for the Church, and other humanitarian causes, is truly edifying.

Serious problems arise for gay men if they are not happy with their homosexuality, and may even feel resentful that nature has made them this way. Some of them seem to be ashamed about it too. Perhaps this is not surprising in view of the fact that it was regarded as reprehensible in the Bible, (Leviticus 18: 22, and 20:13, as well as St. Paul's Letter to the Romans 1: 26, 27.). It was criminalised too in British law in the 19th century. It has been judged in a harsh negative way more recently within the Catholic Church, including the depressing document *The Catechism of the Catholic Church,* which emanated from the Roman Curia in the 1980's.

In short, a place in the Catholic priesthood is still the best hiding place for reluctant gay men, because Church Law still forbids the ordination of married men (except for former Anglican priests). The bishops' refusal to initiate the ordination of married men is as stubborn as ever. That is what I meant by giving this chapter the title, "The Bishops are Currently Evading their Responsibilities". It is the only satisfactory way of explaining, why an otherwise conscientiously pastoral bishop would amalgamate parishes, or close churches, rather than seek the Pope's permission to ordain married men in cases of urgency.

In fact, when one reflects on the performance of the Bishops of England and Wales since Vatican II, it is difficult to think of any example of creative leadership. One can only recall refusals to act, as was the case with the National Conference of Priests, where even the theologically neutral unanimous request for a nation-wide pay and pensions structure was ignored. A similar blanket refusal to act, was their reaction to accede to any of the suggestions agreed by the delegates to the Liverpool Congress of 1980, as I have elaborated earlier in this book.

In 1971 a remarkable opportunity for creative leadership was presented to the hierarchy, by the integration of Heythrop College into the University of London. That institution was originally founded by the Jesuits in 1614 in France. After the Catholic Emancipation Act of 1829 the college moved to England, as did the houses of many other religious orders. In the middle of the 20th century it was located in the village of Heythrop in rural Oxfordshire. The Jesuits judged that its remarkable teaching staff, and extensive library could serve a much wider clientele if it were moved to a large city with a university. With great skill the Jesuits negotiated its removal to London, and what was more significant, it was incorporated as a constituent college of London University by charter on 14th May 1971. Cardinal Heenan welcomed them into Westminster diocese, but other than that he seemed to leave them to their own devices. Eventually they were housed in a former teacher training college in Kensington Square which had been conducted by the sisters of the Assumption. It was an ideal building and location. Quite soon its student numbers made it the largest theological faculty of any university in the country, which was an indication that many people find denominational theology more satisfying than Christian theology in general. The future of the college seemed set fair in the 1970's.

However the changes in Catholic attitudes since Vatican II had repercussions on the college. As I have noted at several points in the course of this book, it soon became clear that the Council had rendered obligatory celibacy for the secular clergy as being theologically unjustifiable. Indirectly that raised the question as to the desirability of celibacy as a component of the life of religious orders. I will treat of the matter more fully in the next chapter. From the 1970's though, recruitment to religious orders started to decline dramatically. As far as the Jesuits were concerned there was one year in the 1980's when their English noviciate received no novices at all, for the first time in the entire history of the English province. It was clear that their original assumption that the Jesuits could always provide the teaching staff, could no longer be assumed.

That was the point at which the English and Welsh bishops should have realised that Heythrop College in London University was a national treasure, serving the whole Church in this country, and that they should jointly help to finance it. Sadly, it seems that such a creative response to the problem was never envisaged. The college's financial difficulties became more and more serious. Various schemes were mooted to save it, but they all come to nothing. In 2019 the college closed, and with its demise the Catholic Church in this country lost one of its most valuable institutions.

After serious reflection, I can recall only one creative measure to have emerged from the initiative of the English and Welsh hierarchy since the Second Vatican Council, namely Cardinal Hume's obtaining Pope John Paul II's permission to ordain convert married former Anglican clergy. And he did not suffer dismissal from his post for that initiative!

CHAPTER SEVEN

RELIGIOUS ORDERS

The Origin and Development of Religious Orders

Religious orders of men and women have been among the most important institutions of the of the world-wide Church, since time immemorial. Yet it is equally clear that Jesus did not found any of them, nor did he command that they should be set up after his earthly mission was over. In short, they are a creation of the Church itself, and let it be remembered, a perfectly legitimate creation, wholly consonant with the Church's mission. Having made that point clear, it is instructive to note that Jesus did make one statement about the kind of renunciation, which found its institutional embodiment in monastic communities. It is in Matthew 19:29, "Everyone who has left houses or brothers or sisters or father or mother or children or lands, for my name's sake, will receive a hundredfold, and inherit eternal life" (and in slightly different words, in Mark 10:29). Brocard Sewell, himself a Carmelite Friar, noted something like the unravelling of this idea, in his study of the decline in recruitment to the religious orders in the latter part of the 20th century. "The religious are sincere hard-working men; but with the contemplative element in their vocation falling into increasing dis-esteem, and the lack of anything creative to replace it, it is not surprising that many of them are now asking exactly where the relevance of their life is to be found".[1]

Their theological validity has to be affirmed deliberately, because the early Protestants repudiated them as somehow illegitimate institutions, because they had not been created by Christ himself, and so did not feature in the New Testament.

The variety and number of religious orders in the modern world, all owe their existence, ultimately to the first monks in Egypt. Initially the different houses were independent, but quite soon they began to link up in groups, presumably for mutual support, encouragement, and inspiration.

Historians are agreed that it is not possible to pin-point the exact place and date of the first monasteries, because of the lack of evidence.[2] It is clear however that what we would now describe as monastic communities were in existence in Egypt, in the second half of the third century. It has been suggested that they might have copied the model of the Jewish Essene communities. Much is now known about the community at Qumran, which was destroyed by the Romans in 70 AD, in the suppression of the Jewish revolt. The remarkable preservation of their copious writings has yielded a clear picture of their way of life, which bears a remarkable similarity to Christian monasteries. But a direct link has not so far been established.

After Constantine's decree of toleration for the Christians, the monasteries multiplied and were founded outside Egypt. In Egypt itself, the biographies of St. Pachomius and St. Anthony record their having been founders of several monasteries. In that epoch there was a very definite pursuit of self-imposed corporal penances, to compensate for the recent cessation of the persecution of Christianity, thereby removing the ever present danger of suffering the agonies of martyrdom.[3]

Inevitably the existence of monasteries gave rise to the existence of superiors, and rules of life, to canalise the energies of the monks, and to avoid the chaos which could have arisen within an un-structured group of religious enthusiasts. Rules like that of St. Basil, appeared among the monks of what is now Turkey, and is still in use among the Greek Orthodox monasteries. The rule of St. Columbanus (latter part of the 6th century), was observed by the Celtic monasteries of Scotland and Ireland, and elsewhere. The existence of the monasteries at such an early date, and so far from Egypt, indicates how popular was the institution, and how well suited to the religious ideals of large numbers of high-minded Christians, both men and women. For Western Europe however, the rule of St. Benedict superseded all others. He produced it in its definitive form at the monastery of Monte Cassino in Italy, probably in the decade 530-40. In the 8th century Charlemagne commanded its adoption by all monasteries in his empire soon after 787, when he had received a copy of the Rule.[4]

The adoption of a rule by a community of monks inevitably gives rise to their living under obedience. This raises problems which had to be faced because if it gains too much influence, the results are harmful. Basically obedience can be described as one person's activities being directed by another person's wishes. In family life, it starts in a healthy manner when children are still infants, and by parental guidance they learn the skills of life. Much of that programme is imitation, and indeed subconscious imitation too. For the good of the child's personality, the actual commands should be restricted to the minimum such as the avoidance of dangers. For example, "Don't touch the gas taps on the cooker", or "You must hold my hand when we cross the road."

For adults, independent choice of activities is normal, and consonant with the possession of a spiritual soul capable of intellectual knowledge, self-conscious introspection, freedom, and personal moral responsibility. Within the family, joint decisions can be worked out by dialogue, but in a wider society the harmonious functioning of communities, does require obedience to rules and laws. This applies obviously in the work-place, except for the very small number of self-employed people. In the wider society, rules or laws have to be made by local or national governments. They may vary from the requirement to drive on the left-hand side of the road, to paying taxes to the government. St. Thomas Aquinas classified obedience as one of the subsidiary components of the wider virtue of justice.[5] As a consequence of its being in the realm of justice, infringements of obedience can arise when citizens act with insufficient conformity, or by acting in a manner which is too obedient. That latter consideration accounts for the almost incomprehensible cruelty in World War II, when thousands of German police and soldiers transported millions of Jews to the extermination camps. They were too obedient to the Nazi government.

St. Benedict treated obedience, as an edifying form of discerning the will of God. Chapter 5 of the Rule is devoted to it, thus: "The first degree of humility is obedience without delay... But this obedience itself will then be acceptable to God and pleasing to men, if what is commanded be not done timorously, or tardily, or tepidly, not with murmuring of the raising of objections. For the obedience which is given to superiors is given to God."

This apparently demanding form of obedience is counterbalanced by the abbot's duty of accountability in chapter 64 of the rule. "Let the abbot when appointed consider always what an office he has undertaken and to whom he must render an account of his stewardship; and let him know that it is his duty rather to profit his brethren than to preside over them."[6]

The emphasis on accountability is reassuring, because that duty is singularly absent from the activities of most other authorities in the Church, namely parish priests, and bishops, whose five-yearly *ad limina* visits to Rome are largely tokens of inspection. Worst of all are the various departments of the Roman Curia at the Vatican, which have no system of accountability built into their pattern of work.

Returning to the classification of Aquinas, an example of offending by excessive obedience was made clear to me in a conversation with a Benedictine monk, in the immediate aftermath of Humane Vitae. He disagreed with the condemnation of artificial birth control, but acquiesced in practice because, to use his own words, "It is now on the abbot's conscience, not mine". No one may shift moral responsibility from his own conscience to that of another person, even his religious superior.

A less serious form of excessive obedience concerns the religious dress code. For example, if a 17th century pope had approved the rule of an order of nuns, the design of the religious habit would also come within its ambit. It is clear from everyday observation, that with the passage of time, the sisters were totally inhibited from altering the design of the habit, so that by the 20th century, their style of dress had become bizarre in the extreme. There can be little doubt that it then constituted a deterrent for young women who might otherwise have considered joining them.

Modern psychology strongly suggests that there is an inherent weakness in the human personality. We are rather too willing to surrender our moral autonomy and responsibility, and hand over the decision making to others. This was illustrated by the notorious experiment of Stanley Milgram. In 1969 he advertised in a local newspaper for volunteers who would be paid four dollars to take part in a scientific experiment. On arrival at the university, they were told that it was an experiment to test the effectiveness of corporal punishment in the process of learning. They were also told that they would be selected at random to be the teacher or the pupil. Their task was simple. If the pupil made a mistake, the teacher would administer an electric shock.

In reality they were being subjected to a very different experiment. They were invited to take from a bowl slips of folded paper bearing on the inside the words Teacher or Pupil, and having made that blind choice, they were instructed to act out that role. Actually, all the slips of paper had the word Teacher. Those who took on the role of 'Pupil' were all professional actors, who had been selected in advance. They were told to act as if they were in pain, if they received an electric shock, for giving an incorrect answer. The pupil actors were strapped into their chairs, to prevent them moving when the "shocks" were administered. Several supervisors in white coats and carrying clip boards, were present to oversee the exercise.

The "teachers" were instructed to administer an electric shock every time a pupil made a mistake. Actually, no electricity was in the apparatus, although the switch was marked with varying voltages from 15 (relatively harmless) up to 450 volts (which would be life-threatening). The charade commenced with the teachers administering 15 volts for the first errors, and then it started to increase. The pupils protested vocally at the supposedly low voltage shocks, but when the shocks became stronger, they cried out in pain, and struggled desperately to get out of the chair, but the straps were too strong. As the agonies appeared to get worse, some of the teachers started to show reluctance to continue. At that point the supervisors told them to continue not with threats, but with instructions such as "Continue please", or "The experiment requires that you go on". At 330 volts the pupils slumped back in the chair, apparently unconscious.

The overall results were highly disturbing. In the first experiment the volunteers were men, and 40 of them took part. None of them refused to administer shock treatment, and a horrifying 26 of them went all the way and administered possibly fatal shocks to the apparently comatose body slumped in the chair. The experiment showed that in certain circumstances, people would act with complete subservience to a supposedly competent and legitimate superior. The experiment was repeated several times by Milgram with minor variations, but the results were always virtually the same. When it was reproduced in other universities, the same results were reproduced. It demonstrated an extremely disturbing trait in human nature.[7]

The consequences of the absence of any control or obedience in a group's activities, was brought home to me in the course of a holiday with members of my extended family. Obviously, obedience was not an issue, but it demonstrated to me just how difficult it is to agree on the simplest kind of joint activity where all the participants are equal. Four families were sharing a large house in the Scottish Border region. One day at breakfast with about 16 people round the table, there was a discussion as to whether, as a group, we would visit the Farne Islands off the coast of Northumberland or go to Edinburgh where the Festival was taking place. That suggestion gave rise to a second range of choices because so many plays and concerts were available, but some of the party did not want to see Shakespeare's King Lear. The discussion lasted for about half an hour, with no consensus emerging. Eventually individual families simply went their separate ways that day, but without rancour, since no matter of principle was at stake.

A more serious example of the necessity for some kind of rule and obedience to it, was the experience of a group of high minded, intelligent conscientious objectors at the start of World War II. They decided to do their bit for the country by agriculture, which in that time of crisis was called, 'digging for victory'. Accordingly, they rented a house with a small holding attached to it. As soon as work commenced, they had to face practical decisions about contributions to the rent, and what standard of purchased food should they buy until the produce of the small holding would supply most of their needs. Then there were the detailed questions of which crops to cultivate on their land. Next came the decisions about domestic duties, who would do the cooking, and the dish washing, and did they really need a spotlessly clean house. Their joint discussions became more and more adversarial. Every member of the group was motivated by strongly held moral principles. After a few months the group became riven by bitter dissensions, and eventually split up, with all of them going their separate ways.

I feel that the examples presented in the preceding few paragraphs show that some degree of structuring is necessary in the lives of monasteries, and indeed of other religious orders. Perhaps the best evaluation of obedience is to regard it as a safety net, so that the monks do not have to waste too much valuable time, for example discussing the menus for the week's lunches and suppers. They have far more valuable activities on which to devote their time and energies.

Generally speaking, in religious orders their members, men and women, now take vows of poverty, chastity, and obedience. The practice of poverty emerged slowly out of the initial requirement in St. Benedict's rule that everything in the monastery should be shared, and that no monk should possess anything which he would claim as his own. Chapter 33 of the Rule treats of it in the context of private property, which for a monk, was considered by St. Benedict to be a vice. Chapter 33 begins with the words "This vice especially ought to be utterly rooted out of the monastery. Let no one presume to give or receive anything, without the abbot's leave, or to have anything as his own, anything whatever, whether book or tablets or pen or whatever it may be:"[8]

In other words, the first step towards the clear pursuit of poverty was common property. Everything in the monastery was owned collectively.

Within that arrangement there were latent some elements which were a danger to the achievement of its aim of detachment from material goods. First of all, the monks enjoyed total material security, which seems to have made some communities insensitive to the real poverty and insecurity of the majority of lay people in the Church. I have noted earlier in this book the Jarrow and Glasgow Protest Marches to London during the depression of the 1930's. No monks or friars, or secular priests for that matter, accompanied those men as a gesture of solidarity, and sympathy.

The Catholic Church in Great Britain at that period was keen to keep out of politics. It did not seem to have occurred to the religious authorities that if they had marched with the unemployed men, it would have constituted an act of witnessing to the truth. When Jesus was before Pilate, he stated "For this I was born, and for this I have come into the world, to bear witness to the truth." (John 18: 37).

At some point in their history many monasteries became rich, despite any deliberate policy on their part to acquire large amounts of money. The economist, Ronald Brech now deceased, proposed a theory for generating profit in commercial enterprises. Paradoxically, in a totally different context it explains how the monasteries became rich despite any attempt to do so. Brech's theory was simple. If a company wishes to generate profit, their first objective must be to serve the good of the community, i.e. find out just what kind of shoes the public really need. The second objective is to aim for efficiency in the factory. If those two objectives are being pursued, the profit will emerge automatically. Applying that theory to the mediaeval Cistercians for example, one can see that the welfare of their community motivated their farm work, without their even having to choose it deliberately. The second condition, efficiency also took care of itself. None of the monks was trying to avoid the foreman's scrutiny. And as is well known, they became rich without ever having intended to do so. As the middle ages drew to a close, their riches and those of other houses like them, provided an irresistible temptation to King Henry VIII to confiscate them, in order to pay for his disastrous French wars. Similar confiscations occurred in other nations, as for example in France at the time of the Revolution.

The wealth of the monasteries could have been avoided, if the religious orders had followed the advice of St. Francis of Assisi. His original intention had been that his followers should live in houses which they did not own, and literally beg for money, in order to make them completely detached from wealth. He expressed his wishes clearly in the First Rule:

"The brothers shall appropriate nothing to themselves, neither a place nor anything; but as pilgrims and strangers in this world, serving God in poverty and humility, they shall with confidence go seeking alms. Nor need they be ashamed, for the Lord made himself poor for us in this world. This is that summit of most lofty poverty which has made you, my most beloved brothers, heirs and kings of the kingdom of heaven."[9]

It is useful to reflect on the social context of that ideal, namely the proliferation of wealth in western society, particularly in the cities of northern Italy. When St. Benedict composed his rule, in the aftermath of the collapse and destruction of the Roman Empire, the nations of western Europe were not rich by any measure. For the spiritual life of the monks, and to combat selfishness, the abolition of private property was the key to detachment from wealth. In the 13th century the situation had changed completely, because of the increase in wealth in Italy and other parts of western Europe.

In the lifetime of St. Francis, so many men joined his movement that the primitive ideal of begging resulted in near chaos. In the first five years of the movement approximately five thousand men had joined St. Francis. At the General Assembly of 1221 another five thousand sought admission.[10] An expansion of such speed had never been seen before, nor since, in the development of any other religious order. It was clear that something practical had to be decided concerning their attitude and buildings and money.

The first realistic measure to deal with ownership was enacted by Pope Gregory IX in 1230. He decreed that the Franciscans in any given province could designate a 'spiritual friend' who was not in their order, who would own property and allow them the use of it. A few years later that principle was taken a stage further by Pope Innocent IV. In 1245, by the bull "Ordinem Vestrum" the actual ownership of the Franciscans' houses, and other property like books, was vested in the papacy, who allowed the friars to make use of them.[11] The artificiality of such an arrangement is clear. As the author Lawrence himself remarks in that context, those who have enjoyed the amenities of an officers' mess, or a university college, have all the advantages of a comfortable life, with none of the responsibilities of its upkeep.

Despite the artificiality of the legal solutions, it must be remembered that the ideal of St. Francis was so powerful, that it has never been lost to view in the life of the Church. All subsequent religious orders have included the vow of poverty in the admission of their novices, and it has influenced their buildings, furnishings and general tone of their lives. Probably as an ideal it is more effective, than trying to legislate precisely for such an intangible objective in human conduct. As I noted above, the hard work and honesty of the monks resulted in their becoming rich despite their desire to shun wealth, and the comforts which it could bring with it.

If the pattern of life in religious houses was becoming too comfortable, and reform was needed, reformers seem to have found it more effective to create new religious orders, rather than attempt to bring the older monasteries back to their primitive idealism. Early in the second millennium there were some spectacular new arrivals within the family of religious orders. The Camaldolese monks were founded in 1012, the Carthusians in 1084, and the Cistercians in 1098. It is something of an over-simplification, to say that they seem to have planned their reform of the spiritual life, by increasing the hardships incumbent on their members. But there is an element of truth in that observation. Many years ago, I knew a family who had a son, who was a Carthusian monk at Parkminster in Sussex. Once a year his parents and siblings were allowed to visit him. I recall clearly his mother describing the hardships of their life. The monks who lived like hermits in small single occupant houses round the cloister, met several times a day in the chapel to sing the divine office. That exercise also took place at night, and the night office lasted from midnight until 3 o'clock in the morning, when the body is most powerfully craving sleep. During Lent when the fast was most strictly observed, the monks assisted at the night office like zombies. His mother did not use that word, but it epitomises the semi-dazed condition which she described, as they walked to the chapel and back to their small houses, in a state of acute hunger and sleep deprivation.

A similar attitude to inflicting pain on the body can be seen in the life of the 13th century German mystic, Henry Suso. It is reported of him that he wore an undergarment next to his skin, containing 150 sharp metallic spikes.[12]

It is with great reluctance that I will write the next few paragraphs, because those heroic men tolerate a life of privations, which I could not have endured. Yet, it is not the individuals whose conduct I am questioning, but the institutions. One must also remember that until very recently, any criticism of priests or nuns, or indeed any practice sanctioned by the Church, was frowned upon. It was regarded as akin to blasphemy. Undoubtedly that attitude favoured the practice of concealing serious misdemeanours by the clergy in the matter of the sexual exploitation of children in the latter part of the 20th century. Open and frank discussion in the pursuit of truth, is the most healthy attitude to all aspects of the Church's life. As I noted above, and repeat again because of its importance, when Christ was on trial before Pilate, he stated "For this I was born, and for this I have come into the world, to bear witness to the truth". (John 18: 37).

Returning to the reflections on the bodily discomforts enjoined by the rule of the Carthusians, (and other orders like them) one must ask if a regime of such self-imposed hardships, really does enhance the love of God and neighbour? The endurance of martyrdom, and the tortures which accompanied it, have always rightly been admired in the lives of those heroic Christians. But for an individual to inflict severe pain on him or herself is of questionable value. One can find little justification for it in the Bible. For example, Psalm 100: 1 & 2 reads "Acclaim the Lord, all the earth, serve the Lord gladly, come into his presence with songs of joy". Serving the Lord with joy is a constant theme in the Book of Psalms. The theme of suffering in the Psalms is always associated with sin, or vendettas. Both of which themes are presented as experiences to overcome or avoided. The pursuit of holiness as described in the gospels and epistles is an exercise of love, joy and sensitivity to the invisible (and obviously unwritten) inspiration of the Holy Spirit. A few extracts from the epistles will illustrate the point. In Romans 14: 17 -19, St. Paul states "The Kingdom of God does not mean food and drink but righteousness and peace and joy in the Holy Spirit; he who thus serves Christ is acceptable to God and approved by men". And again, in the same letter,15:13 "May the God of hope fill you with all joy and peace in believing, so that by the power of the Holy Spirit you may abound in hope". Galatians 5:22 echoes the same atmosphere, "But the fruit of the Spirit is love, joy, peace, patience kindness, goodness, faithfulness, gentleness, self-control." Self-inflicted punishment or pain is not promoted in the Old or New Testaments.

Modern progress in psychology has made the present generation wary of any attitude or activity, which suggests self-hatred. Indeed, it seems to be agreed that for the development of a healthy emotional balance in an individual's personality it is important that they have enjoyed the rich experience of intimacy, both in infancy, and in adulthood. This resonates with a well-known adage about the life of grace, namely "Grace perfects nature, it does not destroy it".

At the end of this chapter, I will describe the way of life of a newly founded religious order, which has adopted a highly original way of life which seems to have solved many of these problems.

Meanwhile there are other aspects of the traditional religious orders which must be examined. How should we understand the present situation and relevance of this vast family of institutions whose lives have enriched the life of the Church and society over the centuries, until crises confronted of all of them in the latter part of the 20th century.

The Occupations of Monks and Other Religious Orders

Over the course of their long history, the monks and other religious orders, have devoted themselves to a variety of specific occupations, which have benefitted the whole

Church, and indirectly the human race, because they were inspired by the values of the gospel.

The first and most basic arose out of the necessity of feeding their own communities. The monasteries were for the most part economically self-sufficient, growing their own food. Farm work and other manual occupations were recommended by their rules for a well-balanced life. Incidentally these areas of work, enhanced the status of manual work, which in the days of the Roman Empire, was performed by slaves, unless of course it was in the individuals' own homes and small-holdings.

With the passage of time a subtle change came over the manual work. For most of their history, the agricultural work of the monasteries was performed by the lay brothers. However, a change came about after the Black Death. Prior to that pandemic the numbers of lay brothers had been declining steadily, and by 1360 they had all but disappeared.[13] The number of choir monks had also been severely reduced by the Black Death. Large numbers of monasteries then rented their extensive agricultural lands to tenant farmers, and they drew an income from those rents. The general pattern of life which emerged after the Black Death had subsided, was that of fewer monks in large buildings with a steady income. It did not augur well for their future.

In addition to agricultural work, a totally different form of occupation was more or less thrust on them by their daily pattern of communal prayer.

Their liturgical life required texts of the bible and the Mass, for which the monastic scriptoriums provided the ideal place for their production. As the documents were for the glory of God, care was taken that they should be objects of beauty. Many of the manuscripts which have survived are objects of quite extraordinary beauty. In fact, some of them, like the Book of Kells and the Lindisfarne gospels, are sublime works of art, comparable with the artefacts emanating from any period of history. Those works of art led on to the similar pursuit of beauty in sculpture and architecture, in the construction and decoration of their churches. It has been a characteristic of Christianity, whose understanding of the decalogue's prohibition of worshiping graven images, has not inhibited our embracing all forms of pictorial and plastic art in the buildings and other material adjuncts to the liturgy. After Constantine's decree of toleration, Christians in the Roman Empire, quickly adopted mosaics and paintings on wood, depicting Christ, the saints and scenes from the Hebrew bible. In the relatively distant province of Britain, archaeologists have discovered several remarkable religious mosaics, in the floors of what had clearly been house churches, but whose superstructures had been destroyed by the Saxon invaders. In short, the pursuit of beauty in all forms of art is germane to Christianity, whose roots can be traced back to the presentation of the creation of the material world in the first chapters of the Book of Genesis, where it is recorded that God saw that all his work of (material) creation was good. But the monks deserve the credit for being the pioneers who revived the practice of creating beauty in church buildings and their material adornment, in the re-establishing of Christianity in the West, after the collapse of the Roman Empire.

The next development in the monks' sphere of work was the establishment of schools, initially for their own novices, but naturally extending to a wider clientele. Quite simply the monks became the educators of early modern Europe. It is a commonplace of history, that they salvaged from the Greek and Roman cultures their classical writings and passed them on to mediaeval Europe and thence to the modern world. That was achieved initially by their copying the manuscripts, and then teaching their content, in what would be recognisable to the modern mind as schools. They started by teaching children to read and write, and then led them on to more difficult subjects. It is worth noting, that in the middle ages, it was in the convents that women too were able to acquire a really good education. There was no secular counterpart in ordinary society, which provided any education for boys or girls.

Over the centuries, and with the development of civilization, culture, and wealth in Europe, it was inevitable that the organization and programme of the schools would become more sophisticated, culminating in universities. These institutions were not created directly by the monks, but their distinctive independence was the direct consequence of their being ecclesiastical institutions. The development of an ecclesiastical legal system with its own courts, helped the clergy on the undesirable path to becoming a privileged class, which I have discussed in Chapter Three. But it also meant that their schools and universities were outside the jurisdiction of the local kings. Moreover, as the universities came more and more under the control of the international religious orders (like the Dominicans) which were exempt from the control of the local bishops, the combination of those two areas of freedom was the basis of what we now call academic freedom. In the middle ages, no other network of organisations, such as the universities, had as much liberty.

The Benedictine monks have always been teaching in schools, and as far as the English Benedictine Congregation is concerned, that tradition survived the Reformation, by their moving their houses and schools to mainland Europe. At the time of the French revolution they moved back to England (as did other Orders), taking advantage of the first Catholic Relief Act of 1791.

After the Second Vatican Council, when many institutions in the Church were re-appraising the suitability of their occupations, a group of EBC monks turned the spotlight on the recent evolution of their schools. The results were included in the wider evaluation of monastic life, in the book edited by Dom Daniel Rees, *Consider Your Call.* He was assisted by about two dozen other monks. They were named in the introduction, but whose names were not attached to the specific chapters, which they had produced. In Chapter 15, under the general title of "Work" there is an evaluation of the changes in the EBC's schools, over the years. The author draws attention to the fact that they have changed considerably, over the course of an eventful history, and particularly in response to the needs of the Catholic community in England, which expanded rapidly after the Catholic Emancipation Act of 1829. I quote his words verbatim. "In the 20th century a justifiable response to the needs of the time, brought about a transformation, in several cases, of small Catholic schools run by the EBC houses into larger national and public schools. Such independent Christian schools have contributed greatly to the course of education and the general good of the Church".[14]

The writer of that passage shows no awareness that after the decision had been made to imitate the English public schools (even to the absurd custom of "fagging" for example), the underlying influence on the ethos of those schools would be the English class system. This is widely recognised as a corrosive effect on English society, because of its cultivation of a sense of exclusive privilege in a minority of the population. Actually, I recall a conversation many years ago, with a former pupil of one such school, in which he informed me that the head-master (a monk) stated publicly that the model for that school was Eton.

The same writer also failed to see that the astronomically high fees which they charge, confine the pupils whom they admit, to the richest small section of society. In other words, they are re-enforcing the socially corrosive class divide which was already strongly entrenched, and harmfully so, in the English nation.

Altogether it was not a re-assuring assessment of Benedictine schools and should be borne in mind when we come to analyse the almost complete drying up of monastic vocations from those schools in the 21st century.

After the Council of Trent, many religious orders were founded specifically for the purpose of education. Their schools were for both boys and girls, and the teachers comprised literally thousands of sisters, brothers, and priests.

Another activity associated with religious orders, including the monasteries, was the care of the sick. In the late middle ages, the practice of that care had been organised and institutionalised into hospitals, which were a distinctively Christian institution in the course of human history. In practice, their advent upon the history of Europe had to await the creation of religious orders, who alone could provide the personnel for staffing them free of charge, and shoulder the other financial costs entailed in the work. They were also assisted by confraternities of lay people who devoted their spare time and money to assist in the work of those hospitals, as an expression of their Christian commitment.

At the close of the 15th century England had approximately 470 hospitals. That figure is deceptive, because many of them had accommodation for as few as three patients. The average size was for about ten patients. Only in London were "real" hospitals to be found, such as existed in other nations. They were St. Thomas's, founded c.1215, and St. Bartholomew's, founded in 1123.[15] At that time the city of Florence had more than thirty hospitals, with an average of about one hundred beds each. All prominent Italian cities had similar numbers of hospitals.

King Henry VIII's suppression of the religious houses brought ruin to the whole system. The process began in 1536 with Parliament's passing the Act for the Dissolution of Smaller Monasteries. That was followed in 1539 by the Act for the Dissolution of the Greater Monasteries. By the following year all religious houses had been disbanded and their wealth, which was considerable, had been claimed by the king. As the motive was pecuniary greed, the social consequences had not been thought through by the authorities. A considerable amount of the erstwhile monastic wealth was acquired by those, who collaborated in their dismantling, but the majority of it came to the crown, to pay for King Henry's disastrous wars with France. The humanitarian outcome was a disaster. The number of surviving hospitals nationwide shrank to two. They were St. Thomas's and St. Bartholomew's in London. It is possible that a third survived in Norwich, but the evidence is not conclusive.[16]

Another occupation on which the monks bestowed their devoted energies was preaching the gospel to the pagan nations. I have noted it earlier in Chapter One, when the adoption of Christianity was being presented to the pagan Anglo-Saxon settlers in Britain, for example, it was the preaching of the monks which provided the necessary information and instruction. When the evangelisation had been completed, the routine care of souls was entrusted to resident married parish priests, and the monks went back to their minsters.

Taking a long-term view of the achievements, initially of the monks, and later of other religious orders as well, one cannot but admire the scope of their activities. In addition to their central spiritual role, their other activities provided all of what would now be designated as social services, education, and culture in general. Every element of it was intrinsically connected to their religious dedication. The secular governments simply did not have the money to spend on such refinements of civilization. Their role was limited to protecting their populations from enemies. That is to say, building city walls and castles to defend them from external enemies, and organizing law courts and judges to protect the innocent from internal enemies.

The role of religious orders in society underwent a profound change in the 18th century and onwards, in those countries which experienced the industrial revolution. Briefly, it created unparalleled wealth, which was eventually taxed by governments, which enabled them ultimately to accept responsibility for educating, free of charge, all the children in their respective countries. In the 20th century the same system was directed to providing national medical care for all citizens, also paid for out of taxed revenue. In a fairly short space of time, relative to the long history of religious orders in the Catholic Church, those developments rendered the work of many orders superfluous. It was a situation that many of them found difficult to adjust to.

In the latter half of the 20th century, when the welfare state was well established, in Britain for example, its functioning had inevitable repercussions on the customary way of life of religious orders in general. For many of them, their rigid adherence to the pattern of life, set for them by the Council of Trent in the 16th century, had rendered them seriously out of step with the authentic progress of the modern world. The most obvious examples were first of all their hospitals, in which patients had to pay for their care. Complications arose too for their schools, which reduplicated the institutions of the State, except for those which charged fees, which entailed further problems for religious orders whose members were vowed to poverty.

A searching examination of the reappraisal of their role, was published in 1970 by Fr. Brocard Sewell, himself a Carmelite Friar, under the title of *The Vatican Oracle*. 1968 was a crisis year for religious orders. For example, in one of the Franciscan provinces in Italy, 92 student friars left the order, in a body, in protest against the authoritarian and paternalistic way in which the affairs of their province were conducted. In the same year, in the U.S.A. something like eleven thousand members of religious orders in general, opted out of their communities.[17]

Moving on from the period, which was covered by Brocard Sewell's book, the Jesuits too found themselves in difficulties. In England in the 1950's they were perhaps the most thriving religious order, with approximately 500 men in the English province. However, in one year, early in the new millennium, for the first time in their history of more than 400 years they received no novices. Sadly, that was not an uncharacteristic blip in their pattern of life. By the year 2015 the novitiates of England, Ireland, Belgium and the Netherlands had been amalgamated into one institution, located in Ireland, but receiving very few novices. Clearly, they are unable to sustain the volume of work and institutions of the previous generation. In the year 2016, I recall a conversation with a priest of the English province of the Franciscans, in which he informed me sadly, that their numbers in England were down to a mere twelve, and that their once flourishing theological centre in the university of Kent had been obliged to close down.

Religious orders in general are now faced with a serious problem of finding work which is compatible with the ethos of the consecrated life, and which the members find satisfying. At the risk of some over-simplification, one could perhaps suggest that the work must be compatible with charity, and with the silence and recollection which the life of prayer requires. This would seem to rule out hospitals and schools, which can be conducted by the state, and by lay people in religious schools which have the financial backing of the state, as is the case in Britain. Clearly this demarcation does not apply to nations outside Europe and North America, in which the governments cannot or will not provide universal free education and medical care, which is the case in most of Africa, and large parts of Asia. I am confining this book to the situation of the Church largely in Europe and north America, where the recruitment to religious orders has virtually ground to a halt.

In the developed world there has been one remarkable innovation, which has reversed the drying up of vocations, namely the creation of a new religious order, which is totally compatible with the social conditions of the developed nations. It is the order known as the Brothers and Sisters of Jerusalem. The community was founded on All Saints Day, November 1ˢᵗ, in 1975, at the church of St. Gervais, in Paris. The initiative had come from Fr. Pierre-Marie Delfieux, formerly chaplain to the students at the Sorbonne, and it was welcomed by the Archbishop of Paris, Cardinal François Marty.

Their originality consists in their living in rented accommodation, i.e. they do not own the buildings. This is more realistic than the solution to the same problem in the early days of the Franciscans. As I noted above, initially, the Franciscan houses were owned by various friends of the order. That was replaced by the simpler pattern, by which the papacy became the owner of all the Franciscan houses. That solution was extremely artificial. It did not really align the friars with poor people, because the popes were most unlikely to evict them!

Furthermore, all the members of this new order have part-time, work in the ordinary labour market. They seek jobs of a humble sort, which will not absorb too much of their energy and attention. For the rest of the day, they can devote their attention to study and prayer, including the singing of the divine office. The significance of these arrangements is that they share the two major insecurities of the working class, namely uncertainty about their source of income, and similar uncertainty about their tenure on their homes. As they do not own the places where they live, it is most unlikely that they will ever become rich in the future.

The positive side of the vision is that they can witness to the gospel in the normal places where the poor people work. This opens up to them a remarkable flexibility to embrace any opportunity, which might occur to advance the cause of Christianity. All artificiality has gone from their lives. They wear ordinary clothes except when they are celebrating the liturgy in their chapels.

At the time of their founder's death, early in the new millennium, approximately one thousand men and women had joined that order.

EPILOGUE

Having analysed the state of crisis in the Church in Europe, and Britain in particular, it is clear that the hopes inspired by Vatican II have not been fulfilled. I trust that the foregoing chapters will have made clear the basic causes for this. It is the harmful direction in which those who wield authority in the Church, have directed their power. To repeat what I have stated many times in the course of the narrative, it is the simple fact that obligatory celibacy provides the perfect concealment for gay men, who are reluctant about their sexual orientation, or ashamed of it, and who wish to hide it. Secondly, principal locus of this over centralised power is in the Vatican, which monopolises more power than is good for the Church.

It is a commonplace of ordinary experience, that immature gay men enjoy eccentric display in their clothing and surroundings. The buildings of the Vatican City were designed by the most renowned architects of the Renaissance period, and the ceremony enacted there (not unlike Buckingham Palace) is frankly theatrical. The Swiss Guards are still wearing the gorgeous uniforms designed for them by Michael Angelo in the sixteenth century. In short, it is the perfect stage for immature gay men to live out a fantasy life of artificiality. It is significant, that from day one of his pontificate, Pope Francis chose to live in the room in the modest boarding house in the Vatican City, which he had occupied when he arrived in Rome for the conclave, which unexpectedly elected him as pope.

What is the solution to this problem? At the time of writing the concluding pages of this book, in the spring of 2020, the Amazon Synod completed its work. On the question of ordinations to the priesthood approximately three quarters of participants voted in favour of ordaining mature married men. However, as I noted above, Pope Francis studiously avoided all mention of married clergy in his official confirmation of the Synod's decisions. Possibly Pope Francis considered that more preparation was required for the secular clergy world-wide, to prepare them for the change. Considerable psychological problems could arise, when they realise that their lives of emotional emptiness had no authentic spiritual value. After that, the outdated law of compulsory celibacy will unravel steadily as more and more national hierarchies petition the pope to end it for their countries.

In the preceding chapters I have outlined numerous institutional changes, which if adopted could turn the Church into a dynamic positively inspired community, for the glory of God, and the service of the human race. Will these changes be embraced?

To answer that question, I will shift the focus of this epilogue to the specific task of aiding the human race in its global problems. Humanity is currently (2020) beset by several really serious problems which threaten every nation on this planet. First of all is the exponential increase of the world's population, which is currently about doubling every thirty years.

This leads on to the task of feeding all these people, when all the world's most productive agricultural land is already under cultivation.

Parallel with those two problems is that which menaces all nations on earth, namely that of climate change brought about by the steady heating of the planet.

How will the political leaders cope with such challenges? To judge by past history, there is a distinct danger that leaders of the most powerful nations in the world will resort to warfare, to seize for their own countries sufficient land on which to produce food for their own people. Given that several nations in the world possess nuclear weapons and inter-continental rockets to carry them to their targets, there is a distinct possibility that most destructive war ever seen in history, could breakout.

Tragically it must be admitted that the abolition of warfare, or the curtailment of its most savage aspects, have eluded a solution for the whole duration of humanity's recorded history. The First World War (1914–1918) was described by its supporters, wishing to find a justification for it, as the war to end all wars. The result was just the opposite of that facile description. The technological advances which had made that war even more cruel than its predecessors, rendered the subsequent wars in that century even more brutal. A satisfactory solution to humanity's propensity for warfare is still nowhere in sight.

The second major problem is unique, in the sense that over-population has never before occurred in the planet's history. It was identified in the latter part of the 20th century. Its causation is relatively clear. It is the combination of the presence on the planet of a population which is already close to the upper limit of the world's capacity for food production. This is aggravated by the fact that this total population is now doubling its numbers in roughly every 30-year period. In 1992 the World Development Organisation published a report which stated (among other things) containing the dire warning that "Between 1990 and 2030 the world's population grows by 3.7 billion, food production will need to double, and industrial output and energy use will probably triple world-wide."[1] Scientific medicine has provided effective medicines for many diseases which were fatal in the past. In a simpler context the modern knowledge of biology and bacteriology, has taught us the importance of keeping drinking water separate from drainage water. This too has enabled millions more to survive childhood and live to a normal old age. Increasing the area of farm-land admits of no such simple expedients.

Modern science and technology have enabled many people to make their lives more comfortable by heating their homes, schools and offices by a variety of methods. Burning coal and wood has been known for centuries. The discovery of oil has accelerated heating of buildings, and indirectly the whole planet, because the majority of vehicles are now powered by oil. By vehicles I include aircraft, ships, trains, cars and lorries as the most common. The exhaust gasses of the world's vehicles, and central heating systems, not to mention industry, are raising the temperature, of the whole of the world's atmosphere. To put this problem in its real context, it is important to remember that the world's atmosphere is a very thin layer of fresh air surrounding our whole planet, but just about fifteen kilometres in height! Compared with the earth's diameter at the equator, fifteen kilometres is such a minute fraction that it cannot realistically be expressed as a percentage: it is so far below even one per cent.

The organisations which ought to be grappling with the heating of the planet are the secular governments of nation states, because the remedies will require legislation. The extent of the problems is so vast, and so urgent that education and persuasion, which worked wonders for the significant reduction of the habit of smoking, for example, are simply inadequate, for the drastic changes in life-style which will be required to halt global warming. For example, one vastly widespread practice, which could be abolished without damage to national economies is the practice of holiday flights. In northern Europe, for example, every summer millions of people fly to the Mediterranean, to spend their holidays in the sunshine and hot weather of that region. All those holiday-makers could make the journey by car, or better still by electric trains, entailing far less generating of heat than is caused by the aircraft. But it would entail the loss of one day at the start and end of the holiday, by the slower method of travel. Most of the electors in the democracies of Europe would never forgive their politicians, if they legislated for the deprivation of two days pleasure in that scenario.

Although some nations in Europe have succeeded in controlling their emissions of CO_2 and general heat into the atmosphere, the majority of the world's nations have not. Some of them, like China for instance, feel entitled to catch up on the material comfort of the erstwhile colonising nations of Europe, like England and France. Not surprisingly they resent being lectured on the matter by the comfortable nations which do not have to make great sacrifices to keep within safe levels of overheating the planet. In brief, it is almost certain that with current practices of fuel consumption, the majority of nations on the planet will be unable to stem the steadily increasing global warming.

The two most populous nations in Asia, China and India, are preoccupied with lifting their vast populations out of poverty and providing them with a minimum of civilized living standards. In the U.S.A., surprisingly there are a dangerously large number of politicians who still deny climate change. In Latin America the existence of shanty towns around most of the large cities is an indication of the problems of acute large-scale poverty, which are the immediate concern of their politicians. Even in the best organised democracies the politicians' horizons rarely extend beyond the next election. The majority of them are preoccupied with their careers, and very few are prepared to give a high priority to climate change. All of this raises the possibility that it is already too late in 2020, for the world's politicians to agree on measures to control global warming.

Early in the new millennium, in 2012, I recall attending a packed meeting in a London theatre, which was addressed by a leading scientist in the field of global warming, Professor Stephen Emmott. He considered all the options for survival. That is to say, prohibition of further use of coal, oil, and all fossil fuels. Only electricity is harmless to the environment, and that would have to be generated by hydro-electric systems, by wind farms, solar panels, and perhaps nuclear-powered generating stations. Though the latter method might be so expensive as to be impractical. This means that cars lorries and ships too, would have to rely on electricity, and this would require the improvement of batteries. Clearly aircraft are out of the question, since it seems almost impossible, at present, to design batteries to enable them to be powered by electricity, despite some success with small planes carrying only one person

Discipline in the sphere of energy consumption will be hard enough, but the sharing of food will be even more challenging. I noted above that the most productive agricultural land is almost entirely being cultivated already. Yet the world's population is doubling roughly every 30 years. The problem is obvious, but the solution is not so clear. Ultimately there will have to be a world-wide system of food rationing. But how to organise it on an international scale defies the imagination. At the end of that meeting in the London theatre, Professor Emmott stated with obvious sadness, that the problem was already out of control, and he saw no practical hope of a solution being found.[2]

In the new millennium research into global warming continued apace. Early in 2020 the American journal "Advances in Atmospheric Sciences" published the report of a team of scientists whose overall consensus was that the world's oceans are heating constantly. Prof. John Abraham of Minnesota pointed out that the heating of the oceans is more reliable than measuring air temperatures. Severe hurricanes such as *El Nino* can have a distorting effect on air temperatures, whereas the temperature of the oceans is unaffected. In summary, the results show that the rate of heating of the oceans between 1987 to 2019 is four and a half times faster than the period 1955 to1986. This causes the ice caps of North and South Poles to melt, with the result that by the end of this century the oceans are expected to rise by one metre. This would be sufficient to ensure that cities close to the sea, like New

York, will be knee deep in water all the year round. At this point one hopes that even the most intransigent deniers of global heating will have to acquiesce to the findings of scientists. A sea level rise of this magnitude will be sufficient to displace 150 million people world-wide. These findings were confirmed by other independent organisations, such as the US National Oceanic and Atmospheric Administration.[3]

The same trend in global warming is also displayed by the atmospheric temperature. Temperature recordings are collected by the UK Met Office (with the University of East Anglia), by NASA and NOAA in the USA, and by Europe's Copernicus Climate Change Service. In summary, their overall agreement is that the last five years, and indeed the last decade were the hottest in 150 years of measurement.

Britain is due to host a UN climate summit in Glasgow in November 2020. In that context the UN Secretary General Antonio Guterres is urging nations dramatically to increase their pledges to cut carbon emissions, since we are currently on course for global temperatures to rise to a disastrous 3 to 4 degrees. Bob Ward, at the Grantham Research Institute on Climate Change at the London School of Economics, concludes that "Even if we succeed in limiting warming to 1.5 degrees, this would not be a safe level of warming for the world. Therefore, we must aim to cut global emissions to net zero as soon as possible".[4]

The sobering facts, noted in the previous paragraphs, explain why an increasing number of scientists are already stating, that the human race as a whole has already passed the point of containment of the planet's fatal overheating.[5]

We are now at a point (2020) where the character of the problem is changing. It is no longer one of innovative technologies and economics. Machines like wind farms and solar panels are well understood. The most pressing problem in the early part of the twenty first century is one of sharing equitably the relatively scarce resources, particularly of food, among a steadily increasing world population. Fundamentally it has now become a moral problem. The wealthy nations of Europe and America should not criticise poorer nations elsewhere. In those countries where the governments cannot or will not organise old age pensions or similar measures for social security, the only remedy for poor people to provide for old age, is to have at least four children to ensure that a couple of them might still be alive in middle age to look after their parents when they are too old to work. This means that it is essentially a moral problem, involving peoples' motives for selfish or altruistic behaviour. How can the world's wealthiest nations be persuaded to share the food available, with countries which even now cannot produce enough for the basic healthy diet of their citizens? The world's politicians have known all the relevant facts for at least twenty years. Their practical initiatives up till the present, have been so inadequate to the scale of the problem, that it is safe to conclude that the politicians are incapable of guiding the world to a satisfactory solution. A radically different path must be adopted if the world is to be rescued from terminal over-heating.

The interconnected problems of global over-population, and limited food production are literally gigantic. But one possible solution for both, is surprisingly simple in principle. Of the two components of the problem one cannot be changed substantially, but the other can. Namely, the world's food production cannot be increased indefinitely, because all the serviceable arable land is already under cultivation. Advances in the technology of agriculture may be able to increase the output marginally, but that is all.

The second component, population increase, can be controlled. To oversimplify somewhat, in the future families will have to limit their size to just two children, since that is the number for replacement, and not for uncontrolled expansion. This limitation may cause surprise and offence to some readers, but it is the only solution. Couples who would like to have a third child will have to be taxed severely, and should any aspire to a fourth child, their taxation will have to be literally punitive. Minor factors in the process are that some couples will be unable to produce children because of infertility. A small minority of couples may not wish to have a family. Taking account of these variants, this plan is fundamentally capable of solving the problem, of the potentially exponential expansion of the human race. I realise that some people will find this hard to accept. However, it must be borne in mind that bringing up two children is psychologically healthy, and the children are happy. The lonely life of an only child is avoided. Many couples in Britain now choose freely to limit their families to two children.

Needless to say, the richer nations of North America and Europe will have to subsidise the poorer nations to adopt this pattern of family life. First of all, we must give them enough money to provide old age pensions for their citizens. Admittedly this will be difficult. Another moral consideration is relevant at this point. It will have to be accompanied by practical safeguards to ensure that local politicians and administrators in the receiving nations do not line their own pockets. This will remove the basic need for them to produce large families. Next we must subsidise their education, so that they can help themselves.

As to the wider class of inter-related problems, namely the complimentary causes of global heating, their ramifications are more complicated. Having stated that the overall problem of sharing is a moral problem, the solution which I will offer for this problem may cause some surprise to the readers of this book. The answer lies in religion, and I will be perfectly frank. Of all the world's different faiths, only Christianity has a realistic chance of leading such a gigantic undertaking.

The famous "nonconformist conscience" achieved it in the recent past. I will describe it in one well documented incident in the life of the poet Robert Graves. The family lived in London, and the young Graves was a boarder at Charterhouse School situated at Godalming in Surrey. In his first letter home, at the start of a new term, Robert related to his parents an incident in the journey which he clearly regarded as a success. The school had chartered a special train, exclusively for their pupils, which would travel from Waterloo station to Godalming without any intermediate stops. He had arrived rather late at Waterloo, calculated that he did not have time to buy a ticket, and judged that in the crowd of school-boys he could slip past the ticket inspector undetected. It worked. When the train stopped at Godalming, he employed the same stratagem and for the second time in that journey, he slipped through the barrier without a ticket. Back in London his father opened the letter while he was eating breakfast. (At the end of the nineteenth century the first post in London was delivered really early). Reading of his son's having travelled without a ticket, he was extremely indignant. He put down the knife and fork, left the house, and travelled straight to the ticket office at Waterloo. There he purchased a child's one-way ticket to Godalming. He made his way straight to the nearest litter bin, tore the ticket into small pieces, threw them into the bin, and went home to finish his breakfast.

Some readers may find that incident slightly comic, but the attitude was widespread in the nation. It was so influential that it gave rise to the British law courts' reputation for incorruptibility. This trust has lasted until the twenty first century, and civil law-suits from other countries are still brought to Britain for resolution, because of that repute.

So let me elaborate on my confidence that Christianity can achieve this goal. The basic task of sharing limited food resources is a main-stream objective of the bible. It occurs in the Hebrew bible. In the first chapter of Genesis. God declares that the material world is good, and indeed, very good. This is an extremely important pronouncement because in some of the world's religions, their concentration on the goodness of the spiritual element in reality, causes them to deprecate matter, even to the point of treating it almost as an illusion.

In the writings of the prophets, and in the Psalms there is a shift to the moral duty to share the world's commodities, like food and clothing with poor people. In the gospels that perspective has moved into the central focus. The forward-looking accounts of the Last Judgement of human beings in Matthew 25: 31-46, focus the substance on which people will be judged, as the sharing or withholding of food, drink, clothing and shelter. The straightforward description of the Last Judgement is also backed up by the lessons in parables such as the poor man Lazarus, who was denied food by the rich man at whose gate he lay suffering (Luke 16: 19-31).

The social context in which those warnings and parables were spoken by Jesus, and recorded soon afterwards by the evangelists, was one of individual personal contacts. In the modern world, responsibility for many of those activities has laudably been shouldered by the state, such as their providing the NHS and social services. They are financed from taxed money, which in well organised nations, derived from re-distributive systems of taxation. It is imperative that such institutions are adopted by other nations, especially the poorer ones, which will have to be subsidised financially, as a temporary measure by rich countries. In that scenario it is absolutely essential that the money is channelled to the alleviation of poverty, and not into the pockets of corrupt government officials. In other words, the success of such international support is essentially a moral matter comprising generosity, and honesty.

Granted that morality has taken over centre-stage as the principal force, as the only influence strong enough to shape human behaviour in taming global heating. The next stage along this path is to realise that morality must be guided by religious principles. Because Christianity is the only world-wide organisation which acknowledges original sin, and is capable of overcoming its dire influence, and because time is short, I suggest that Christianity should assume the lead in this undertaking.

Common sense, common decency and similar high-minded human endeavours, are all inadequate to meet the urgency of the challenge presented by global heating.

If any readers are in doubt, let me add just one more illustration. In January 2020, Jewish communities throughout the world were marking (but not celebrating) the liberation of the concentration camp of Auschwitz by Russian soldiers in 1945. The sympathy of all civilized people, world-wide was focussed upon the survivors who were still alive, and on the memory of the millions who did not survive. Naturally there were high profile events in the State of Israel. But at the same time the Israeli government was conducting its own form of persecution of the Palestinian people, as they were gradually and insidiously taking possession of the Palestinians' territory. Admittedly the expedients used against the Palestinians were not as brutally cruel as those which the Nazis employed at Auschwitz and other camps. Yet, the total disregard of the rights of the Palestinians, such as making them pay (yes, with cash) for the demolition of their own homes to make way for Israeli "settlements" and the connecting roads, displays an inexcusable form of cruelty. If they could not pay, they were forced to demolish their own houses with their own hands. Have we learnt nothing from history?

To return to the practicalities as to how religious individuals and organisation should set about changing national policies, starting with existing structures, let me repeat that it is essential for people of good will enter politics to safeguard the honest and efficient running of such enterprises as the NHS. That is why I have stated earlier in this book, and I repeat it now, that all committed Christians have a duty to be actively involved in politics, which has to be party politics. The situation in Great Britain in the decade after 2010 is a perfect paradigm to learn from. The policies of the Conservative government, masquerading as "austerity" have withheld adequate money from those organs of government, such as the NHS and social services, to an extent which is frankly immoral. When the corona virus pandemic hit the nation in 2020, it was discovered that the NHS woefully lacking in essential protective clothing for nurses and doctors. In another area millions of citizens have been reduced from poverty to destitution by the new system of universal benefits. Yet another cruel policy was their refusal to build council houses and flats, which has created a new wave of homelessness, evidenced by hundreds of individuals sleeping on the streets. The callousness of the system in borne out by details such as requiring people who have lost their jobs, to wait six weeks before the first payment of unemployment benefit. After six weeks many of them will have defaulted on rent!!

From what I have written in the previous paragraphs, it will be clear to my readers that conscientious Christians will have to select with care, which party to support or join. Facing such a choice goes against the practice of the Catholic Church, in Great Britain, for almost two centuries. After the Catholic Emancipation Act of 1829, the Catholics gratefully entered the mainstream of national life, but were careful not to "rock the boat" by drawing attention themselves by identifying with divisive political issues. Keeping a low profile was the custom, but after nearly two centuries a more pro-active policy is required of us. Ensuring the adequate financing of institutions like the NHS will require careful choice, and deep personal commitment. Inevitably, committed Christians will be involved in conflicts with their fellow citizens. Is this a Christian way of acting? My answer must be Yes. Indeed, Jesus foresaw it and warned his followers in sobering words: "Do not think that I have come to bring peace on earth; I have not come to bring peace, but a sword. For I have come to set a man against his father, and a daughter against her mother, and a daughter in law against her mother-in-law; and a man's foes will be those of his own household. (Matt. 10: 34-36).

The decision-making process for issues such as those described above, was worked out realistically by the Liberation Theologians in Latin America, shortly after the Second Vatican Council. It is called Conscientization, and I described it at some length in Chapter One, in the same context as this point, namely political reform based on Christian morality. Groups of Christians should be discussing political and social issues in the national or local communities. The first stage is to ascertain whether the issue entails a moral decision or not. For example in the installation of street lights, what is a reasonable spacing of each one from the next? Clearly it is a practical decision, which does not entail moral considerations. On the other hand, the question as to the case load of probation officers is a highly moral issue. At this point the second stage of conscientization comes into focus, namely finding a satisfactory moral solution to the problem. If the probation officers are over-loaded with too many discharged prisoners (as in Britain at the time of writing), they will be unable to give any of them the care, which they must have if they are to be helped back to an honest pattern of life.

The Christian response to such situations will have to be, that they will give their support to the political parties which are prepared, when in government, to raise taxes and divert the money to employ an adequate number of probation officers. (And obviously to bring it back from being a commercial organisation, to its being under government supervision, where there is no question about profit for shareholders.)

The principles of conscientization, applied by committed Christians, will have an even more vital role to play when the problems being faced are those of global heating. I have outlined above that the sacrifices which will be demanded, of the wealthier inhabitants of our planet, are so severe that democratically elected parliamentarians will simply not have the moral courage to enact them. This is where religion enters the scene, because this source of motivation is the only one strong enough to convince voters about the importance of the severe measures of collective self-denial, which must be adopted.

In a book of this kind, there is insufficient space to weigh up all the world's religions, in order to assess their suitability to face the practical issues of global heating. For the sake of brevity, let me say that it is my conviction that the Catholic form of Christianity is the best equipped to grapple with climate change. The reasons are quite simple. From the earliest period of its history, Catholicism, as its name implies, has been aware of a world-wide responsibility. In the 21st century it has viable communities in the vast majority of countries world-wide but is independent of all secular governments.

This sense of world-wide consciousness was apparent in the 1960's in the Second Vatican Council when about 3000 bishops from all over the world met to do business. In a slightly different perspective, it was seen again in the creation of new Cardinals in the autumn of 2019, since most of them were from small countries from every continent. Symbolically it showed that the psychological atmosphere of being centred on European culture, was on the way out.

The central challenge in the equitable sharing of the world's resources, is not as difficult as it might appear at first sight. The money is there among the wealthier nations. It depends on how they now spend it. These nations can make meaningful economies by spending less on weapons of war. No more aircraft carriers, or nuclear submarines, armed with inter-continental rockets with nuclear warheads.

Religion has an irreplaceable role, as the motivator, and collective moral conscience. Normal self-interested political persuaders are clearly inadequate to motivate the kind of collective magnanimity that is required in these gigantic acts of collective generosity. Not only will the wealthier nations have to give money to poorer ones, but considerable measures of self-sacrifice at home will also be necessary. So, I repeat that total commitment to religious motivation is indispensable.

The role of Catholicism among the various Christian Churches is at present problematical. The damage done to our reputation by the well-publicized sex abuse scandals has undoubtedly shaken public confidence. Hopefully this disgraceful episode in the Church's history is well on the way to rectification. If the reforms which I have outlined in the preceding chapters are implemented satisfactorily, the Catholic Church could assume the role of world-wide moral leadership, on account of its global outreach, noted above.

Having spoken of my confidence in the Catholic Church's potential to espouse the cause of climate change, let me add that ecumenical relations between all Christian Churches are so well advanced, that it is certain that other Churches, (many of which are quite simply national Churches), will follow the lead of Catholicism, if they have not entered upon that path already! Some readers may be puzzled or sceptical about my confidence in the Churches' ability to lead the world out of the danger of self-destruction or global heating.

The conclusion that follows from the previous few pages, is that in the midst of the world's dramatic crises of over-population in an over-heating planet, the Catholic Church should have found that is has an indispensable role to play, on the world stage. I gave to Chapter Two of this book the title "Catholicism's Lost Opportunities". By contrast, in the early years of the 21st century, it is the only world-wide organisation which can fill the role of gigantic moral persuasion. This may seem an overconfident claim to some of my readers. Yet, on reflection it is hard to think of any other organisation which could discharge this role. The International Red Cross does not have the qualitative amplitude. If one thinks of agencies of the United Nations, like the World Health Organisation, their role is

by definition too restricted. The realisation among
Catholics, that our Church is uniquely qualified to fill this
role, could provide the motivation to shake off all trivial
preoccupations, like dithering about ordaining married
men. The awareness of being indispensable should
provide the psychological motivation to rise to the
demands of the crisis. The Second World War supplies
a useful lesson. After Dunkirk, the country went through
a complete collective change of attitude to the war. It was
apparent to practically everyone in the nation, that Britain
alone was left to resist Hitler, whose ruthless
expansionism, with its subsidiary evils, like exterminating
the Jews, just had to be stopped. The nation underwent a
collective conversion to shouldering the complete
responsibility for saving the free world from Hitler. And
let it be remembered, that was well before Russia and the
U.S.A. were drawn into the conflict.

But let me assure my readers that my confidence does not
repose solely upon my trust in the competence of the
Churches' human leaders and bureaucrats. Above all, we
have the divine promises of God's protection and
guidance for his Church. The clearest indicator for this
trust is the farewell message of Jesus at the end of St.
Matthew's gospel, (28: 18–20) "All authority in heaven
and on earth has been given to me. Go therefore and
make disciples of all nations... and lo, I am with your
always, to the close of the age". There are parallels in
Luke 24: 49, John 16:33, and elsewhere.

The confidence in divine guidance and protection, has
been a constant feature of the Church's history. General
councils always begin with prayers for the guidance of the
Holy Spirit, and that is why their decisions on doctrinal

matters, have always been regarded as permanent and irreformable.

I think that it is legitimate to detect instances of such supernatural guidance in the Church's recent history. When Pope Pius XII died his successor was the aged archbishop of Venice, Cardinal Roncalli. I recall clearly that when I heard the news, my heart sank, as I thought to myself, "What hope is there of any updating of the Church with such an ancient pope?" Yet after about a year in office, he announced the summoning of a General Council. The pope himself attributed his decision about the Council to the guidance of the Holy Spirit. There had been no preliminary consultations, nor feasibility studies. The rest is history. That Council's enactments gave the Church the plan for a total renewal of its mission, and the means to engage constructively with the modern world's problems. After the death of Pope John Paul I, the Polish cardinal Woytila was elected as pope, and began a conservative reaction.

This showed itself principally in selecting known conservatives as bishops. That unfortunate policy was re-enforced by his inserting one of the conditions for candidates to the episcopate the fact that they had to be supporters of the birth control encyclical *Humanae Vitae,* as I noted earlier in this book. In assessing the damage inflicted on the international episcopate, one has to reckon with two equally depressing but connected factors. Namely, was the candidate so lacking in theological acumen that he did not see that the document was flawed. Alternatively, was he so ambitious for promotion that he compromised his perception that it was wrong, in order to become a bishop. By the end of a long pontificate Pope

John Paul II had been able to renew the majority of the international episcopate, many of whom were compromised. He also appointed the majority of the cardinals who would elect his successor.

After the death of John Paul II, and the resignation of Benedict XVI, many in the universal Church waited glumly for the election of another reactionary pope. The election of the Argentinian Cardinal Bergoglio was utterly unforeseeable. Years before, he had moved out of the archbishop's palace in Buenos Aires and lived in a small apartment in a working-class suburb of the city. Each morning he travelled to the diocesan office on the tram, rubbing shoulders with the other workers. Once elected to the papacy it was no real surprise that he refused to take up residence in the Vatican Palace, but remained in the simple room in the modest guest house where he had been lodged for the duration of the conclave. He also takes his meals in the self-service restaurant in that same guest house. The rest is history, as this edifying pope does his best to reform the Church along the lines of Vatican II.

As a totally committed Christian, I feel fully convinced that the elections of the two reforming popes can be regarded as acts of God's guidance of the Church. I think that it is equally reasonable to count on the divine guidance of the Church, if it is taking the lead, morally, in educating the world's citizens in the scale of generosity which will be entailed in the collective choices that must be made, if our planet is to survive as the home for all forms of life.

Initially, in the title of this book, I asked if Catholicism was reformable. I trust that my readers, who have followed the line of reasoning employed in the development of this narrative, will have seen that reform is possible. My own personal conviction that reform is not only possible, but capable of realisation in the near future, depends upon the divine promises of support for the Church, which are explicit in the New Testament.

NOTES

INTRODUCTION

1. Numbers from *The Tablet* 4 July 2020.

2. Bullivant, Stephen. *Mass Exodus: Catholic Dissafililiation in Britain and America since Vatican II*, Oxford 2019, 29.

3. Bullivant, Stephen. *Mass Exodus*, 36.

4. Boff, Leonardo. In the Vienna based journal, *Kirche In* April 2020.

5. Congar, Yves. *Vraie et Fausse Réforme dans l'Église*, Paris: Éditions du Cerf, 1950.

CHAPTER ONE

1. Bede. *Ecclesiastical History of the English Nation*, Eds. Judith McClure and Roger Collins, trans. Bertram Colgrave, Oxford, 1969, 95.

2. McDade, John. Published as 'Ministry in a Post – Religious Society Can we do it at all'. In *New Blackfriars*, March 2019, 215.

CHAPTER TWO

1. Thomas, Hugh, *The Slave Trade*, 126, 146.

2. Guttiérrez, G. *In Search of the Poor of Jesus Christ*, New York (1999), passim, is mainly about Bartolomé de las Casas. Brading, David. *The First America: The Spanish Monarchy, Creole Patriots, and the Liberal State*

1492 - 1867. Cambridge, 1992, Chapter 3 contains a summary of the life of Bartolomé de las Casas.

3. *Karl Marx and Frederick Engels: Collected Works.* 'Theses on Feuerbach', number 11, Vol. 5, London: 1976, p. 5.

4. Lean, G. *God's Politician*, London,1980, 89.

5. Spicq, C. *La Théologie Morale du Nouveau Testament*, Paris, 1965, Vol. I, 353, 354.

6. Berr, Héléne. *Journal*, London, 2008, 202.

7. Clark, Christopher. *The Sleepwalkers: How Europe Went to War in 1914*, London 2012.

8. Clark, C. *The Sleepwalkers*, 392, 394.

9. Clark, C. *The Sleepwalkers*, 405.

10. Grass, Gunter. In *The Guardian*, 6 May 1995.

11. Roberts, Andrew. *The Storm of War*, London, 2009, 553.

12. Giridharadas, Anand. *Winners Take All: The Elite Charade of Changing the World*, London, 2019. Quoted in *The Guardian*, 22 January 2019. On 22 July 2020, The Guardian also reported that the wealth of Jeff Bezos (creator of Amazon) increased by $ 13 billion in one day, bringing his total fortune to $ 189 billion, on a par with the GDP of small nations like Greece and New Zealand.

13. St. Augustine, *Confessions*, Book 1, Chapter 1.

14. Halik, Tomás. *The Night of the Confessor*, New York, 2012, 85.

15. Stern, Fritz. from his obituary, in *The Guardian*, 3 June 2016.

16. Franzen, Jonathan. Quotation from the review of his book *The End of the End of the Earth*, in *The Guardian* 10 Nov. 2018.

17. Lenton, Tim. In the journal *Nature*, Nov. 2019, quoted in *The Guardian*, 28 Nov. 2019.

18. Hitchens, C. writing in *The Guardian*, 16 June 2007.

19. Figes, O. *A People's Tragedy*, London 1996, 773.

20. Monbiot, George. Writing in *The Guardian*, 11 October 2005.

21. *The Guardian*, 13 September 2018.

22. Pochmann, Marcio's researches, quoted by Leonardo Boff, writing in *Kirche In* July 2019.

CHAPTER THREE

1. Basseville, M (ed.), *Études sur le Sacrement de lOrdre*, (quoting from *Codex Theodosianus*, XVI, 26), Paris 1957, 127.

2. Basseville, M. (ed.) *Études*, 129.

3. Congar, Y. 'The Historical Development of Authority in the Church' in *Problems of Authority*, Todd, J.M. (ed.) London 1961, 135.

4. Cooke, Bernard. *Ministry to Word and Sacraments*, Philadelphia, 1976, 544.

5. Hefele, K. and Leclercq, J. *Histoire des Conciles*, Paris 1908 - 194, Vol. 1, 191.

6. Hefele, K. and Lecercq, J. *Histoire*, Vol. 1, 414.

7. Gelasius, Pope. Letter 14, 'To the Bishops of Luciania'. Quoted in Theile, A. E. *Epistolae Romanorum Pontificum Genuinae*, Brunswick 1867, Vol. 1, 371.

8. Stultz, Ulrich. *Die Eigenkirche als Element des mittelalterischgermanischen Kirchenrechtes*, Basel 1895. Translated by Barraclough, G. as Mediaeval Germany, Oxford 1938, Vol. 2, 35 - 70.

9. Abbott, Walter. (ed.) *The Documents of Vatican II*, New York 1966, p. 73.

10. Vogels, H. J. *Celibacy-Gift or Law*, Tunbridge Wells 1992, 76.

11. Damasus, Pope. *Ad Gallos Episcopos*, M.P.L. Vol, 13, cols. 1181 – 1194.

12. Ranke-Heinemann, U. *Eunuchs for the Kingdom of Heaven*, London 1990, 110.

13. Ranke-Heinemnn, U. *Eunuchs*, 110.

14. Alberigo, J. et al. *Conciliorum Oecumenicorum Decreta*, Bologna 1973, 198.

15. Vatican II, *Presbyterorum Ordinis*, § 16, Abbott 565.

16. Vatican II, *Gaudium et Spes*, § 49, Abbott 253.

17. Vatican II, *Gaudium et Spes*, § 87, Abbott 302.

18, Pius XI, Pope. *Casti Connubii*, Rome 1930, "Acta Apostolici Sedis, 22, 542.

19. Dominian, Jack. *Marriage: The Definitive Guide to What Makes a Marriage Work*. London 1995, 54

EXCURSUS ONE

1. *The Guardian*, 28 Sep. 2018.

2. *The Tablet*, 23 March 2019.

3. Martel, Frédéric. *In the Closet of the Vatican*, London, 2019, 511.

4. *The Tablet*, 29 Sep. 2018.

5. *Kirche In*, March 2019.

6. *The Tablet*, 9 March 2019.

7. *The Tablet*, 21/28 Dec. 2019.

8. *Kirche In*, July 2019.

9. *The Tablet*, 18 August 2018.

10. Alison, James. 'Caught in a Trap of Dishonesty', in *The Tablet*, 4 August 2018.

11. Alison, James. 'Caught in a Trap of Dishonesty', in *The Tablet*, 4 August 2018.

EXCURSUS TWO

1. Pius XI, Pope. *Quadragesimo Anno*, in Acta Apostolicae Sedis 23, (1930), p. 203. Quoted by Pope John XXIII, in the encyclical *Mater et Magistra* in Acta Apostolici Sedis, 53, (1961), p. 414.

2. English translation by Shaun Whiteside in 2019, published in London by Bloomsbury Continuum.

3. Martel, Frédéric. *In the Closet of the Vatican*, 90.

4. Martel, Frédéric. *In the Closet of the Vatican*, 103.

5. Martel, Frédéric. *In the Closet of the Vatican*, 505.

6. Martel, Frédéric. *In the Closet of the Vatican*, 506.

7. Martel, Frédéric. *In the Closet of the Vatican*, 343.

CHAPTER FOUR

1. Bede, *Ecclesiastical History*, 10.

2. *Kirche In*, May 2020, p. 19.

3. Vatican II, "Apostolicam Actuositatem", § 26, in Abbott, *The Documents of Vatican II*, § 26, 515.

4. *The Tablet*, 14 Sep. 2019.

5. Winter, Michael. *Whatever Happened to Vatican II?* London 1985, 66 - 74.

6.   Lampe, Peter. *Christians at Rome in the First Two Centuries*, London 2003, T & T. Clark International.

7.   Lampe, Peter. *Christians at Rome*, 100 – 103.

8.   Eusebius, *Historia Eccesliastica*, IV. 23, 10.

9.   Radcliffe, Timothy. In *The Tablet*, 12 Oct. 2019, 14.

CHAPTER FIVE

1.   Recently it has been suggested that those letters should be given a later date, but the evidence is unconvincing.

2.   Sweeney, Gareth. 'The Wound in the Right Foot', in Hastings, Adrian. (ed.) *Bishops and Writers*, Wheathampstead 1977, 207.

3.   *Annuario Pontificio*, Rome 2019, 17 – 817.

CHAPTER SIX

1.   Translation in Abbott, W. *Documents of Vatican II*, 407.

2.   *Catholic Directory for England and Wales*, 2010, p. 832. *Church of England Year Book*, 2010, p. 56.

3.   Translation in Abbott, W. *Documents of Vatican II*, 64 & 270.

4.   Translation in Abbott, W. *Documents of Vatican II*, 65.

CHAPTER SEVEN

1.   Sewell, Brocard, *The Vatican Oracle*, London 1970, 155.

2. Fliche, A. & Martin, V. 'De la Paix Constantinienne à la Morte de Théodose'. In *Histoire de l'Église*, Paris 1950, Vol. 3, 303.

3. Hughes, Philip. *A History of the Church*, London 1952, Vol. 1, 140.

4. McCann, Justin. *The Rule of St. Benedict*, London 1951, ix, xiv.

5. Thomas Aquinas. *Summa Theologica*, II-II, question 104.

6. McCann, Justin. *The Rule of St. Benedict*, 33, 35, 147.

7. Milgram, Stanley. *Obedience to Authority*, New York, 1969, passim.

8. McCann, Justin. *The Rule of St. Benedict*, 85.

9. Lawrence, C. H. *The Friars, The Impact of the Early Mendicant Movement on Western Society*, London 1994, 33.

10. Hughes, Philip. *A History of the Church*, Vol. 2, 359.

11. Lawrence, C. H. *The Friars*, 40.

12. Feldmann, Christian. 'Der Mystiker vom Bodensee', in *Kirche In*, March 2020, 32.

13. Knowles, David. *The Religious Orders in England*, Cambridge 1948, Vol. 2, 358.

14. Rees, Daniel. (ed.) *Consider Your Call*, London 1978, 312.

15. Porter, Roy. (ed.) *Cambridge History of Medicine*, Cambridge 2006, 183.

16. Porter, Roy, *Cambridge History of Medicine*, 184.

17. Sewell, Brocard. *The Vatican Oracle*, London 1970, 134, 135.

EPILOGUE

1. Street, A. & Summers, L. *World Development Report,*
   1992, Oxford 1992, 2.

2. In 2013, Professor S. Emmott published an expanded
   version of that lecture as a book entitled *Ten Billion.*

3. *The Guardian,* 14 January 2020.

4. *The Guardian,* 16 January 2020.

5. *The Guardian,* 14 January 2020.

SELECT BIBLIOGRAPHY

Abbott, Walter (ed.) (1966), *The Documents of Vatican II*, New York: Guild Press.

Alberigo, J. et al. (1973), *Conciliorum Oecumenicorum Decreta*, Bolgna: Istituto per le Scienze Religiose.

Annuario Pontificio, (2019), Rome: Vatican Press.

Aquinas, Thomas. *Summa Theologica*.

Augustine of Hippo. *Confessions.*

Barraclough, G. see Stultz, Ulrich.

Basseville, M. (ed.) (1957), *Études sur le Sacrament de l'Ordre*, Paris: Éditions Du Cerf.

Bede, (eds.), McClure, J. & Collins, R. (1969), *Ecclesiastical History of the English Nation*, (trans. Colgrave, Bertram), Oxford: Oxford University Press.

Berr, Héléne. (2008), *Journal*, London: Quercus.

Boff, L. (1993), *The Path to Hope*, New York: Orbis Books.

Brading, David. (1992), *The First America: The Spanish Monarchy, Creole Patriots and the Liberal State 1492 – 1867*, Cambridge: Cambridge University Press.

Bruns, H. (1839), *Canones Apostolorum et Conciliorum Saec. IV-VII* (2 vols.) Berlin: G. Reimer. Reprinted in 1959, Turin.

Bullivant, Stephen. (2019), *Mass Exodus: Catholic Disaffiliation in Britain and America since Vatican II*, Oxford: Oxford University Press.

Chadwick, O. (1975), *The Secularisation of the European Mind in the Nineteenth Century*, Cambridge: Cambridge University Press.

Clark, Christopher. (2012), *The Sleepwalkers: How Europe Went to War in 1914*, London: Allen Lane.

Congar, Yves. (1950), *Vraie et Fausse Réforme dans l'Église*, Paris: Editions Du Cerf.

Congar, Yves. (1961), 'The Historical Development of Authority in The Church', in Todd, J. M. (ed.) *Problems of Authority*, London: Darton, Longman, and Todd.

Cooke, Bernard. (1976), *Ministry to Word and Sacraments*, Philadelpia: Fortess Press.

Damasus, Pope. *Ad Gallos Episcopos*, M.P.L. vol. 13. cols. 1181 – 1194.

Dominian, Jack. (1995), *Marriage: The definitive guide to what makes a marriage work*, London: Heinemann.

Duffy, Eamon. (1997), *Saints and Sinners: A History of the Popes,* New Haven: Yale University Press.

Emmott, Stephen. (2013), *Ten Billion.*

Eusebius of Caesarea. *Historia Ecclesiastica*, M.P.G. vol. 19.

Fagan, S. (1997), *Does Morality Change?* Dublin: Gill and MacMillan.

Feldmann, Christian. 'Der Mystiker vom Bodensee', in *Kirche In*, March 2020.

Figes, Orlando. (1996), *A People's Tragedy*, London: Pimlico.

Fliche, A. & Martin, V. (eds.) (1950) 'De la Paix Constantinienne à la Morte de Theodose', in *Histoire de l'Eglise*, Paris: Bloud & Gay.

Franzen, Jonathan. Review of his book *The End of the End of the Earth,* in *The Guardian*, 10 Nov. 2018.

Gelasius, Pope. (1867), 'Letter 14, To the Bishops of Luciania' in Theile A.E. *Epistolae Romanorum Pontificum Genuinae*, Brunswick.

Giridharadas, Anand. (2919), *Winners Take All: The Elite Charade of Changing the World*, London: Allen Lane.

Gryson, R. *Les Originesdu Célibat Ecclésiastique*, Gembloux: Duclot.

Gutierrez, G. (1993), *In Search of the Poor of Jesus Christ*, New York: Maryknoll Orbis Books.

Halik, Tomás. (2012), *The Night of the Confessor*, New York: Image Books.

Hastings, Adrian. (ed.) (1977), *Bishops and Writers*, Wheathampstead: Clarke.

Hefele, K. & Leclercq, J. (1908-1949), *Histoire des Conciles*, Paris: Letouzy & Ané.

Hughes, Philip. (1952), *A History of the Church*, (3 vols.) London: Sheed & Ward.

Jackson, B. (1990), *Poverty and the Planet*, Harmondsworth: Penguin.

John XXIII, Pope. 'Mater et Magistra', in *Acta Apostolicae Sedis*, 53, (1961).

Knowles, David. (1948), *The Religious Orders in England*, (2 vols.) Cambridge: Cambridge University Press.

Küng, H. (1990), *Global Responsibility*, London: SCM Press.

Lampe, Peter. (2003), *Christians at Rome in the First Two Centuries*, London: T & T Clark International.

Lawrence, C.H. (1994), *The Friars, The Impact of the Early Mendicant Movement on Western Society*, London: Longman.

Lean, G. (1978), *Rich World, Poor World*, London: George, Allen and Unwin.

Lean, G. (1980), *God's Politician*, London: Darton, Longman, &. Todd.

Mahoney, J. (1987), *The Making of Moral Theology*, Oxford: Oxford University Press.

Martel, Frédéric, (2019), *In the Closet of the Vatican*, London: Bloomsbury Continuum.

Marx, Karl. & Engels, Frederick. (1976) *Karl Marx and Frederick Engels: Collected Works*, Vol. 5, 'Theses on Feurbach', Number 11, London: Lawrence & Wishart.

Maxwell, J. F. (1975), *Slavery and the Catholic Church*, Chichester & London: Barry Rose Publishers.

Meadows, D. H. (1972), *Limits to Growth*, London: Pan Books.

Milgram, Stanley. (1969), *Obedience to Authority*, New York: Pinter & Mann.

Moltmann, J. (1976), *Theology of Hope*, London: SCM Press.

Monbiot, George. (2017), *Out of the Wreckage: A New Politics for an Age of Crisis*, London: Verso.

Murphy-O'Connor, J. (1978), *Becoming Human Together*, Dublin: Veritas Publications.

McCann, Justin. (ed.), (1951), *The Rule of St. Benedict*, London: Burns Oates.

McDade, John. 'Ministry in a Post-Religious Society: Can we do it at all?' in *New Blackfriars*, March 2019.

Noonan, J. T. (1967), *Contraception*, New York: The New American Library.

O'Connell, James. 'The Discernment of Morality, Distinguishing Grounds, Guidelines and Laws', in *Theology*, May/June 2001.

O'Connell, Marvin. (1994), *Critics on Trial: An Introduction to the Catholic Modernist Crisis*, Washington: Catholic University of America Press.

Oldmeadow, E. (1943), *Francis Cardinal Bourne* (2 vols), London: Burns & Oates.

Parish, Helen. (2010), *Clerical Celibacy in the West*, Aldershot: Ashgate Publishing.

Piaget, J. & Inhalder, B. (1969), *The Psychology of the Child*, London: Routledge & Kegan Paul.

Pius XI, Pope. 'Quadragesimo Anno', in *Acta Apostolicae Sedis*, 53, 1930.

Pius XI, Pope. 'Casti Connubii', in *Acta Apostolicae Sedis*, 22, 1930.

Porter, Roy. (2006), *Cambridge History of Medicine*, Cambridge: Cambridge University Press.

Ranke-Heinemann, U. (1990), *Eunuchs for the Kingdom of Heaven*, London: A. Deutsch.

Rees, Daniel. (ed.) (1978), *Consider your Call*, London: SPCK.

Rice, David. (1990), Shattered Vows: *Exodus from the Priesthood*, London: Michael Joseph.

Roberts, Daniel. (2009), *The Storm of War*, London: Allen Lane.

Ruyter, K. W. 'Pacifism and Military Service in the Early Church' *Cross Currents*, 32 (1), 1982.

Salmon, P. (1959), *L'Office Divin*, Paris: Éditions du Cerf.

Scheffczyk, Leo. (1981), 'Urstand, Fall und Erbsünde, Von der Schrift bis Augustinus.' in *Handbuch der Dogmengeshichte*, (eds.) Michael Schmaus, Alois Grillmeier, Leo Scheffczyk, Michael Seybold, Band II, Fazikel 3a (1. Teil) Freiburg: Herder.

Sewell, Brocard. (1970), *The Vatican Oracle*, London: Duckworth.

Sipe, A.W.R. (1995), *Sex, Priests and Power: An Anatomy of Crisis*, London: Cassel.

Spicq, C. (1965), *Théologie Morale du Nouveau Testament*, Paris: Librarie Lecoffre.

Stern, Fritz. 'Obituary Notice' in *The Guardian*, 3 June 2016.

Street, Andrew. & Summers, Laurance. (eds.) (1992) *World Development Report 1992*, Oxford: Oxford University Press.

Stultz, Ulrich. (1895), *Die Eigenkirche als Element des mittelalterish-germanischen Kirchenrechtes*, Basel. Translated by Barraclough, Geoffrey, Mediaeval Germany, Oxford: Oxford University Press.

Sweeney, Gareth. (1977), 'The Wound in the Right Foot', in Hastings, Adrian (ed.) *Bishops and Writers*, Wheathampstead: A. Clarke.

Teichmann, J. (1986), *Pacifism and the Just War*, Oxford: Blackwell.

Thomas, Hugh. (1996), *The Slave Trade*, London: Picador.

Vallely, P. (ed.) (1998), *The New Politics: Catholic Social Teaching for the Twenty-First Century*, London: SCM Press.

Vogels, H. J. trans. G.A. Kon. (1992), *Celibacy – Gift or Law?*, Tunbridge Wells: Burns & Oates.

Ward, B. & Dubois, R. (1972), *Only One Earth*, Harmondsworth: Penguin.

Warnock, B. (2001), *An Intelligent Person's Guide to Ethics*, London: Duckworth.

Wills, G. (2000), *Papal Sin: Structures of Deceit*, London: Darton, Longman and Todd.

Winter, Michael. (1985), *Whatever Happened to Vatican II?* London: Sheed & Ward.

Winter, Michael. (2002), *Misguided Morality*, Aldershot: Ashgate Publishing Company.

Woodhouse, P. (1992), 'Environmental Depredation' in Allen, T. & Thomas, H. (eds), *Poverty and Development in the 1990's*, Oxford: Oxford University Press.

INDEX OF SUBJECTS

WS - #0041 - 100822 - C0 - 216/138/16 - PB - 9781784567668 - Gloss Lamination